WESTERN MICHIGAN FOOTBALL

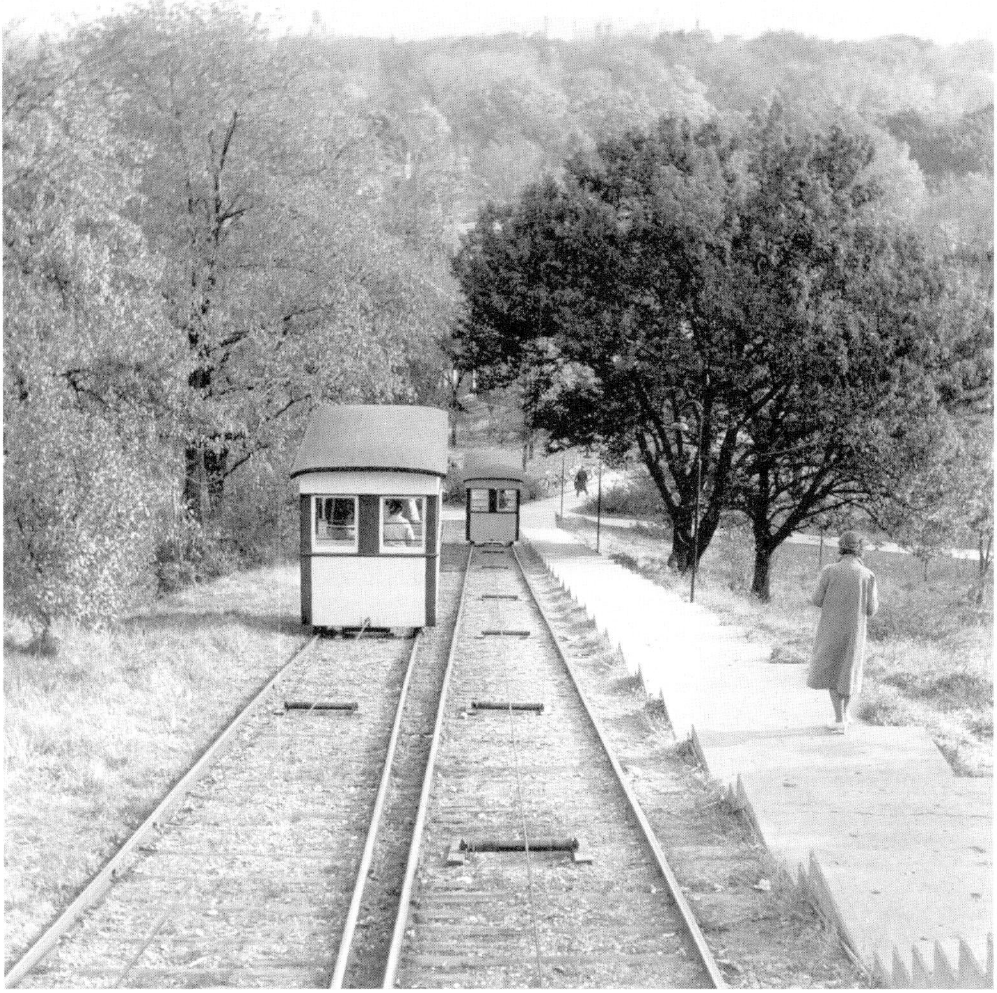

When Western Michigan University was founded, its main buildings were located at the top of Prospect Hill. The campus's most identifying feature in those early days was the set of cable car tracks that guided the trolleys up the hill, carrying weary students to class.

On the front cover: Western Michigan quarterback Tim Lester is shown here. (Courtesy of the Western Michigan University Athletic Department.)

On the back cover: Two players celebrate during a game. (Courtesy of the Western Michigan University Athletic Department.)

Cover background: An early Western football squad poses for a photograph. (Courtesy of the Western Michigan University Athletic Department.)

WESTERN MICHIGAN FOOTBALL

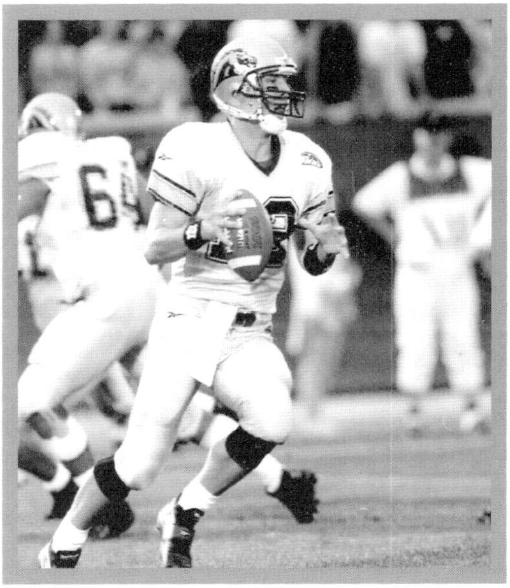

Mark Fricke

ARCADIA PUBLISHING

ISBN 978-0-7385-4088-7

Published by Arcadia Publishing
Charleston, South Carolina

Printed in the United States of America

Library of Congress Catalog Card Number: 2006926902

For all general information contact Arcadia Publishing at:
Telephone 843-853-2070
Fax 843-853-0044
E-mail sales@arcadiapublishing.com
For customer service and orders:
Toll-Free 1-888-313-2665

Visit us on the Internet at www.arcadiapublishing.com

This book is dedicated to the Western Michigan University athletes who played the game, the coaches who guided them, and, most of all, the fans who supported them.

CONTENTS

ACKNOWLEDGMENTS

Proceeds from the sale of *Western Michigan Football* will benefit the Mike Gary Athletic Fund. The "Gary Fund" was established in 1956 and designed to provide benefits for improving sports programs at Western Michigan University (WMU) by providing direct financial support for all varsity men's and women's sports at WMU. Named for Mike Gary, WMU's longtime coach and administrative leader, the fund was the brainchild of a dedicated group of alumni, friends, fans, media, coaches, administrators, and former athletes. The collective gathered in 1956 to formulate plans for donations and disbursements and sought goals of $100 contributions from willing benefactors. Since that time, the fund has grown to receiving over $800,000 annually. Today the Gary Fund has chapters all over the state and provides needed support for student-athletes, state-of-the-art facilities, travel expenses, and equipment for WMU's 16 intercollegiate programs.

There are several people who deserve recognition for their help in this project. This book could not have been accomplished without the help of Daniel Jankowski and his staff at the WMU Sports Information Department, including Adam Bodner and football sports information director Matt Kanan. All player photographs in this book are courtesy of the WMU Athletic Department unless otherwise noted. Thanks also to Sharon Carlson and the staff at the Western Michigan University Archives and Regional History Collection, including Steven Rice, for their assistance in supplying photographs. Nonplayer photographs prior to 1975 are courtesy of the Western Michigan University Archives and Regional History Collection unless noted. Finally acknowledgment is due for Thomas C. Slaughter and Harold L. Ray for their fine publication, *Go Broncos!: The History of Western Michigan Athletics*. Their fine research proved invaluable in assembling this book.

INTRODUCTION

For 100 years, there has been top-notch varsity college football played in Kalamazoo, a town that has comfortably settled into its title of a true college town. Nestled in a southwestern Michigan valley midpoint between Chicago and Detroit, Kalamazoo has been home to the school known as Western State Normal College, then Western State Teachers College, Western Michigan College of Education, Western Michigan College, and finally in 1957 Western Michigan University (WMU) since its establishment in 1903. Perched on a hill overlooking the prominent valley, the college's most dominant early feature was cable car tracks that accommodated the trolleys needed for students to ascend the hill to the school building. Female undergraduates dominated the student body. Less than two dozen males were enrolled in the first year, but that did not stop the desire for athletic competition. Sporting games were popping up on makeshift fields surrounding the campus. Students George Sievers and Archibald Polley looked into creating a team in the new sport of football. The two had been stars on the local high school football teams and hoped to bring the game to the college level. They assembled a squad of 15 potential players but saw all but two players drop out before any games could be played.

Nevertheless, Sievers and faculty advisor Dr. John McManus persisted and eventually aided in the creation of the Western State Normal Athletic Association to oversee football, basketball, tennis, and baseball activities at the college. Promises were made by college president Dwight Waldo to find a paid coach for the football team as soon it could be afforded. With formal backing now in place, the efforts to field a team became more fruitful.

A group of 11 was formed and run through its paces. Uniforms were little more than thick sweaters that lacked any uniformity in color and thin leather helmets. Dr. McManus managed to schedule two games against local high schools. The lack of experience among Western's players overrode the age advantage in the games. Augusta High School and Plainwell High School both dispatched the collegiate 11.

The lack of success failed to quell enthusiasm for the sport. Dr. McManus helped to recruit more players and was able to find some true talent at the team's disposal. The promise of scheduling games against other colleges helped to fuel interest from the student body as well as the surrounding civilian population.

The little school on the hill was now starting to make its mark among other, more established institutes of higher learning. The team, soon dubbed the "Hilltoppers" in light of the location of its main buildings, was now a true athletic team, ready to begin a century of competition. Brown and gold were selected as the team's colors. The level of competition grew from local high schools and small colleges to universities far enough away to require train trips.

As a world war sapped much of the talent, the game continued. Those who played did so for the love of the game, despite restrictions on travel, equipment, and fans. Newspaper headlines were far more interested in the life-and-death struggle against Kaiser Wilhelm II than a game against Hillsdale, even though their boys scored a record 103 points.

But the players struggled on. Not for the glory, but for the game. Through tough economic times, football became an outlet for not only the players' aggressions but also for the fans, who were in desperate need of entertainment. More and more, the players were earning a proud status on campus. The star athlete was gaining more notoriety. New inventions such as the radio had given a new media outlet and, therefore, new opportunities for the latest exploits to be hailed. The sports program grew as well, with new facilities and a new nickname of the "Broncos."

Another world war came, along with another loss of athletes, some of whom would never return. Those that did found a quickly changing world. Television brought new images into the family home. It was now possible for a star athlete to become a household name.

When the 1960s arrived, a new attitude was obvious among the student body, and a renewed attitude was born within the football team. Its efforts were rewarded with the goal of any college football team, a postseason bowl game. Even if it was a fledgling bowl one state away, it provided some measure that things were bouncing in the right direction. The team fired off a couple of winning seasons, including its first back-to-back six-win seasons in 34 years.

Not long after they found themselves flying high with postseason glory, the Broncos found themselves trying to get their feet back under themselves. A pair of losing seasons made things uncomfortable. Talented players would show up on campus to provide a needed boost but would soon be gone, and replacements had to be found.

The Broncos fought back, however. Four straight winning seasons seemed to right the ship, but they soon found themselves needing a win in the season finale to avoid a winless year. At times, the team found itself at the top of the league standings and challenging for the conference crown, other times it was satisfied just to stay out of the cellar. The ball was bouncing, and the Broncos were going along for the ride.

Throughout it all, the Kalamazoo fans showed their support. Record crowds made Saturday afternoon at Waldo Stadium a required autumn activity. Shades of brown and gold speckled the campus, and new songs in support of the team were learned. There was no doubt that Bronco football had grown up. The team moved up to the cherished Division 1-A status and began putting its name up at the top of the national rankings in several categories. It would boast one of the best rushers in the nation, a walk-on turned NFL star, and some of the most exciting football in the state.

Through all the highs and lows, Bronco football was becoming the pride of WMU.

WMU finally took the next step late in the 1980s when it claimed its first outright Mid-American Conference (MAC) title and earned its second bowl trip. More MAC division titles came, and more great players thrilled fans at Waldo Stadium. Some moved on to the NFL, while others became leaders in other fields.

The sport of college football took to a national stage, and WMU was right there for the spotlight. Twice it won the MAC division title and proved week in and week out that it was worthy of the highest levels of competition.

Since its birth as a squad of youthful athletes seeking a bohemian activity to its current place as a major college football program, WMU football continues to respond to the call of its fight song: "Western win this game!"

1

FIGHT ON, FIGHT ON FOR WESTERN 1906–1960

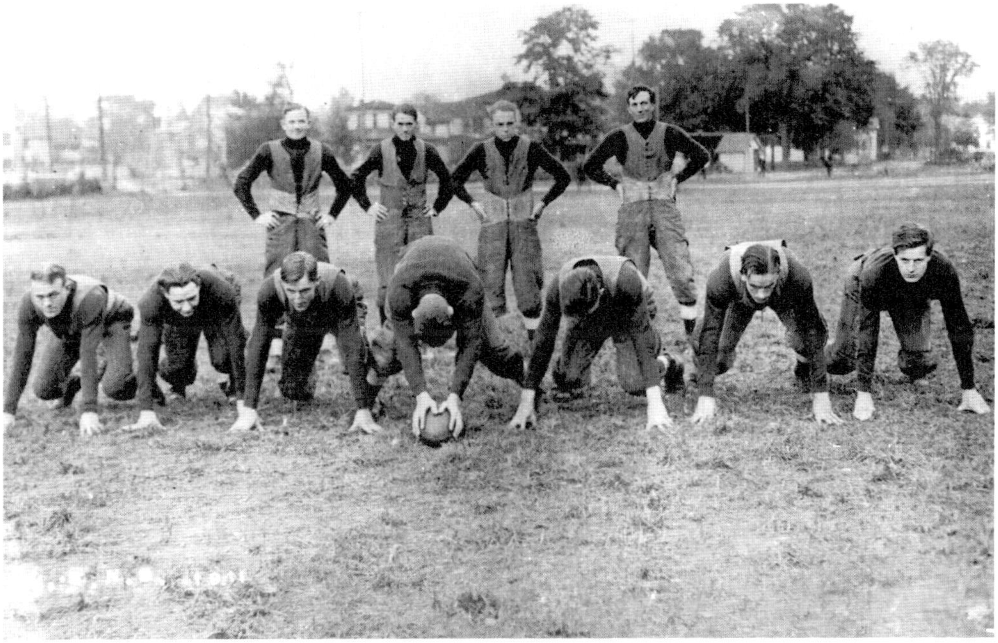

ASSEMBLING A QUALITY FOOTBALL TEAM among a predominately female student body was not easy, but there was talent to be found nevertheless. Western State Normal College was able to show it could compete with programs around the area. The students enjoyed the new outlet as well. School pride could be put on display both in the stands and on the field. Even the local newspapers showed up to report on the game, although those reports usually discussed the latest cheers or clothing choices more than the actual game. After all, football was as much a social event as it was an athletic competition. But the game itself grew as well. Players, coaches, and administrators showed that they could take the game seriously. Higher-level competition was invited while the local players became bigger, stronger, and faster. The Hilltoppers were the pride of Kalamazoo.

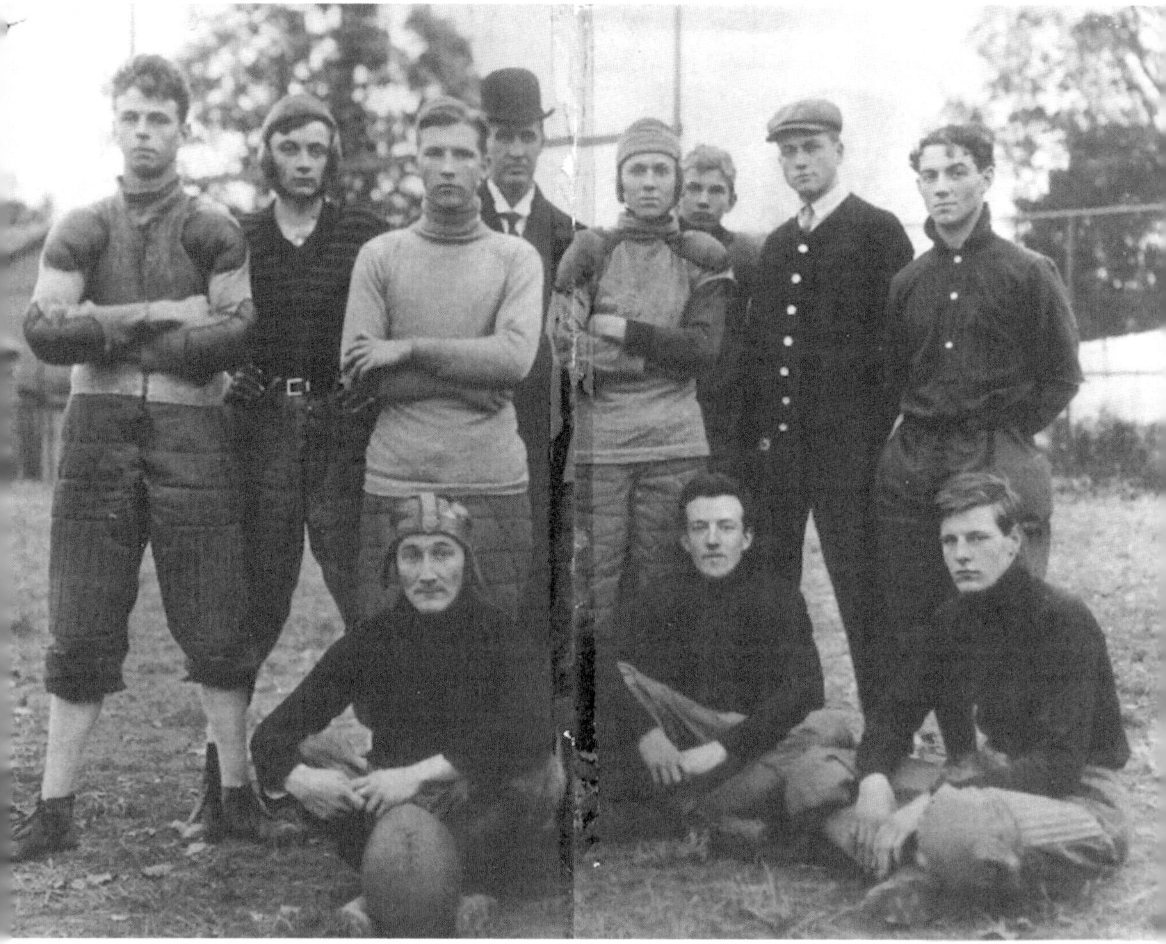

WESTERN'S FIRST VARSITY FOOTBALL TEAM IN 1906 was a team only in the loosest of terms. It had no formal coach, scrambled to find opponents, and barely had enough players to field a squad big enough to compete. There was no lack of familiarity with the game on the campus, however. Football had been played for at least two years on the campus as a club or recreational activity. The squad's lack of experience still hindered it as it lost its first two games against college-level opponents. It lost to Michigan State Normal College, another teaching college on the other side of the state that would later be known as Eastern Michigan University, and fell victim to a squad from Kalamazoo College. It capped the year with the school's first victory, a 21-0 triumph over a prep squad from Wayland High School. The scoring star of Western's inaugural win was Marion Sherwood, who logged two touchdowns in the 21-0 victory.

STUDENT MELVIN "TUBBY" MYERS SERVED as Western State Normal College's first de facto coach in 1906 based primarily on his experience as a star for the state champion Kalamazoo Central High School team. Myers took up the challenge of teaching his peers the finer points of the game and served as the team captain through the 1908 campaign.

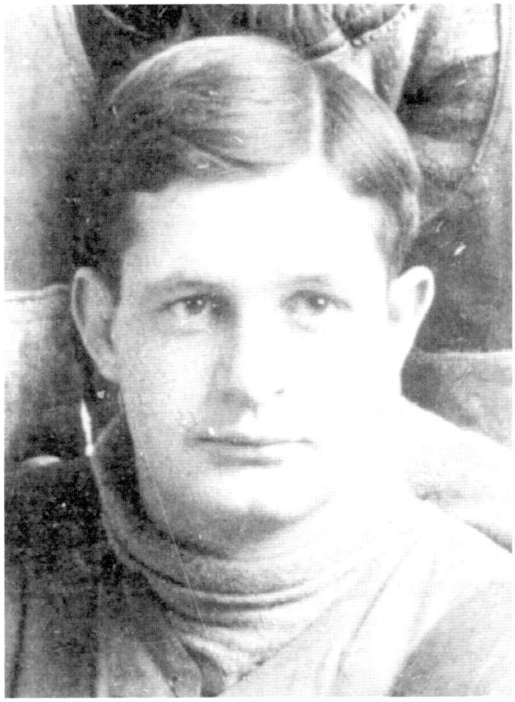

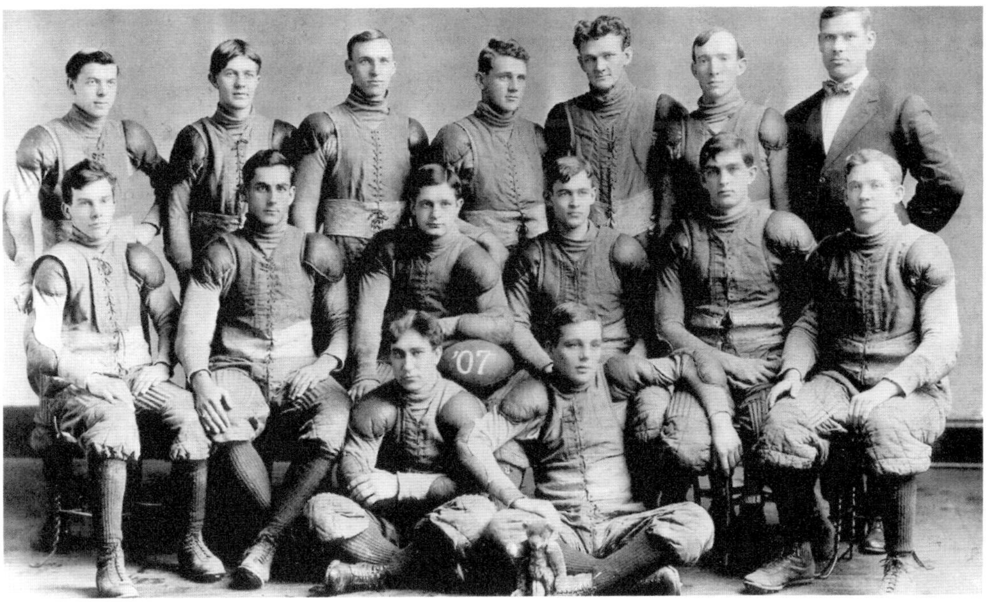

WESTERN HIRED BILL SPAULDING TO COACH the Hilltoppers in 1907, confirming the sport's elevated status at the school. Defensive struggles were the order of that season. Western shut out four of its six opponents but won just three games in light of three scoreless performances of its own. The highest scoring outburst was a 27-0 win over Central Michigan Normal School in the first of a long line of matchups between the rivals.

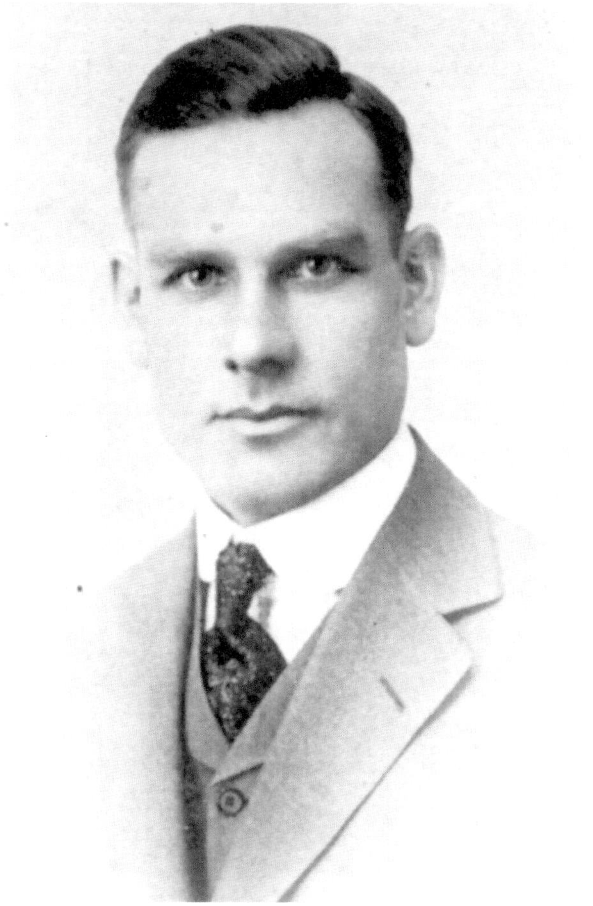

HEAD COACH BILL SPAULDING'S plan of slowing down opponents and keeping the game low scoring paid off in the 1909 season. Western kept six of its opponents out of the end zone, but unlike earlier efforts, its offense stepped up and outscored opponents 194-8. It claimed an undefeated 7-0 record and caused many, both on and off campus, to start noticing the program.

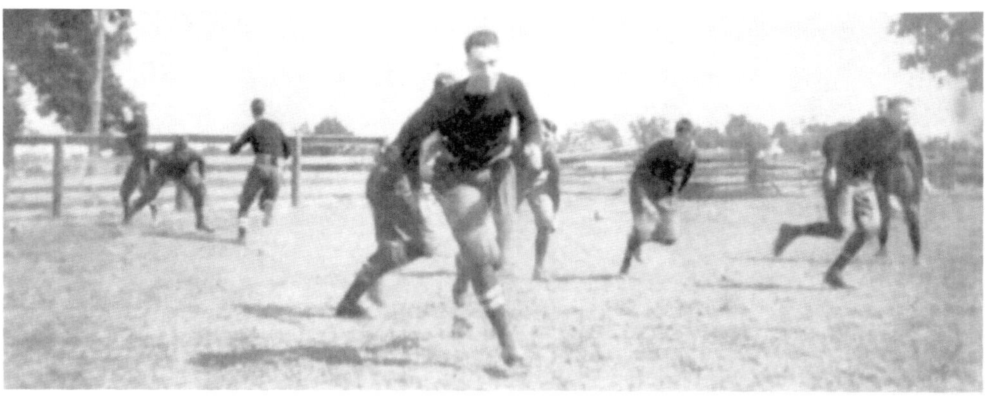

ONE OF SPAULDING'S FIRST ACTIONS WAS TO establish a training camp, dubbed "Camp Baker." Hoping to distance his players from the distraction of the city, Spaulding found he was able to ensure participation in two daily scrimmages, provide the proper nutrition, and guarantee that his players got the proper amount of sleep. Spaulding also made sure there was time for fun activities such as a jump in the nearby lake.

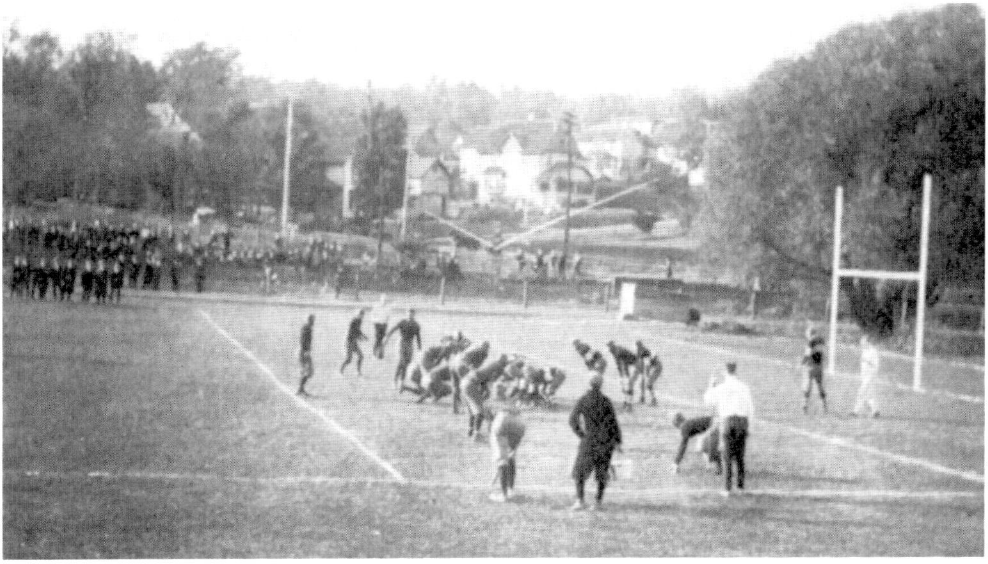

WESTERN'S 1916 TEAM WAS A SCORING explosion unlike anything before or since. Three times that season, Western scored 80 points or more, and it topped the 90-point mark twice. It outscored Indiana State Normal School by a score of 94-0 and blanked Grand Rapids Veterinary College 93-0. Its only loss of the season was a hard fought battle against a squad of Notre Dame freshmen.

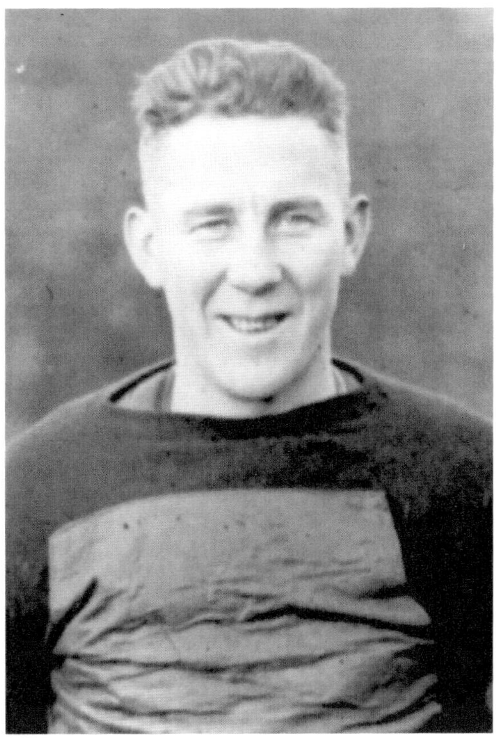

WESTERN'S FIRST STAR PLAYERS WERE A tandem of backfield aces on the 1916 squad. Quarterback Walter Olsen lead the entire nation in scoring with 17 touchdowns and 36 extra points. In a 93-0 rout of Grand Rapids Veterinary College, Olsen scored eight touchdowns and accounted for 52 of the team's total points in that game.

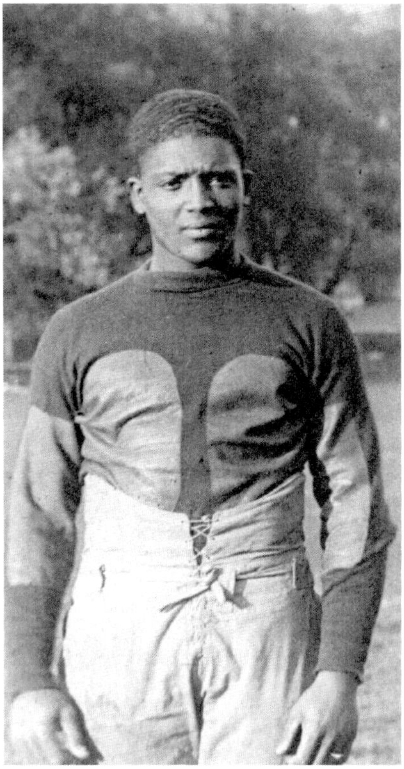

VERSATILE SAM DUNLAP DELIVERED THE SECOND Western punch of 1916 by scoring a school-record 19 touchdowns. He also served admirably as the team's punter. Even legendary Notre Dame head coach Knute Rockne acknowledged Dunlap as the finest punter he had ever seen.

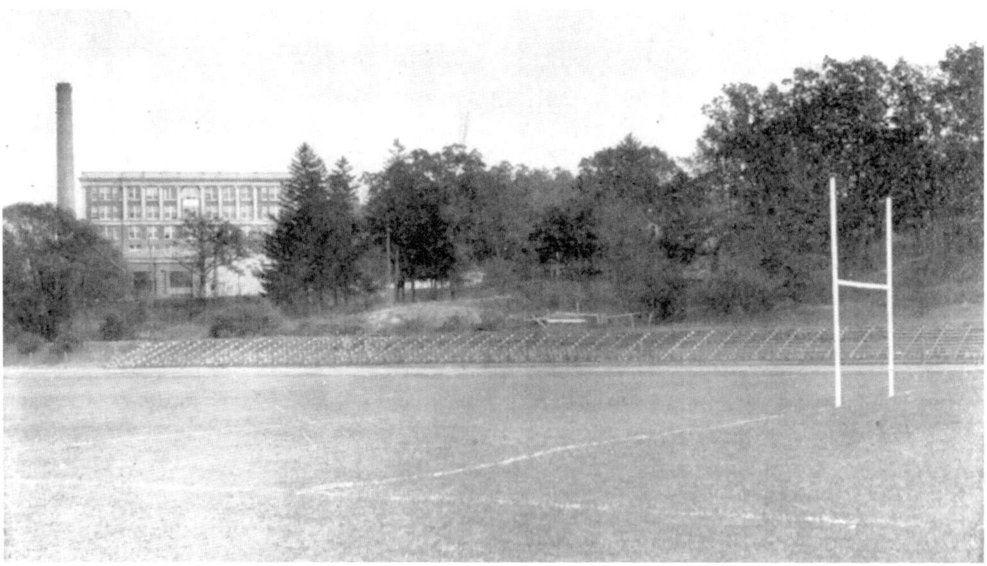

FINDING A STABLE ENVIRONMENT FOR FOOTBALL was not easy for Western. In its first days, Western played many of its home games at Kalamazoo College's field and also utilized the Kalamazoo High School fields. In 1914, Western finally constructed its own field by diverting Arcadia Creek and draining the surrounding land.

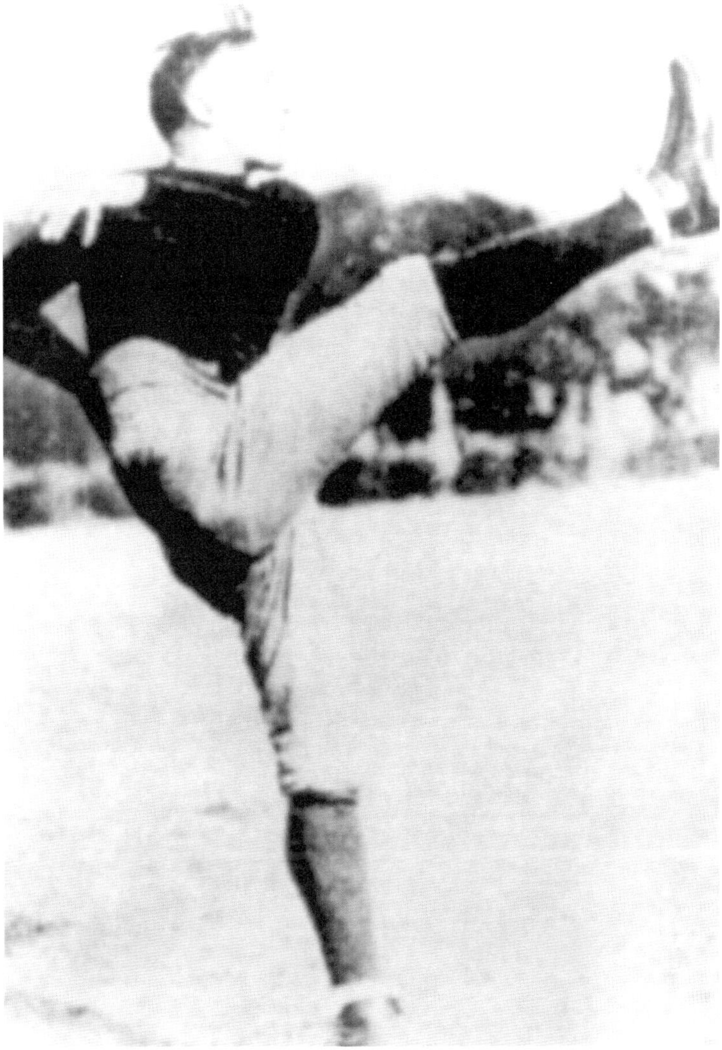

KALAMAZOO BECAME THE SITE OF ONE OF college football's most fabled plays, undertaken by one of the sport's most legendary players. Western played a squad of Notre Dame freshmen players in November 1916. The game was a hard fought battle with both teams missing many scoring opportunities. The Fighting Irish held a slim 7-6 lead late in the game, and they were hoping to put some scoring distance between them and their foe. Star back George Gipp took things in his own hands. He stepped back from the line, took the snap, and promptly executed a perfect dropkick from 62 yards away. Overly eager scribes contorted the story into a heroic last-second action taken to break a tie score. In reality, the score gave Notre Dame its final 10-7 margin with each team wasting a pair of future scoring chances before time ran out. Western would face Gipp again when the Notre Dame varsity played the Hilltoppers in 1919 and 1920. Gipp himself entered college football immortality when illness claimed his life at a young age. His coach, Knute Rockne, extolled his charges to "win one for the Gipper." (Courtesy of the University of Notre Dame.)

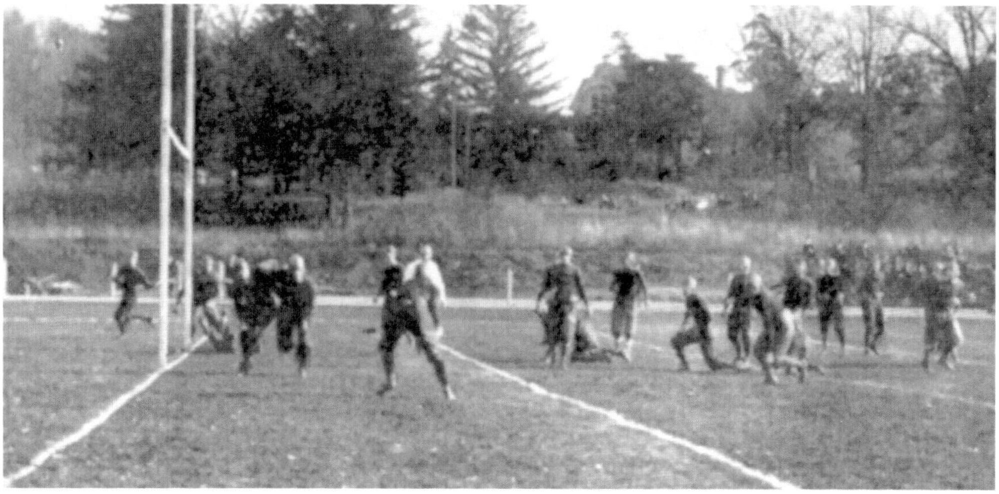

COLLEGE FOOTBALL BEGAN TO UNDERGO significant changes in the early part of the century. New rule changes implemented in 1906 sought to eliminate the brutal nature of the sport and emphasize speed. A more structured change occurred after 1913 when the forward pass entered into prominence. Now colleges, such as Western, had an alternate method of scoring.

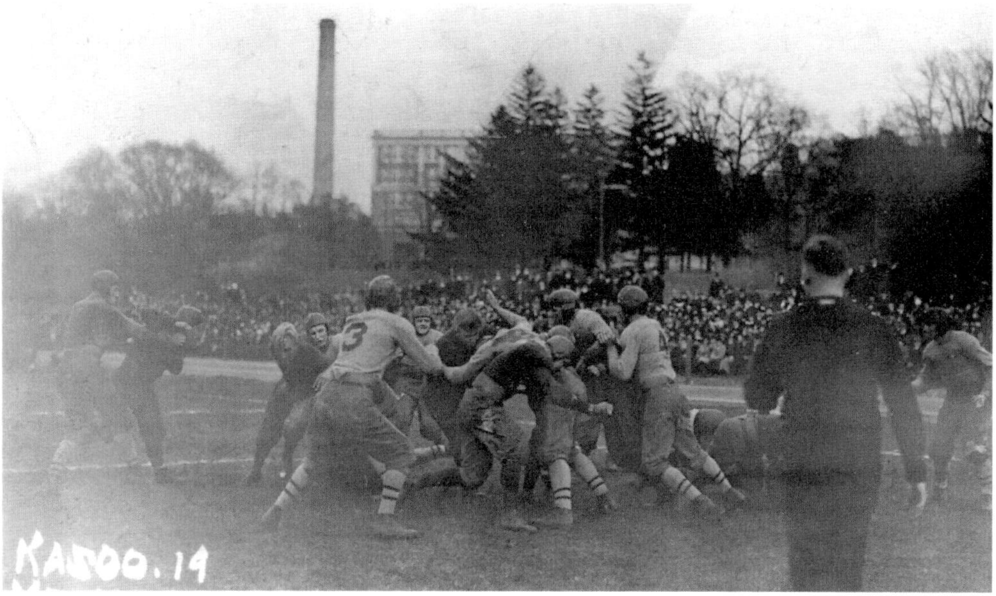

WESTERN STATE NORMAL COLLEGE ENTERED the Roaring Twenties with an impressive track record behind it. With the exception of its very first year, Western experienced just 1 losing season in 13 seasons. Having upgraded its schedule in 1912 to eliminate any high school–level teams, Western saw action against powerful varsity squads from Notre Dame, University of Michigan, and Michigan Agricultural College (later known as Michigan State).

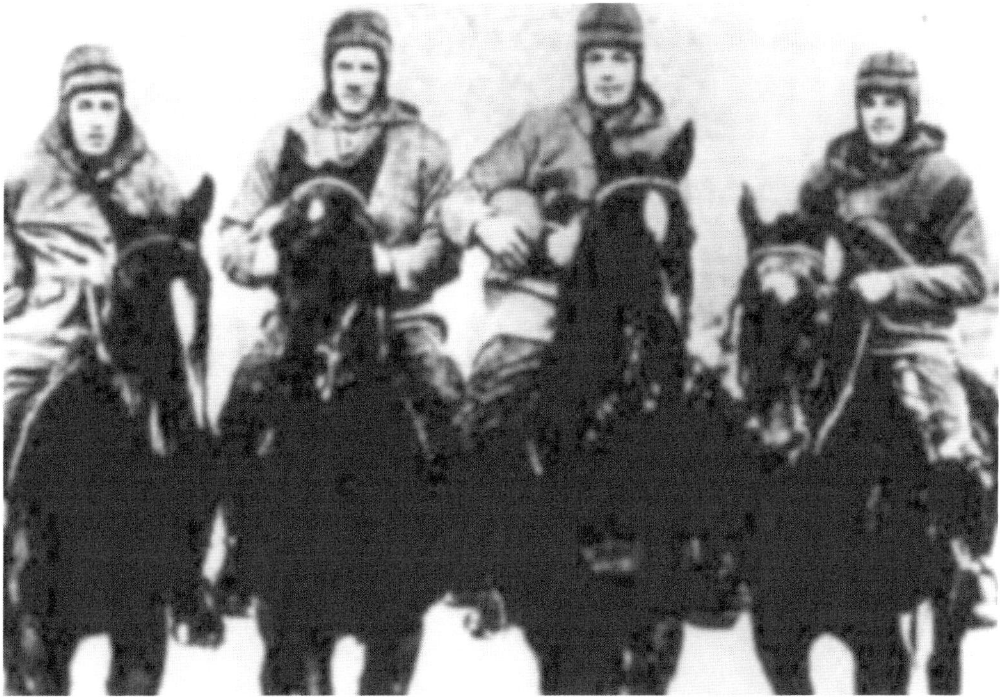

WESTERN ALSO PEPPERED ITS EARLY SCHEDULES with freshman squads from well-known schools. That did not mean that star talent was not on display in Kalamazoo. When Notre Dame's freshman group arrived in 1921, its lineup included the names Jim Crowley, Elmer Layden, Don Miller, and Harry Stuhldreher. The quartet would later be dubbed "the Four Horsemen" and become one of the most famous player groupings in sports history. Western won that game 7-0. (Courtesy of the University of Notre Dame.)

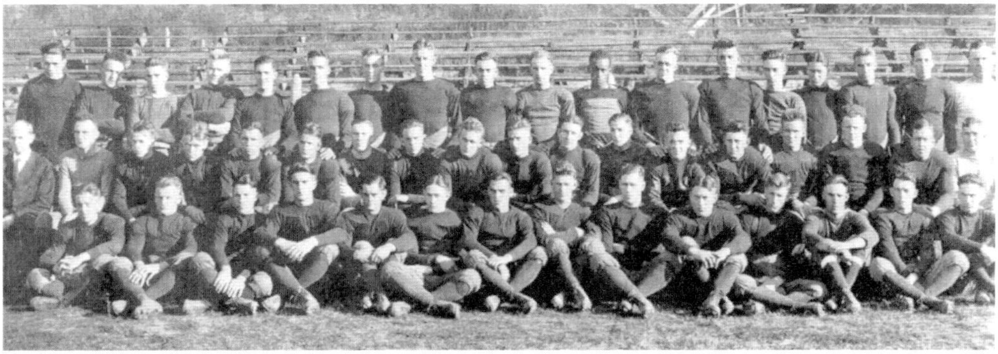

SCHEDULING GAMES BECAME THE BIGGEST ISSUE for Western around this period. Three teams cancelled their games with Western in 1919, fearing the Hilltoppers were too tough. That left a short five-game slate that year and a six-game schedule the next. Western was able to face some major foes in those years. For the only time in its history, Western faced Knute Rockne and the Notre Dame varsity squad in 1919 and 1920.

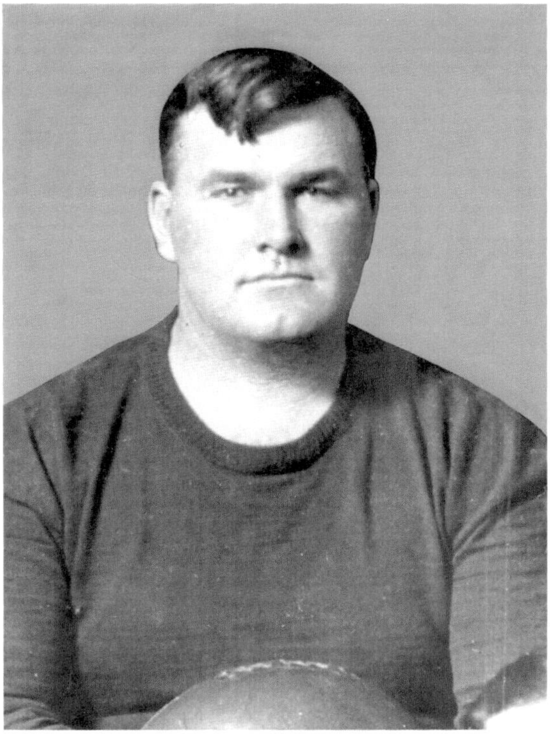

WESTERN'S 1922 TEAM COULD LAY A legitimate claim to being Western's best team ever. It certainly delivered on the scoreboard by completing a perfect season. Behind powerful center Leo Redmond, the team won all seven games and outscored opponents 160-0. The undefeated campaign helped anchor a 16-game undefeated streak that began in 1921 and stretched until the final game of 1923.

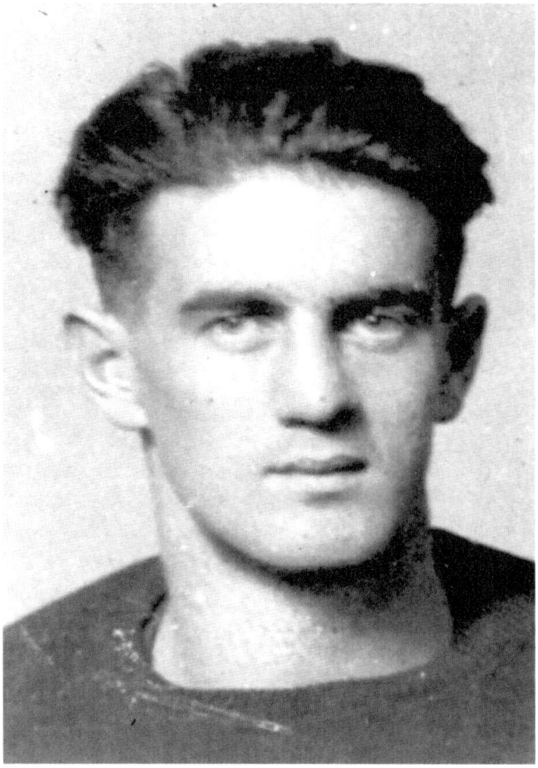

WESTERN HAD NEVER SEEN, AND MAY never see, a player as decorated as Rudy Miller. Miller earned a stunning 14 athletic letters during his time at Western. On the football field, he stood out as one of the best ends in the nation. His talents at catching passes from Harry Potter made him a crowd favorite.

HARRY POTTER BECAME WESTERN'S FIRST nationally recognized player when the legendary Walter Eckersall placed the talented running back on his All-Western honor roll. During his three years in Kalamazoo, Potter's teams went 18-3-1. The talented running back from Muskegon gave the Hilltoppers a blinding rushing attack.

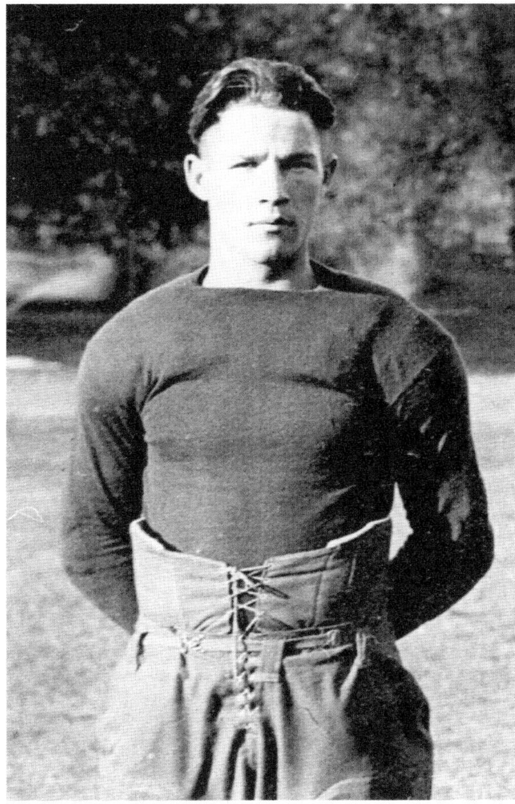

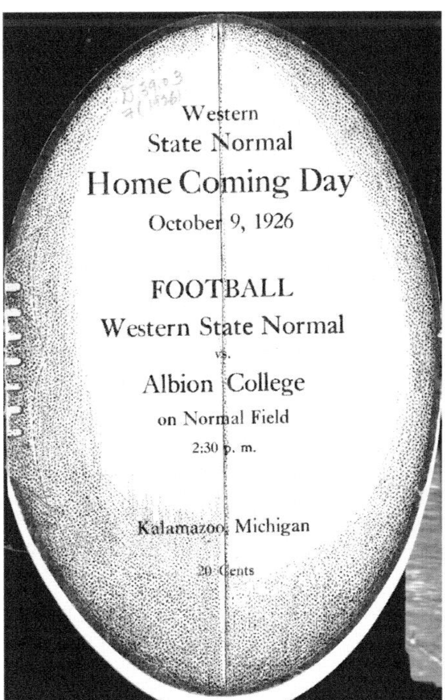

Western
State Normal
Home Coming Day
October 9, 1926

FOOTBALL
Western State Normal
vs.
Albion College
on Normal Field
2:30 p. m.

Kalamazoo, Michigan
20 Cents

THE TRADITION OF THE ANNUAL HOMECOMING game was the biggest social event on Western's campus. Designed as a reunion celebration for former students in hopes of keeping contributions rolling in, the annual football game was the centerpiece of all weekend activities. The games were hardly a homecoming for the football team, however. From 1924 to 1926, Western played only two games on the road.

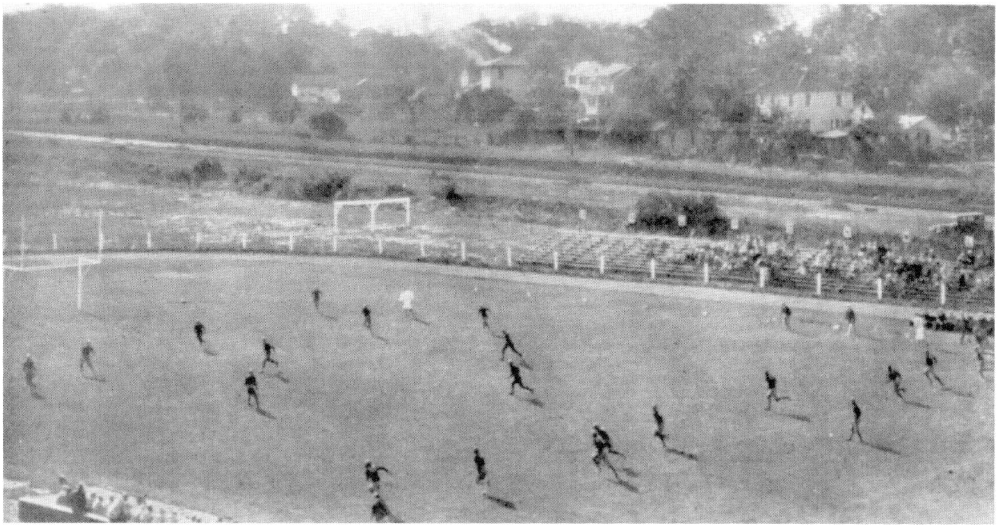

WESTERN SAW SEVERAL CHANGES IN 1927. THE school changed its name to Western State Teachers College and, along with four other schools, joined its first conference, known as the Michigan Collegiate League. Two years into the new alignment, Western claimed a share of its first championship with a 5-2-1 overall record in 1929.

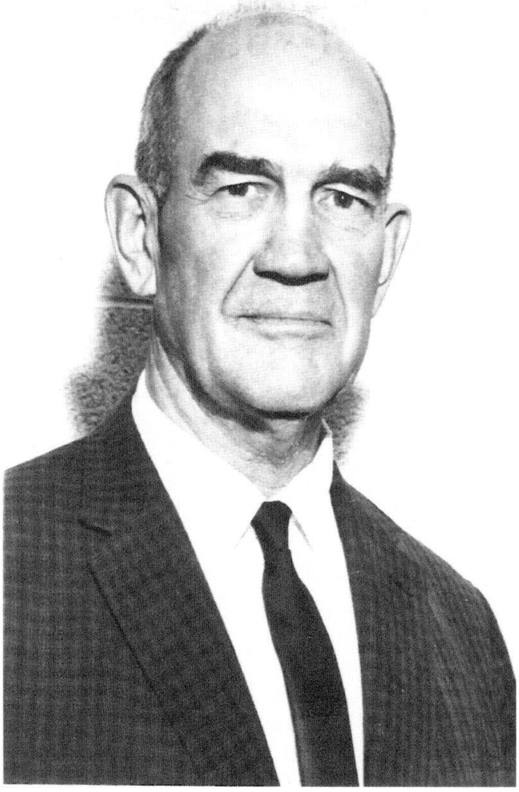

AS THE DEPRESSION ROLLED IN ACROSS the country, Western continued to keep its football hopes alive. New head coach Mike Gary took over the reins in 1929 and stayed on until the outbreak of World War II, leading the team to many impressive years. As a collegian, Gary played at the University of Minnesota, blocking for the great Bronco Nagurski.

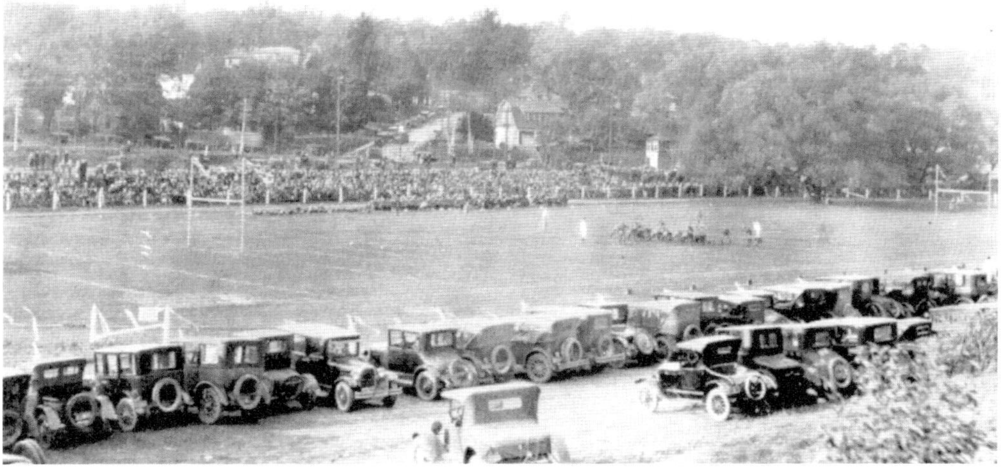

LARGER CROWDS BEGAN TO ASSEMBLE TO watch Hilltopper football games. With the promise of high scoring and quality opponents always present, the demand for seats started to put a strain on the facilities, and talk began to circulate about finding more appropriate accommodations. They would have to settle with what they had for another decade, however.

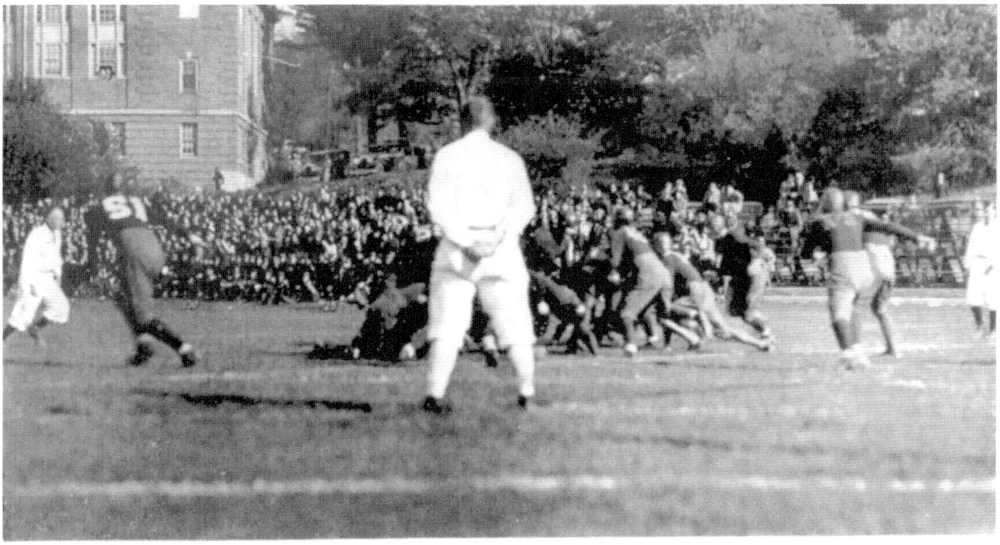

BIESKI DRIVES THROUGH AGAINST NOTRE DAME

WESTERN'S TEAM SHOWED NO SHORTAGE of victories during the 1930s. During the period of 1930 to 1934, the team went a combined 26-7-3. The 1932 edition went undefeated with six straight shutout victories, and the 1934 squad rallied after a season-opening loss to win seven straight games.

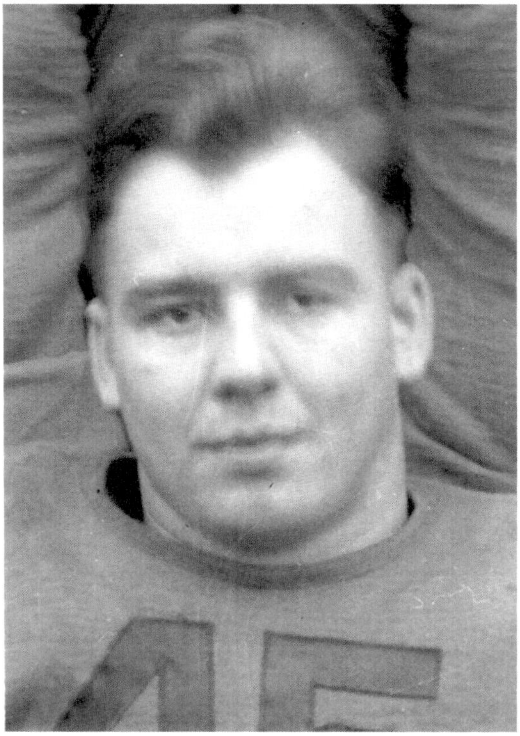

THE FIRST WESTERN STAR DRAFTED INTO professional football was Ray Bray. The Chicago Bears drafted the dazzling guard in the seventh round of the NFL draft. He went on to play for 10 seasons with the Bears and Green Bay Packers and was inducted into the Helms Major League Football Hall of Fame.

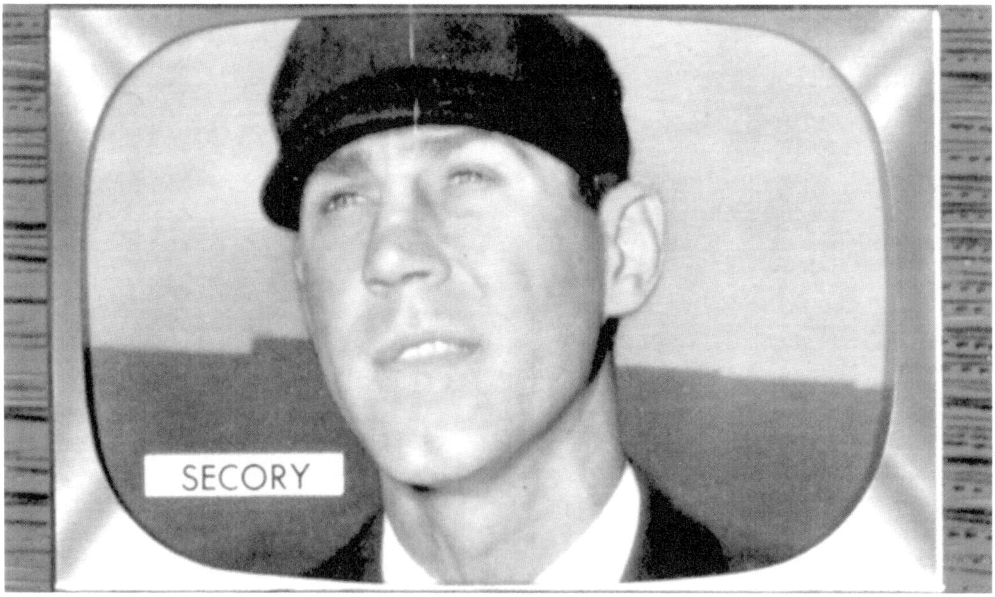

FRANK SECORY WAS A POWERFUL GUARD ON the Hilltoppers' 1934 squad, but he would make his claim in sports on another field. After a career in professional baseball with the Chicago Cubs, Secory went on to be a topflight major-league umpire. His likeness later appeared on a 1955 baseball card, making him the first Western graduate with such an honor.

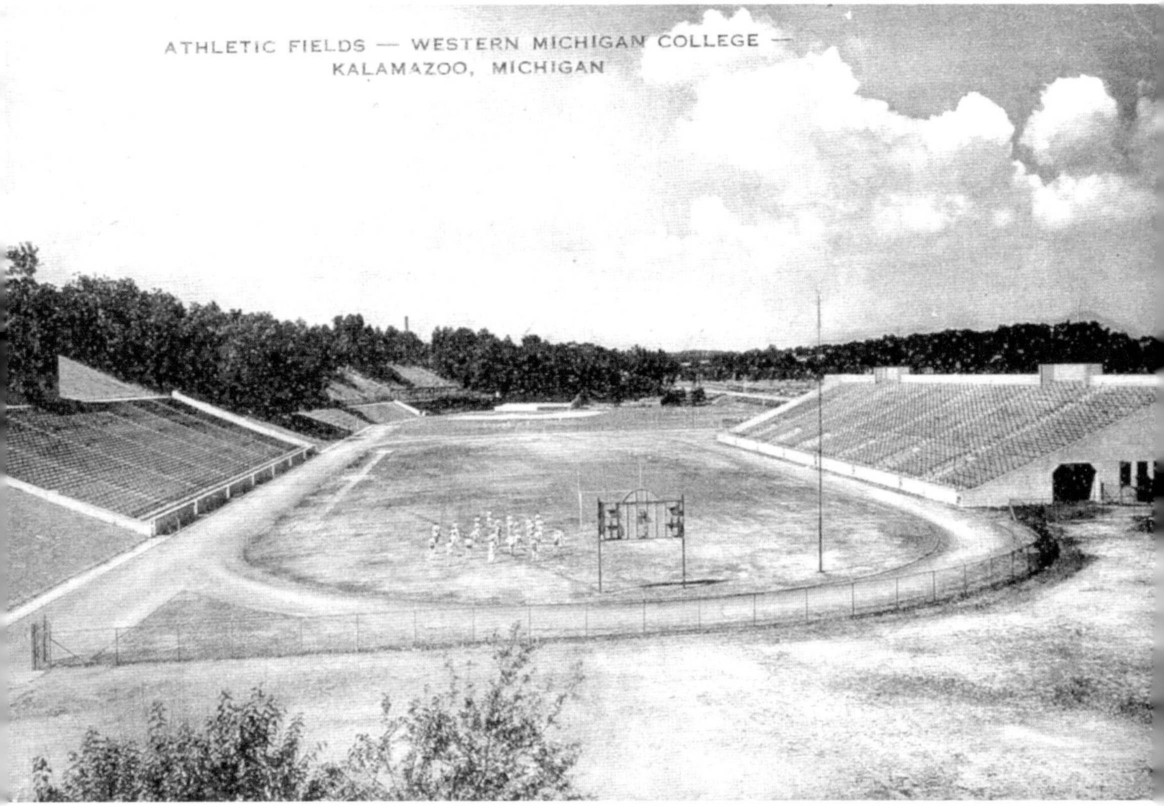

WESTERN REACHED COLLEGE FOOTBALL'S big time in 1939 with the construction of Waldo Stadium. Built through donations and at a cost of $250,000, the 15,000-seat venue featured a modern press box, a running track, and a nearby baseball field. The Western student yearbook hailed the new facility as "one of the greatest improvements to be undertaken at Western State Teachers College." The field was named after Western's first president, Dwight B. Waldo. Western won the first game played in the new stadium, a 6-0 win over Miami University. The dedication game was slated for later in the season against a Western Kentucky State Teachers College squad coincidentally nicknamed the Hilltoppers. A unique admission requirement was put in place for the dedication game. Contributors who had donated to the project were acknowledged with a medallion. That medallion became the required ticket for entrance to the game. Western Kentucky spoiled the festivities by defeating Western 20-14.

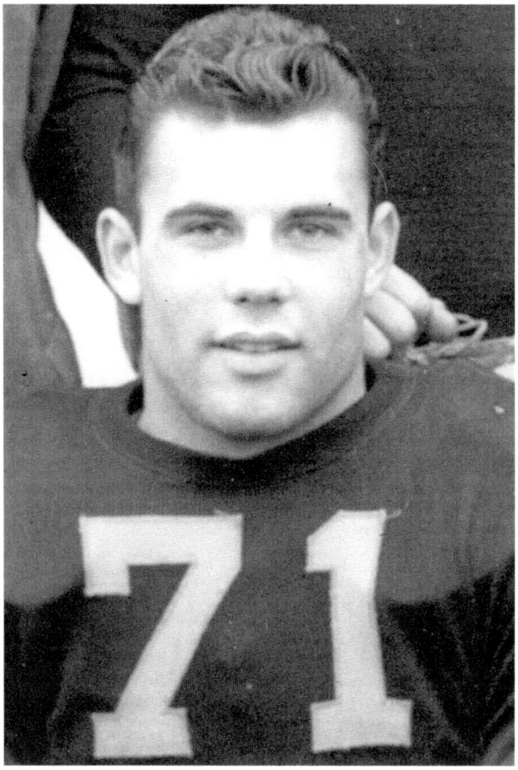

DAVE KRIBS WAS THE HERO IN WALDO Stadium's inaugural match. Kribs was a stellar punt returner on special teams and a team leader in interceptions on defense. But it was his offensive delivery of the game's only touchdown that gave Western a 6-0 victory over Miami in the stadium opener. Kribs ensured a happy housewarming for the new facility.

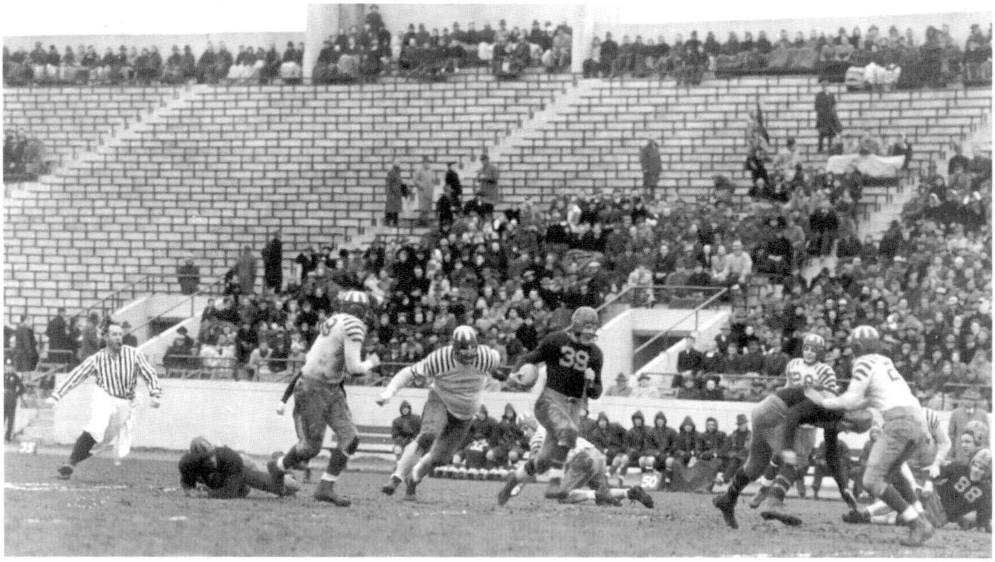

THE YEAR 1939 SAW MORE THAN JUST A CHANGE in surroundings for Western; it also donned a new nickname. Following a community-wide poll, the name "Broncos" was selected as the name for Western's athletic teams. The old Hilltoppers moniker was deemed inappropriate for the growing campus that now spread across the valley.

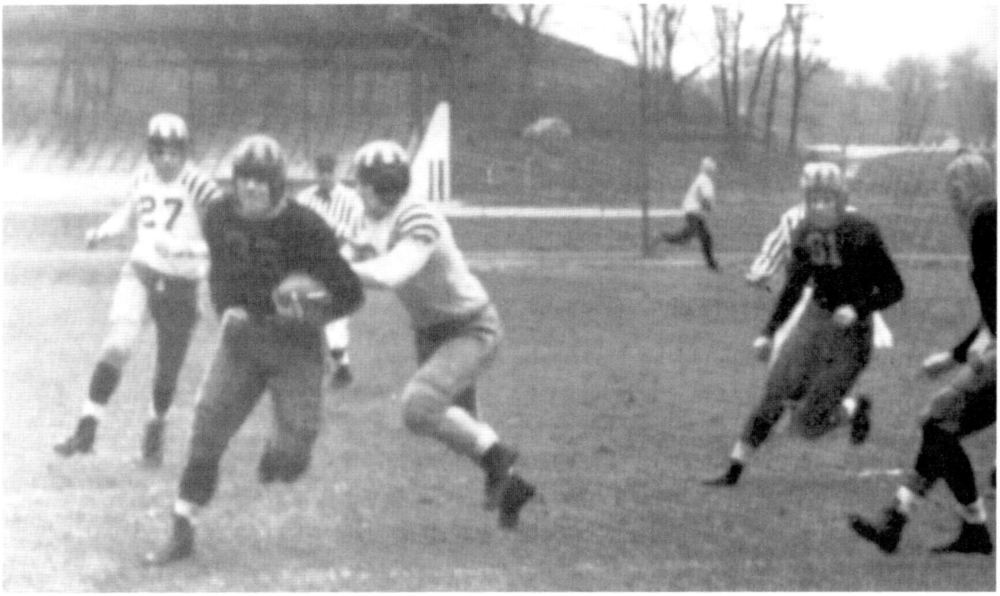

THE BRONCOS' 1941 TEAM PRODUCED ANOTHER of the school's undefeated and untied seasons. No opponent scored more than one touchdown against them, while coach Mike Gary's newly installed T-formation offense rolled up 183 points. At season's end, Western was ranked ninth nationally in total offense.

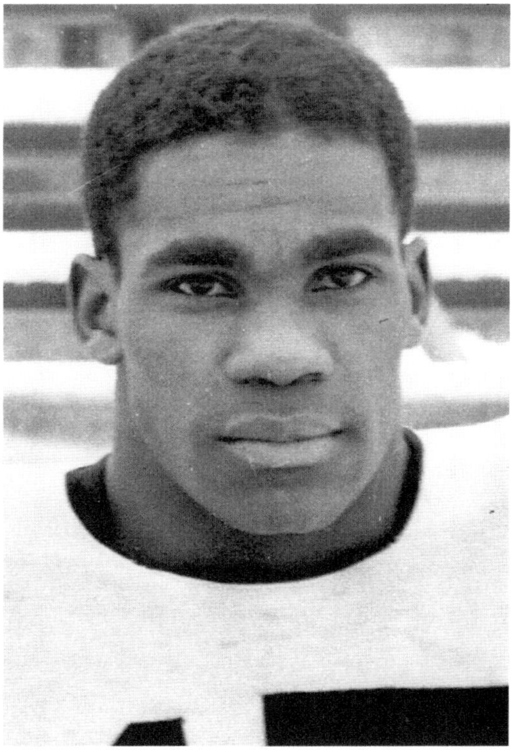

LEADING THE UNDEFEATED WESTERN squad in 1941 was scrappy halfback Horace "Hap" Coleman. He scored 12 touchdowns and averaged seven yards every time he was handed the ball. Coleman was ranked fifth in the nation in rushing in 1941. His 87-yard touchdown run against Toledo was one of the longest in Western history.

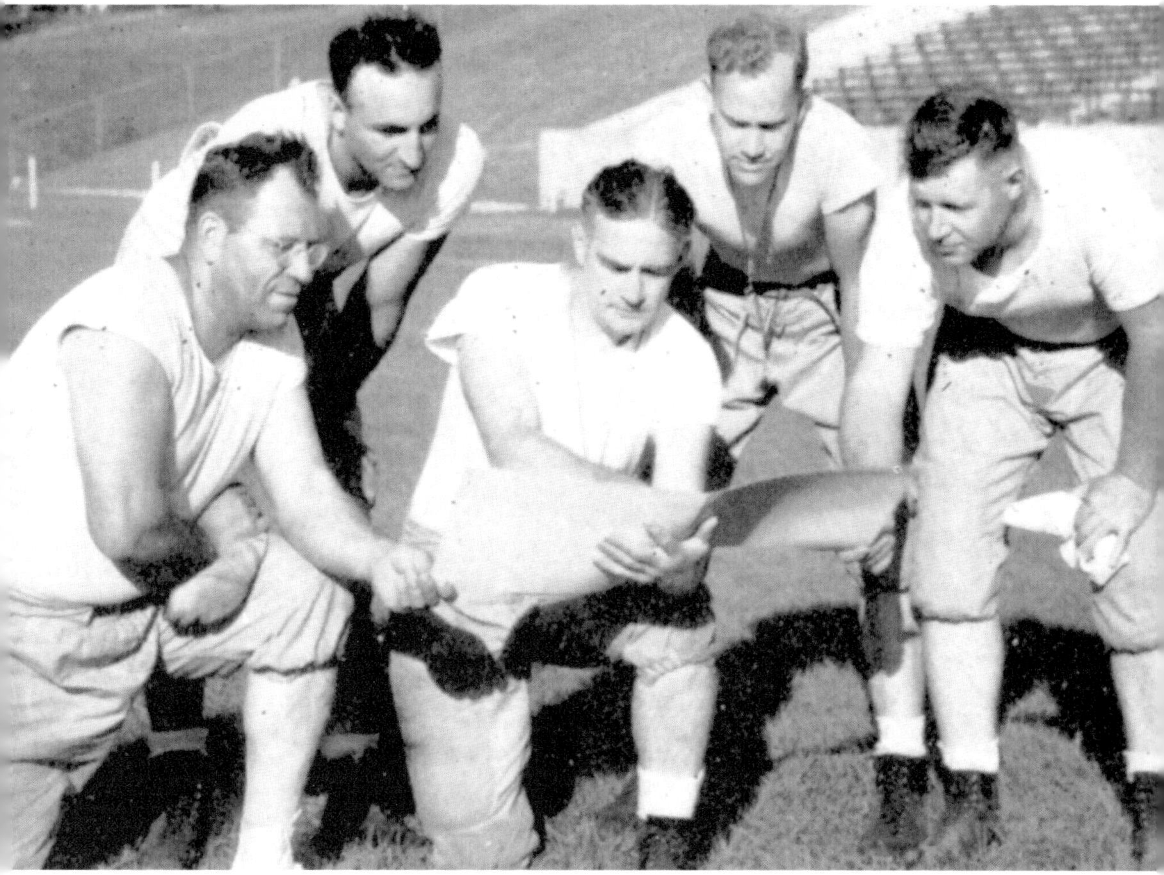

JOHN GILL WAS ONE OF WESTERN'S MOST celebrated players, having starred as a top punter and passer on the undefeated and unscored upon 1922 team. Gill booted a record seven extra points in a 1921 game against Milwaukee State Normal School, and he matched that feat the next year in a game against Earlham College. After his playing days ended, Gill did not stray far. He returned as the head freshman coach for football, basketball, and baseball in 1928 and joined the varsity coaching staff as the backfield coach in 1936. When head coach Mike Gary left the university to serve in the navy at the start of World War II, Gill was elevated to the position of head coach.

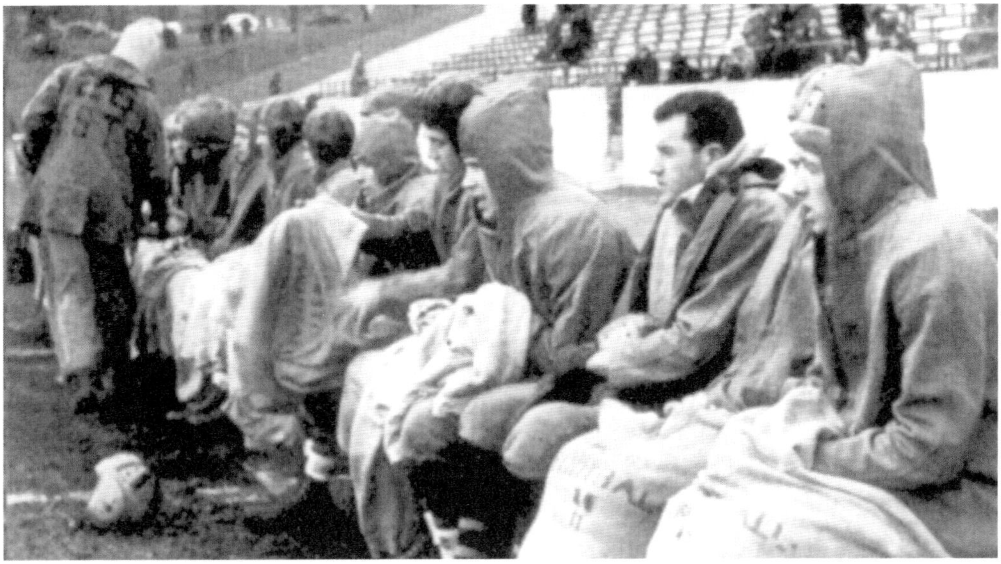

THE WAR YEARS PROVED TO BE TOUGH TIMES for the Broncos. With most able-bodied men heading off to service, the team often had to patchwork squads together from those that remained healthy. By 1943, the team began benefiting from the arrival of a U.S. Navy and Marine Corps reserve unit that provided athletic men, if only for short periods. By 1944, Gill was forced to recruit civilians for the team.

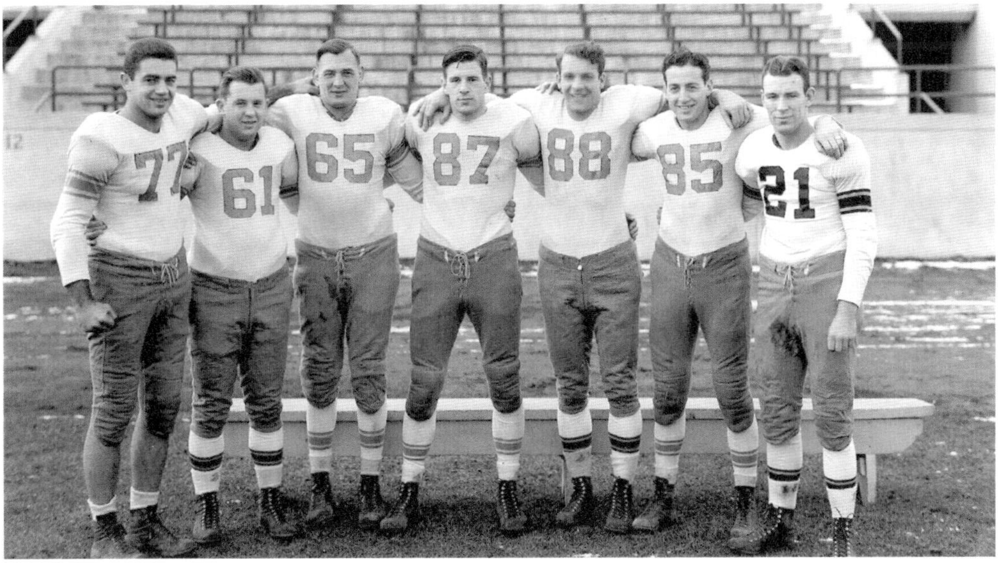

EVEN IN TOUGH TIMES, WESTERN STILL PUT together respectable seasons during the war. From 1941 through 1945, the Broncos never had a losing season. The 1942 lineup bounced back from a season-opening loss to win five straight without giving up more than one touchdown in those wins.

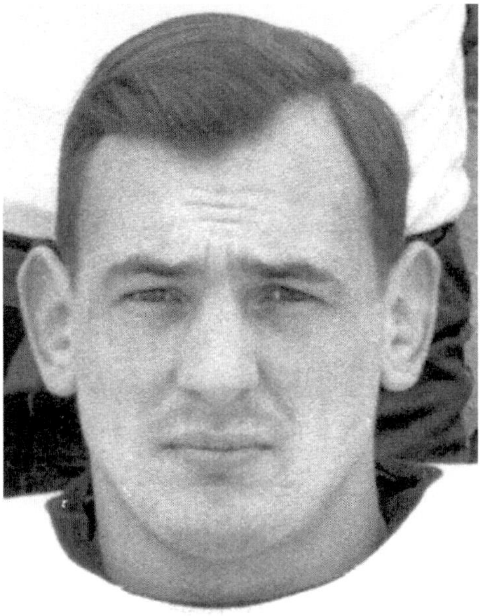

One of the war-year stars for Western was Bill Yambrick. As the two-way anchor for the Bronco line, Yambrick's offensive duties included opening holes for backs like Hap Coleman, while defensively he was required to shut those holes for opposing running backs. His contributions were recognized when he was selected the MVP of the 1942 team.

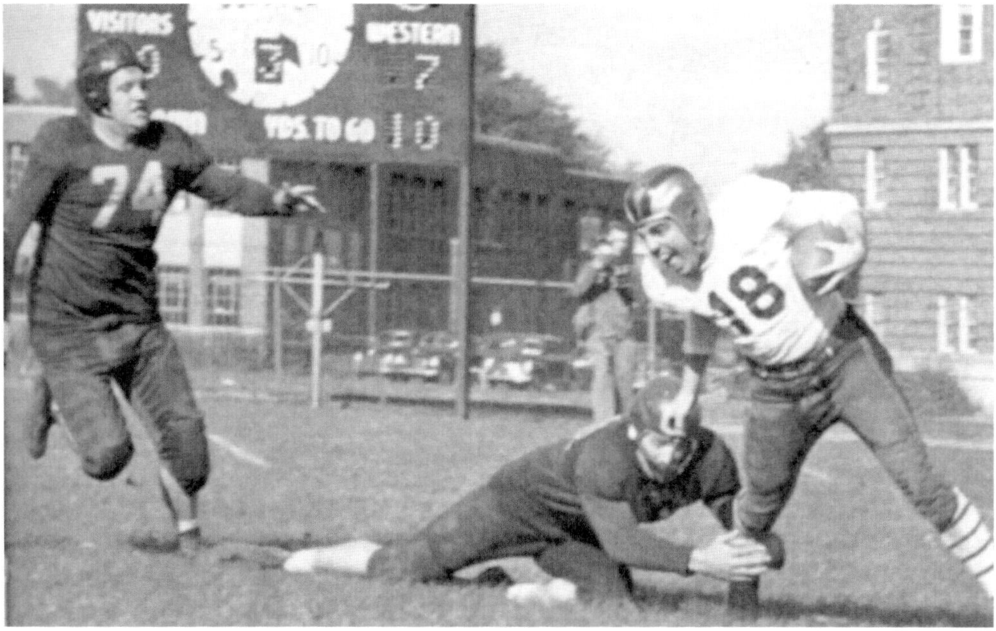

As wartime restrictions cut travel down, Western was forced to look for games against schools closer to home. One obvious choice was Central Michigan College of Education from nearby Mount Pleasant. The two schools had played routinely since 1907 but had not met since 1938. Western defeated Central Michigan 19-0, signaling the start of its fiercest rivalry.

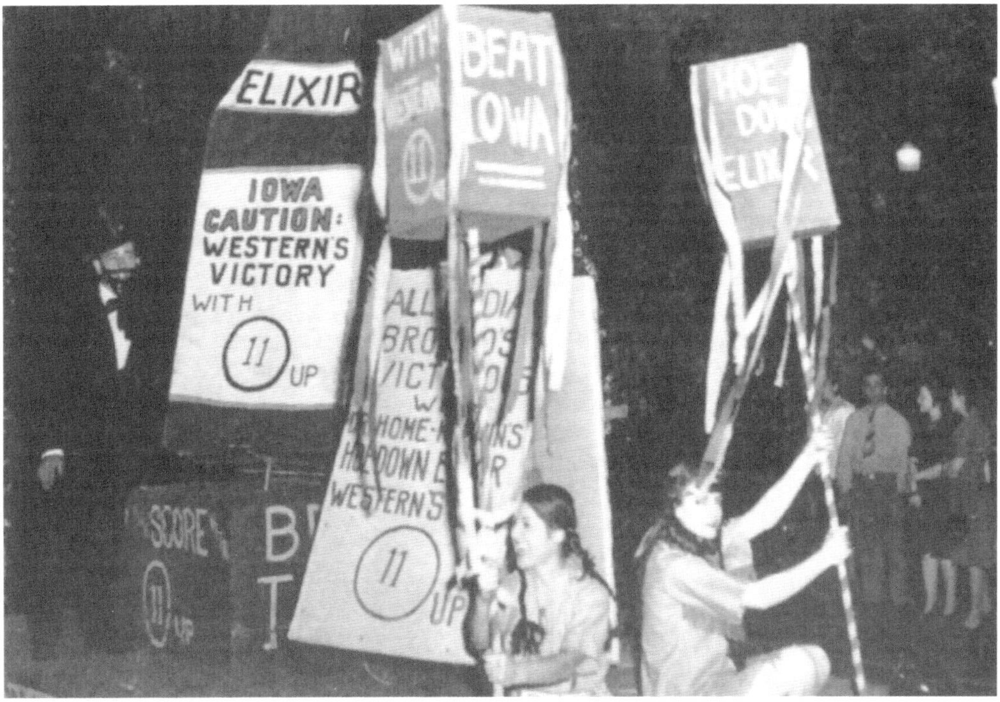

WITH THE WORRIES OF GLOBAL CONFLICT behind them, Western students were free to explore the joys of campus life. Homecoming activities and football pep rallies became the social events of the season. A near-record crowd of 11,000 fans packed Waldo Stadium to watch Western defeat Iowa State Teachers College in 1947.

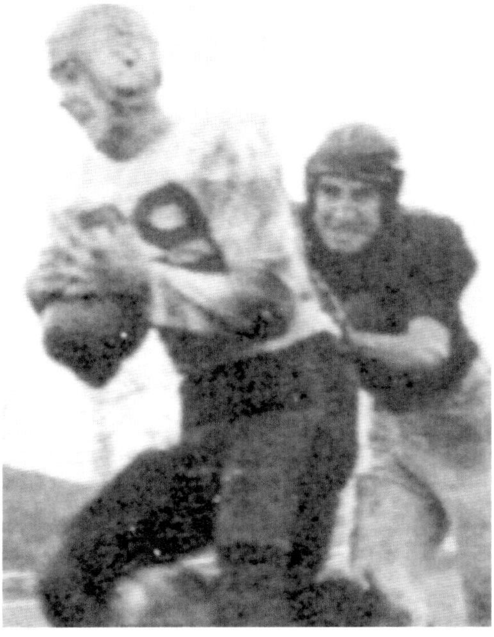

CARL SCHILLER HELPED USHER IN WESTERN'S return to football prominence with a phenomenal senior year in 1947. He became the favorite target of quarterback Nick Milosevich, catching a school-record 47 passes from his end position. Schiller's sure hands helped lift Western to a 5-4 record.

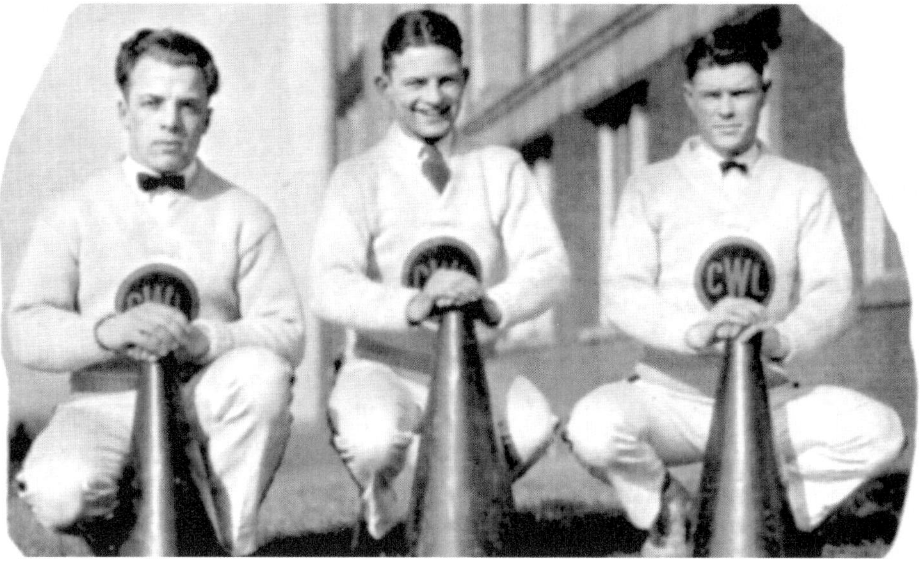

EARLY COLLEGE FOOTBALL GAMES WERE AS much social activities for the fans as they were athletic competitions. The job of keeping fans entertained and involved was the duty of male "yell leaders." Their importance can be noted by early newspaper accounts of games that often spent as much print space describing the yells as they did the game action. An early Western favorite yell was "Hy-lo-zoo, hy-lo-zoo, Western Normal, Kalamazoo!"

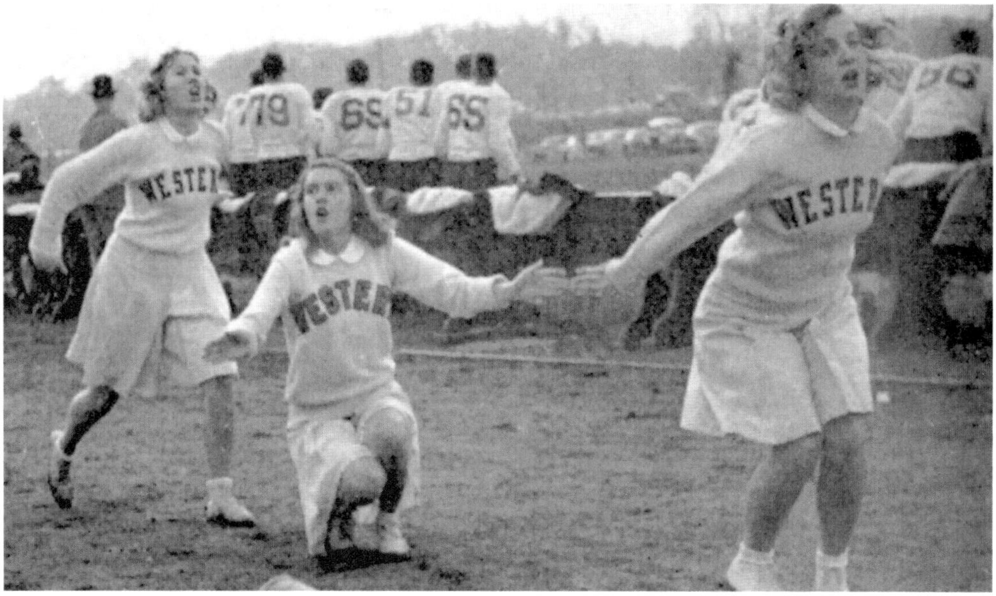

WHEN THE WAR SAPPED ALL AVAILABLE MEN into service, the duty of leading the spectators fell into the hands of coeds. Female students eagerly took up the challenge and, adorned in skirts and school sweaters, rallied the stands with scripted and unscripted cheers.

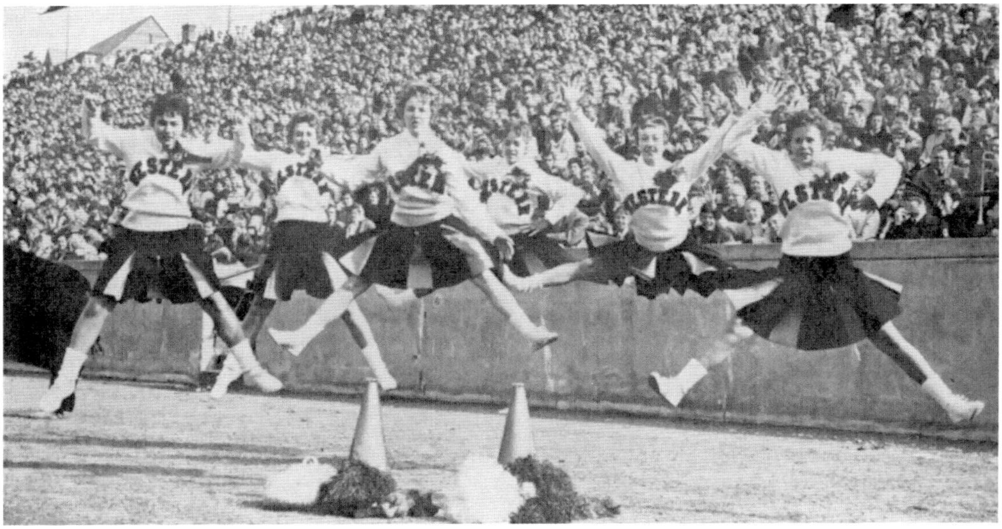

AS FOOTBALL FANS BECAME INCREASINGLY sophisticated, cheerleaders were no longer able to rely on simple yells and cheers to get the fans' attention. Soon jumps, pyramids, and other gymnastics turned the simple act of cheering into an athletic endeavor itself.

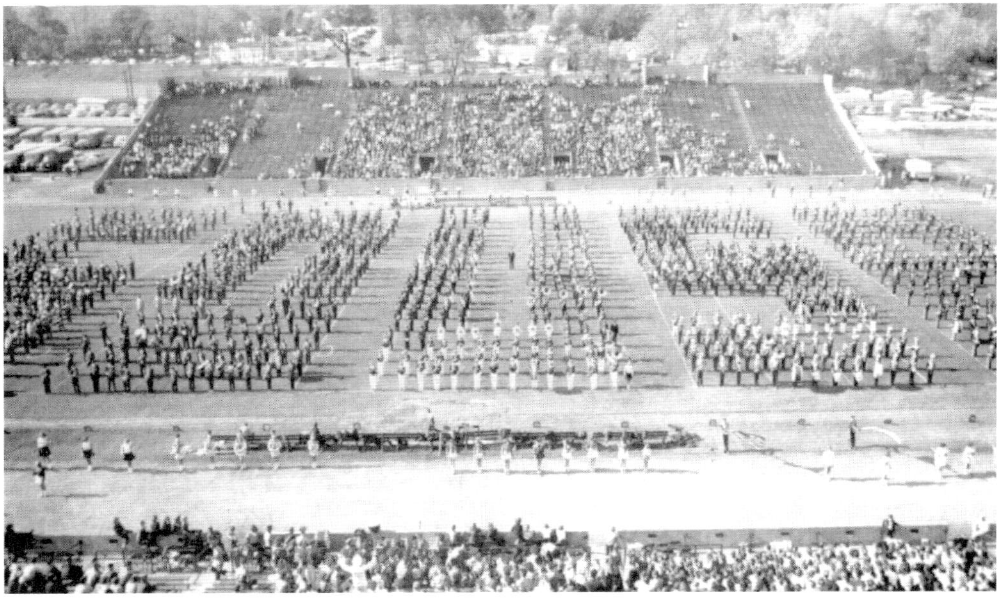

THE BAND PROVIDED THE FINAL PIECE OF THE football game day experience. Performing stirring marches as well as favorite contemporary tunes, Western's marching band was a key component to the halftime experience. In later years, it helped bolster the odd student body tradition of waving to Amtrak passenger trains that passed within site of the stadium during games.

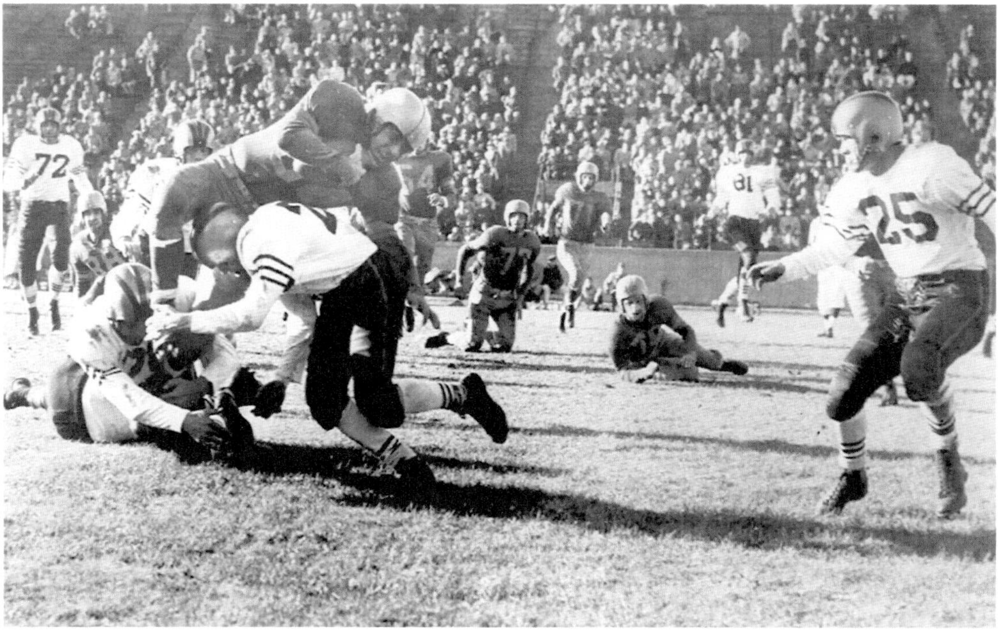

A NEW CHAPTER OF WESTERN FOOTBALL history began in late 1948 when it joined up with Butler University, University of Cincinnati, Ohio University, Wayne State University, and Western Reserve to form the Mid-American Conference (MAC). In its first year of competition, Western finished second in the league with a 3-1 MAC record, 6-3 overall.

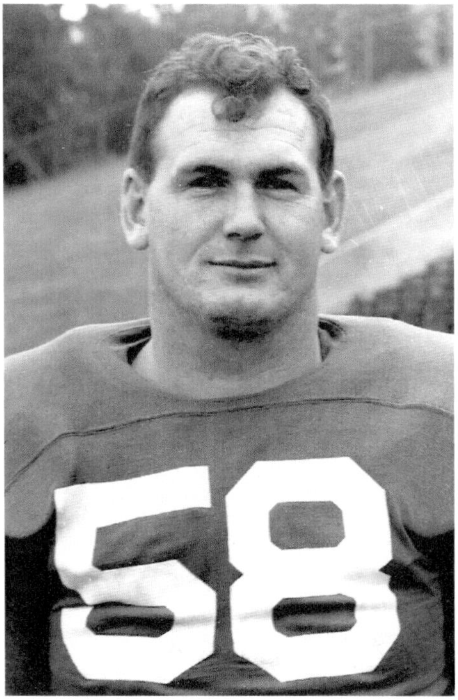

CENTER CHUCK SCHOOLMASTER MADE himself right at home in the new conference by earning All-MAC first-team honors in both 1948 and 1949. He became the first Bronco to earn the league honor by breaking open holes for star fullback Al Bush. He earned four letters while at Western.

WHEN IT CAME TO FOOTBALL LETTERS, NO ONE was more recognized than Art Gillespie. He earned five monograms between 1944 and 1948. He scored 15 touchdowns in his career and turned in some of the longest kickoff returns and rushing plays in school history.

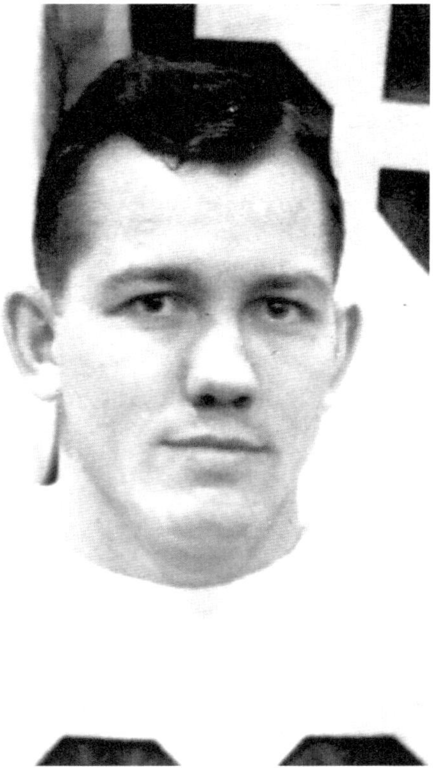

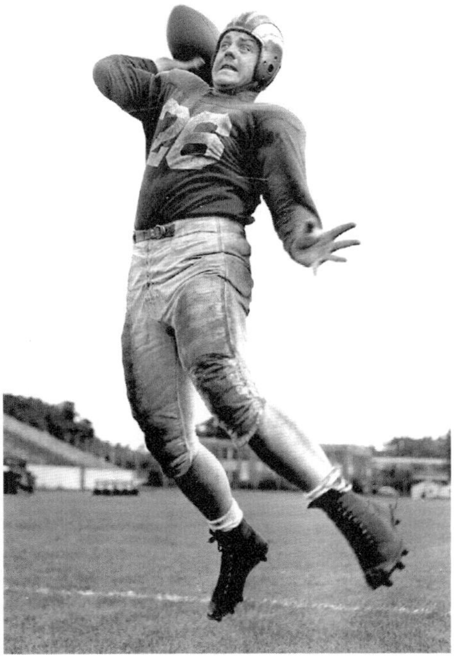

HEAVY GRADUATIONS BEGAN TO TAKE THEIR TOLL on the Western program in the early 1950s. The team managed to avoid losing seasons by going 4-4 in both the 1951 and 1952 seasons but could not avoid occupying the MAC cellar. Western was not without its stars, though. Quarterback Norm Harris compiled 2,064 yards of total offense and set new school standards for touchdown passes in a season (18) and career (25).

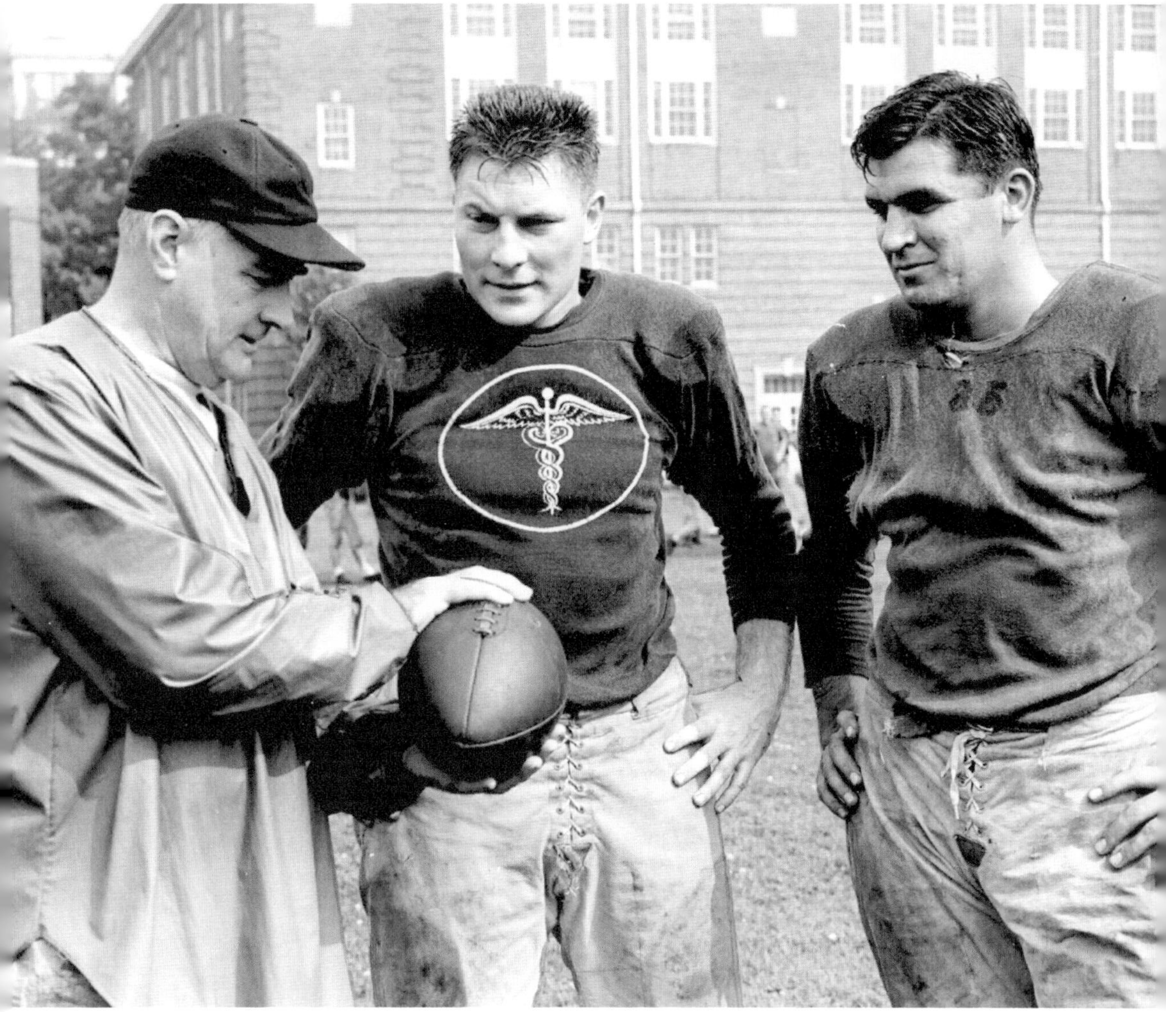

COACH JOHN GILL DECIDED TO HANG UP his whistle following the 1952 season. His departure from the football field did not send him far. He took over the duties of athletic director for the next 17 years. He was dubbed "Mr. Bronco" not just for his stellar playing career or his many years of service to the university. It was Gill who suggested the nickname Broncos for the sports teams. The name was approved and put into use in 1939. In later years, the John Gill Scholar Athlete Award was created in his honor. Gill remained one of Western's most vocal and visible supporters throughout his lifetime.

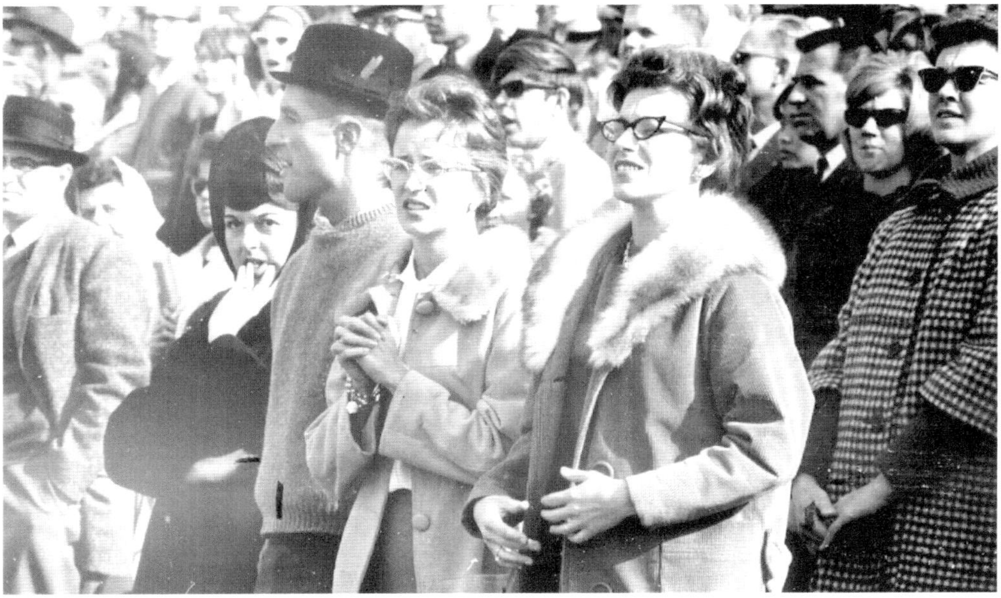

THE DEPARTURE OF GILL SAW DARK DAYS descend upon Bronco football for the rest of the decade. They struggled to get out of the conference basement while failing to record a winning season. Head coach Jack Petosky lasted just four years, compiling a dismal 8-25-2 record. Bronco fans were becoming increasingly impatient for success.

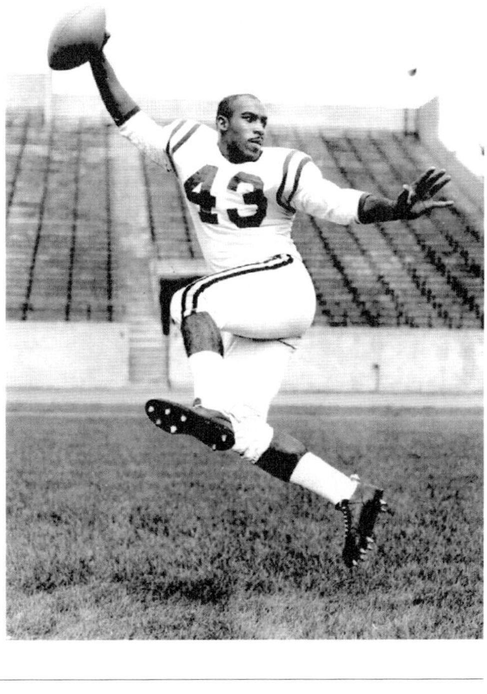

DESPITE THE BRONCOS' RECORD, THE BIGGEST game of the year was always the match against Central Michigan College of Education. A win there would make the season complete. In 1958, Lovell Coleman did everything he could to comply. He rushed for an amazing 279 yards against the Chips. Despite the effort, the Broncos fell one point short 33-32. Coleman finished the year with a record 1,258 yards and averaged over 6 yards per carry.

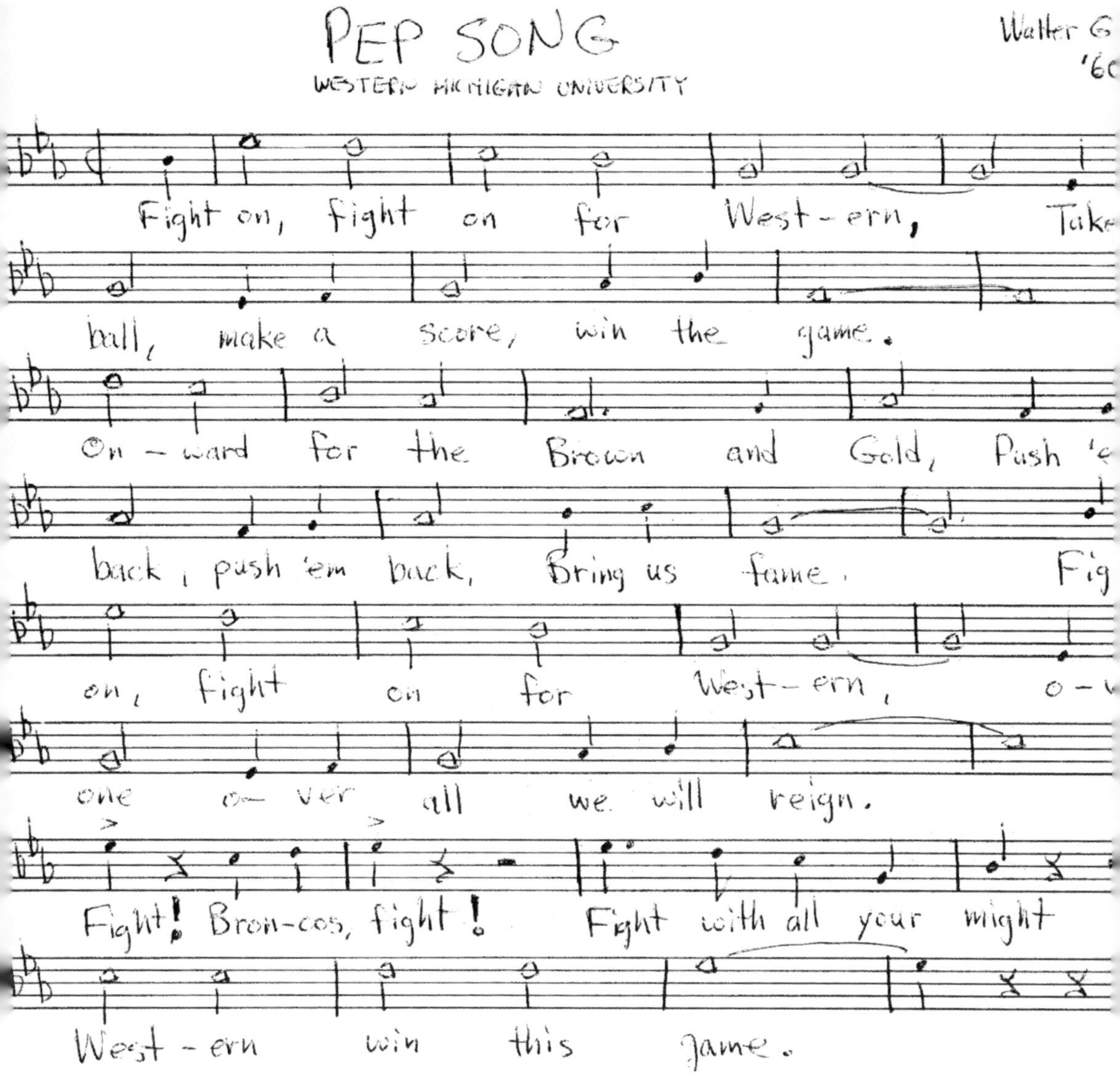

RESPONDING TO A CONTEST FOR A NEW SCHOOL fight song, sophomore physics student Walter Gilbert studied other popular fight songs before submitting his composition. "I . . . realized that good fight song lyrics mention the name of the school, the mascot, and the school colors," Gilbert says. His lyrics stayed with the formula and were quickly selected among many entries as Western's new fight song. For his effort Gilbert won a $25 prize. He also composed the school's alma mater. "It's perhaps ironic that the songs were officially adopted in 1961, the year after I graduated. Therefore, I have never heard them played on campus," Gilbert admits. (Courtesy of Walter Gilbert.)

2

Onward for the Brown and Gold

1961–1987

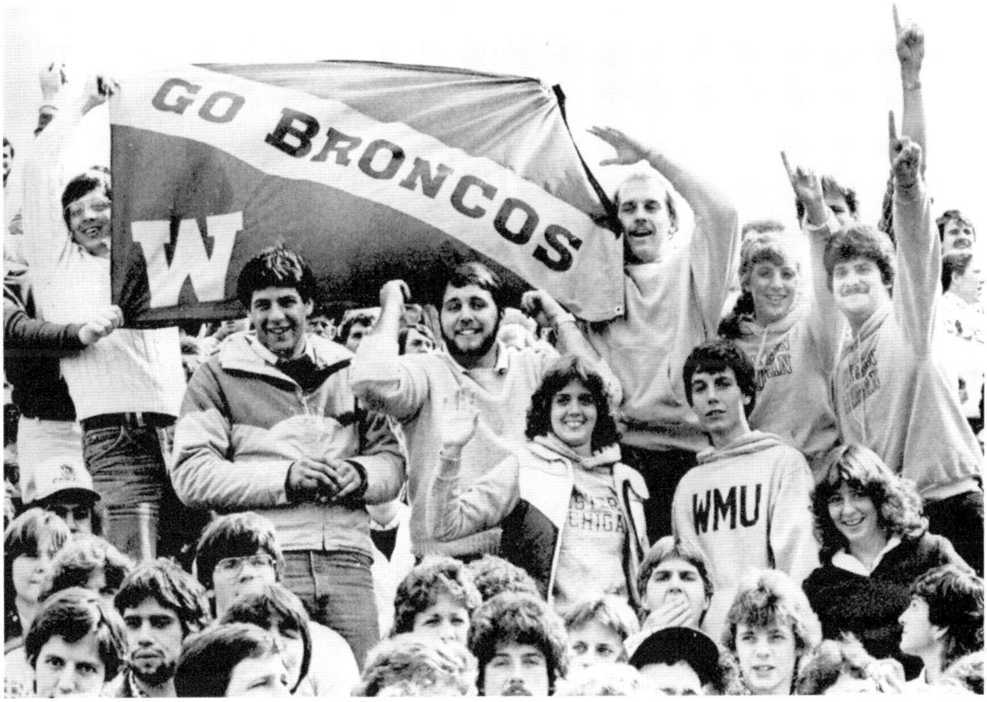

ATTITUDES WERE CHANGING ACROSS COLLEGE campuses through the 1960s and 1970s and Western Michigan University (WMU) was no exception. Protests over civil rights, foreign wars, and women's rights dominated the social agenda for undergraduates when they were not pursuing their educational goals. Still they found a rallying point each Saturday afternoon in the fall. When the Broncos played, the students showed up on Stadium Drive to show their support for the team. The Broncos responded with some of their greatest moments to date. WMU earned its first invitation to a postseason bowl and put together some of the most thrilling games and seasons ever witnessed. As American society was evolving and maturing, so was WMU football.

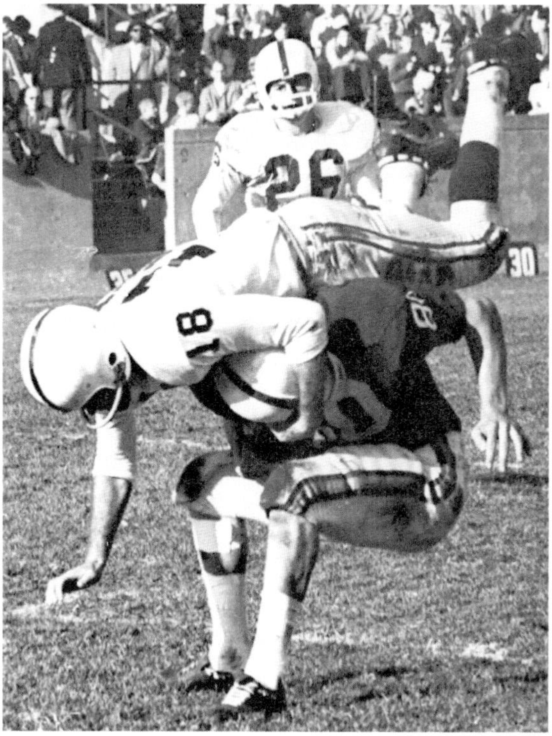

THE WMU TURNAROUND BECAME evident in 1961 when it assembled a fine 5-3-1 regular season record and a 4-1-1 conference tally. The only league loss was to eventual champion Bowling Green State University. Even their out-of-conference losses had a measure of understanding. The Broncos lost to a Utah State team that featured eventual NFL Hall of Famer Merlin Olsen.

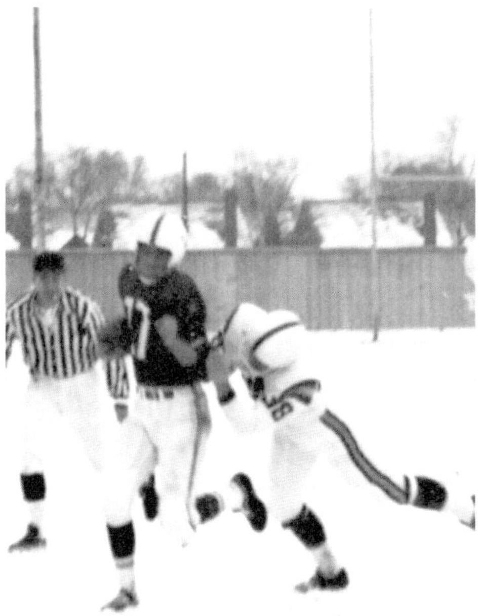

WMU WAS REWARDED FOR ITS SECOND-PLACE conference finish in 1961 with its first ever bowl game invitation. It accepted a bid to face New Mexico in the newly formed Aviation Bowl in snowy Dayton, Ohio. The game was designed to show off Dayton's history of powered flight but ended up showing the area's climatic shortcomings.

UNIVERSITY OF NEW MEXICO WENT UP EARLY with a powerful rushing attack and never looked back, but the Broncos battled nonetheless. Bob White scored WMU's first touchdown on a short plunge. Quarterback Ed Chlebek completed 18 passes for 207 yards, including a touchdown pass. New Mexico took advantage of Broncos turnovers, however, to claim a 28-12 win in what turned out to be the only Aviation Bowl competition.

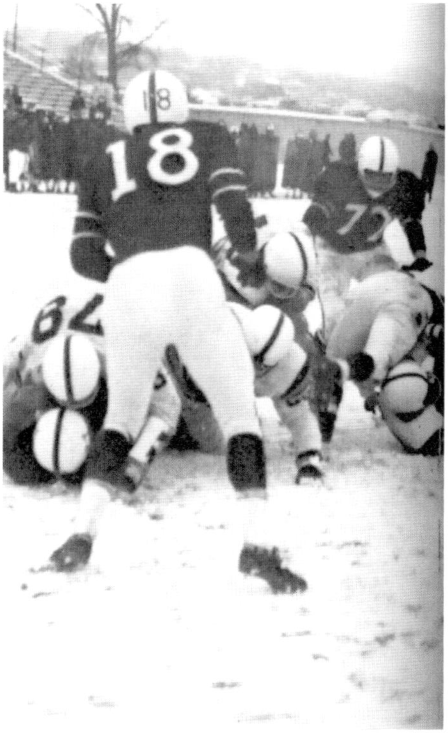

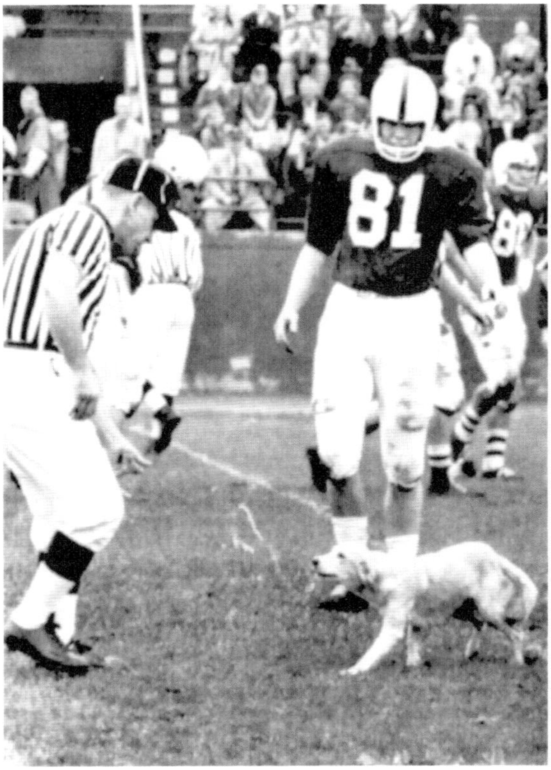

AS QUICKLY AS WMU'S HOPES were raised by its first bowl invitation, the Broncos abruptly returned to the dog days as they fell right back toward the bottom of the MAC standings. Things reached a head in 1963 when the Broncos won just two games and suffered their 10th nonwinning season in the past 12 seasons. A change had to be made.

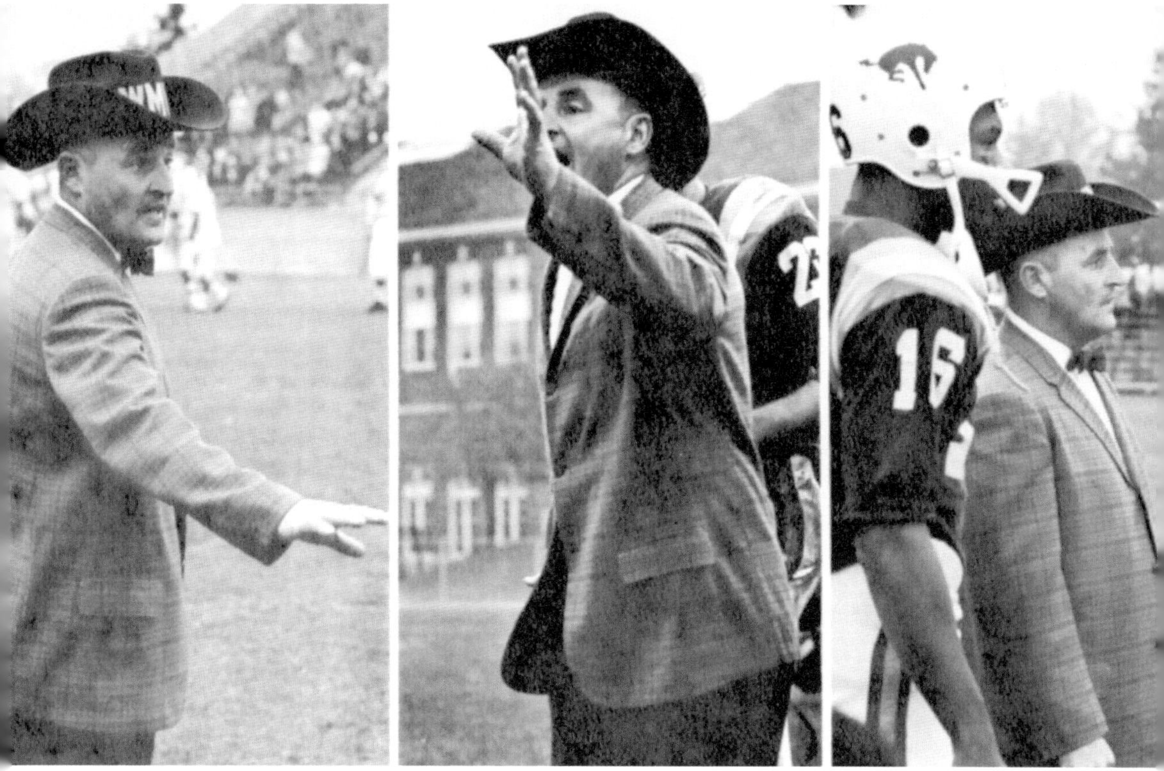

IN HOPES OF REVIVING ITS FLAGGING PROGRAM, WMU hired Bill Doolittle, a fiery former Ohio State quarterback who learned his tutoring skills as an offensive coordinator at Army. His resume included several high schools in Michigan. Sporting an omnipresent cowboy hat and bow tie, Doolittle's personality and enthusiasm showed through, and he quickly endeared himself to the Bronco fans and elicited support from his players. Doolittle's team showed immediate progress in 1964 with a season-opening victory at Louisville, but it struggled the rest of the year to end with a 3-6 record. But losing seasons would be the exception rather than the norm during the Doolittle era. Doolittle had the resources of a new tool at his disposal. Beginning in 1964, WMU offered full-ride scholarships to cover an athlete's room and board as well as all tuition, fees, and books.

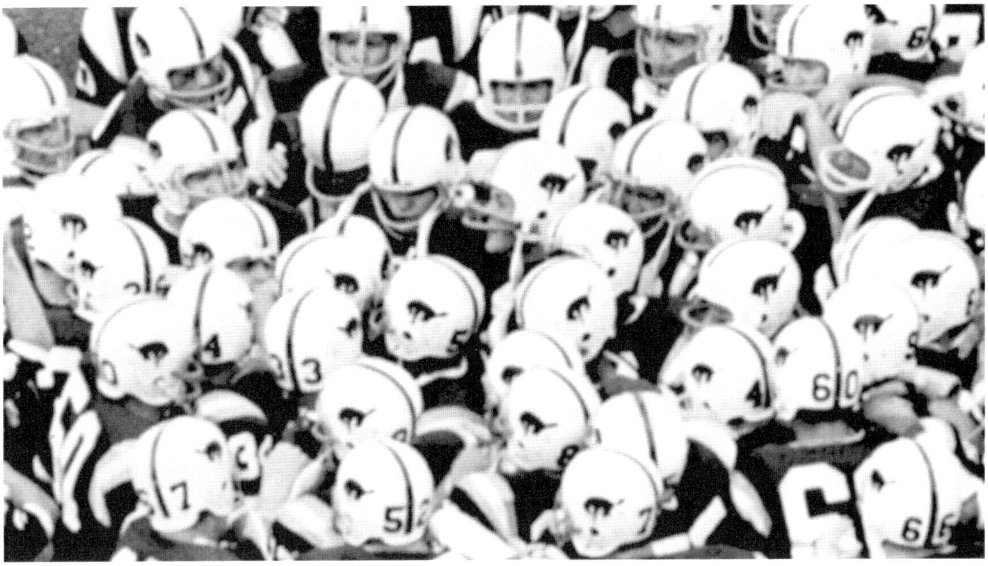

WMU SHOWED THE RESILIENCE IN 1966 when, after losing its MAC opener to Miami University, it went on to win five straight league victories and claimed its first ever share of the MAC conference title. They finished the year with an overall record of 7-3. The campaign success earned coach Doolittle the title of MAC Coach of the Year.

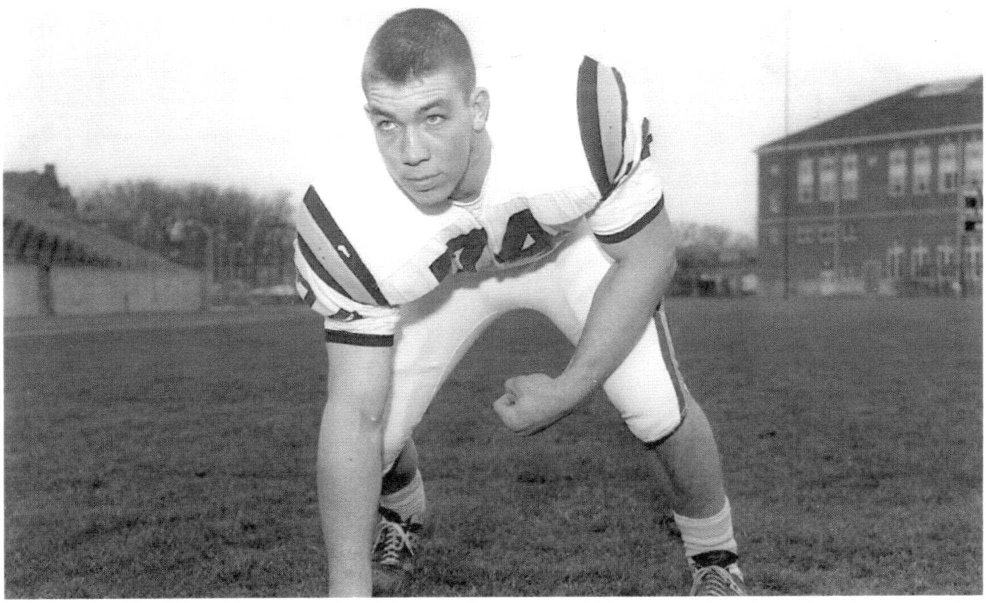

MUCH OF WMU'S RESURGENCE ON THE FIELD was credited to tackle Bob Rowe. He was voted the MAC Most Valuable Player two years straight (1965 and 1966), an unprecedented feat for an offensive lineman. He was also honored nationally as a second-team All-American. Rowe went on to a successful professional career.

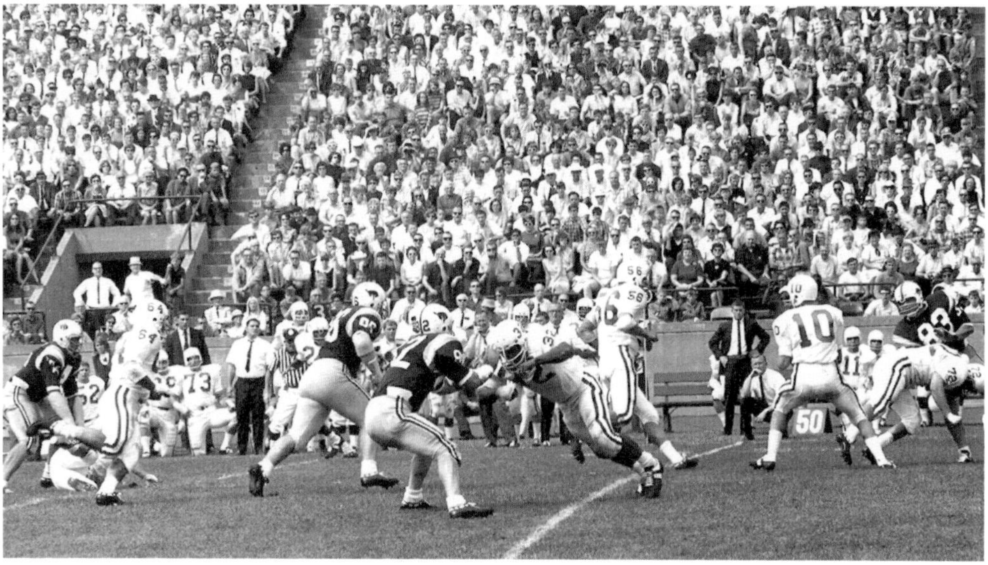

WMU'S RETURN TO COMPETITIVENESS IN the MAC was reflected in the fan support for the team. New records were being set in attendance as more fans flocked to Waldo Stadium to watch the action. The all-time home-record attendance mark was shattered against Miami University in 1967 when 22,093 showed up, only to have that mark broken again two games later with 22,806 on hand for the Kent State game.

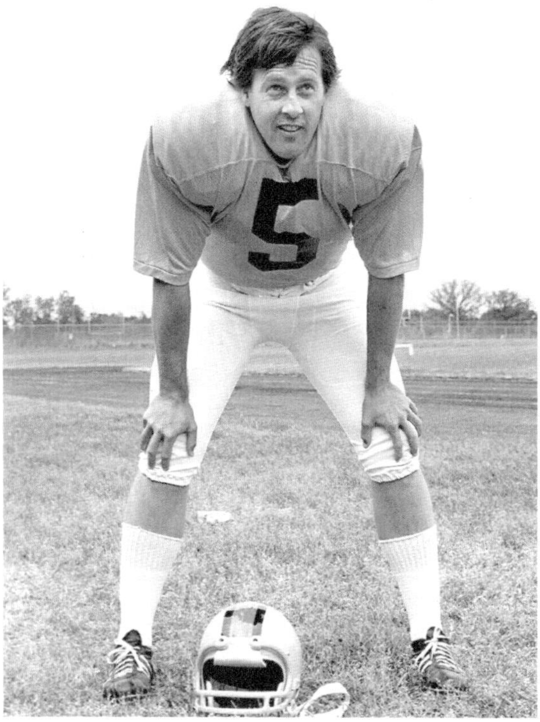

IF EVER THERE WAS A POSTER BOY for WMU's walk-on program, Dale Livingston would be it. After arriving on campus without a scholarship, Livingston proved his skills to the coaches and became one of WMU's greatest kickers. Livingston set team records in career punting average, game punting average, and booted a team-record tying 86-yard punt against Brigham Young University in 1966.

WESTERN EMBRACED A NO-HOLDS-barred game plan, allowing more players to steal the spotlight. End Greg Flaska (right) grabbed nine passes in a single game against Toledo in 1969. On the other side of the ball, defensive back Vern Davis (left) swatted away 13 passes that same year, giving the Broncos a balanced pair of stars.

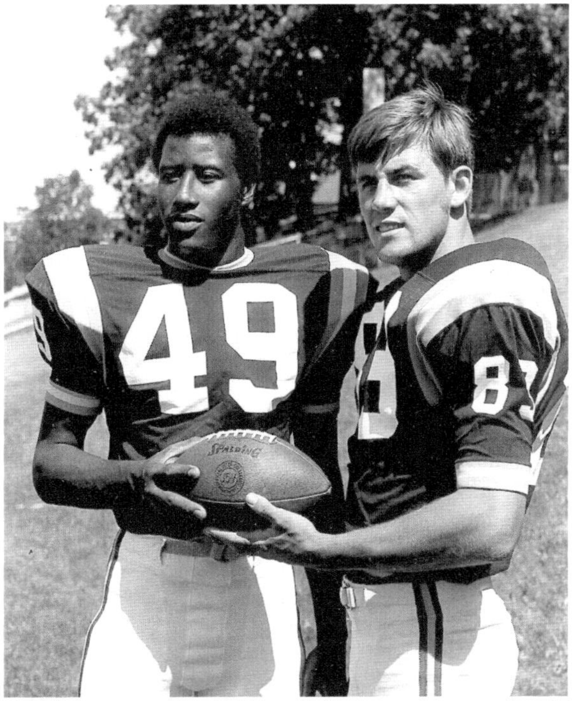

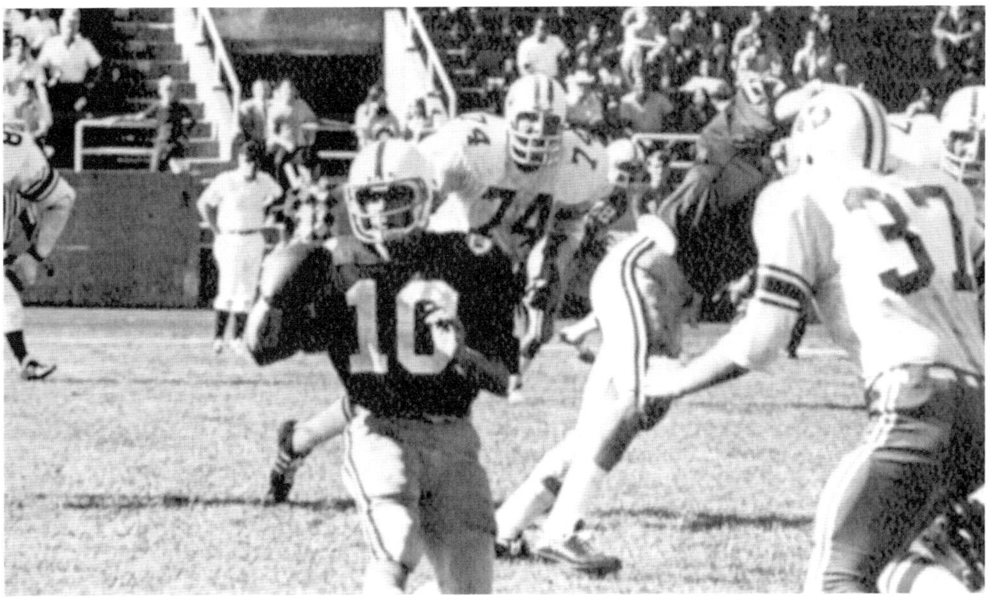

COACH BILL DOOLITTLE MADE CHANGES TO the offensive plan in 1970 when he installed the "Houston Veer" offense. The more run-and-gun approach proved to be a wise move as WMU's offense exploded, and the Broncos had three straight seven-win seasons, losing just one nonconference game in that stretch. Their offense averaged 35 points in their seven wins.

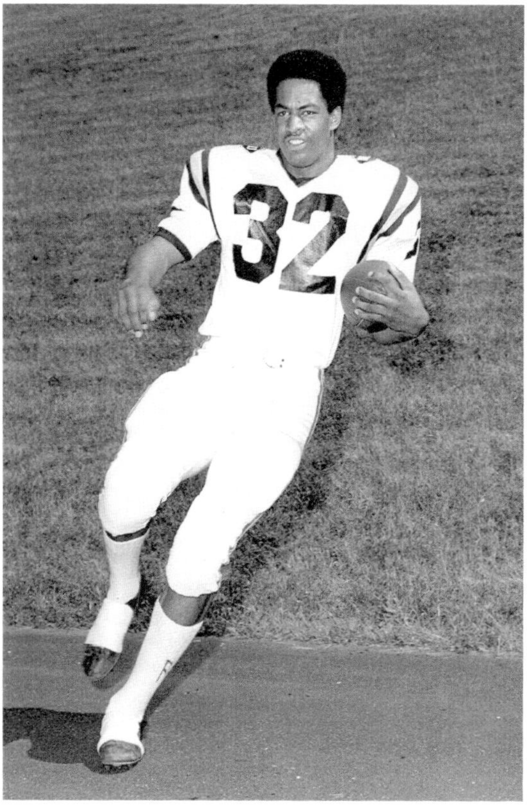

THE HERO OF WMU'S REVAMPED ATTACK was fullback Roger "Ramjet" Lawson. His pounding runs covered 1,250 yards in 1970, giving him the best per-carry average in the nation with 7.2 yards per touch. Riding on Lawson's back, the Broncos finished 10th in the nation in total rushing. Lawson finished his career as WMU's first career 2,000-yard rusher.

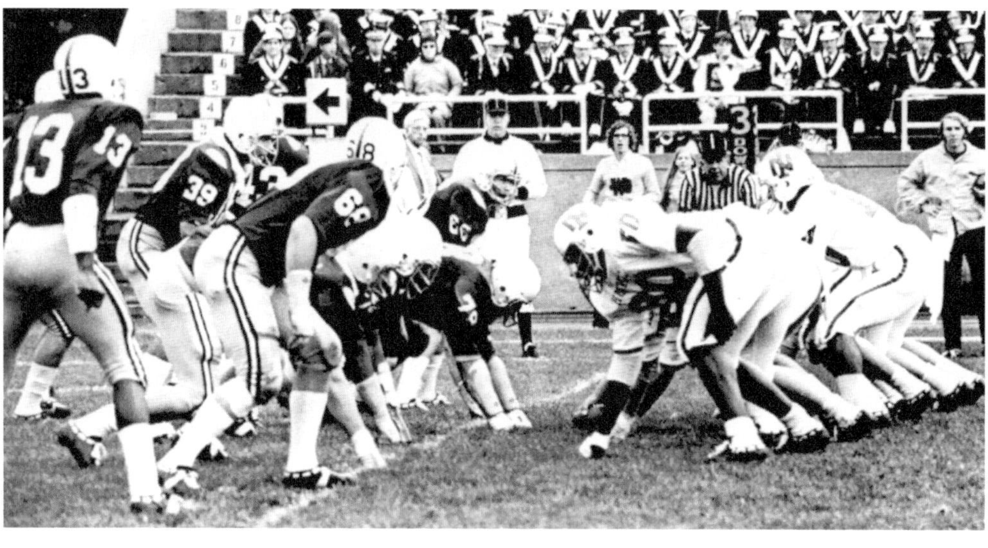

ALTHOUGH WMU'S OFFENSE WAS DOING WELL, it was the defense that received national accolades. The 1971 squad ranked 4th in the nation in rushing defense and 11th in total defense. The 1971 team was even more impressive, finishing second in the nation in stopping the run by allowing under 90 yards per game.

WITH WMU'S OFFENSE NOW IN GEAR, THE BRONCOS still needed some starring performances from their defensive squad. Linebacker Greg Igaz was more than happy to serve in that role against Brigham Young University. He recorded 25 tackles in that game and single-handedly helped shut down the Cougar attack.

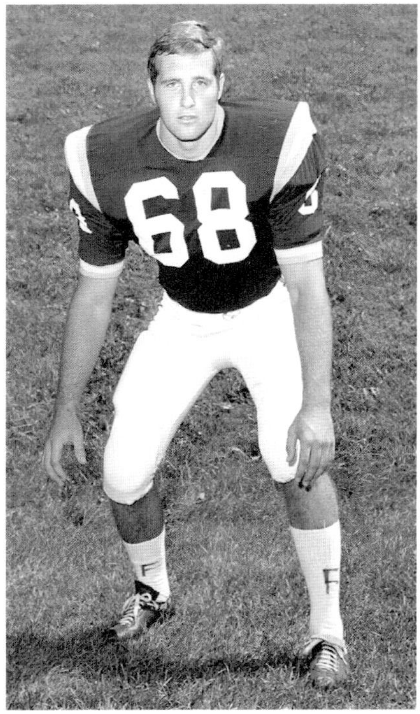

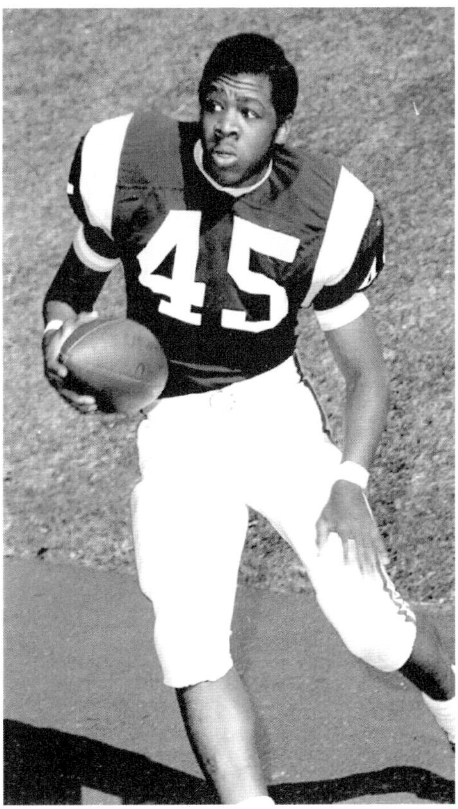

IT WAS BECOMING MORE COMMON TO SEE Bronco names appearing near the top of national performance lists. Running back Larry Cates's ability to find the end zone placed him 16th in the nation in scoring in 1971. He also earned the first of two All-MAC first-team honors that year.

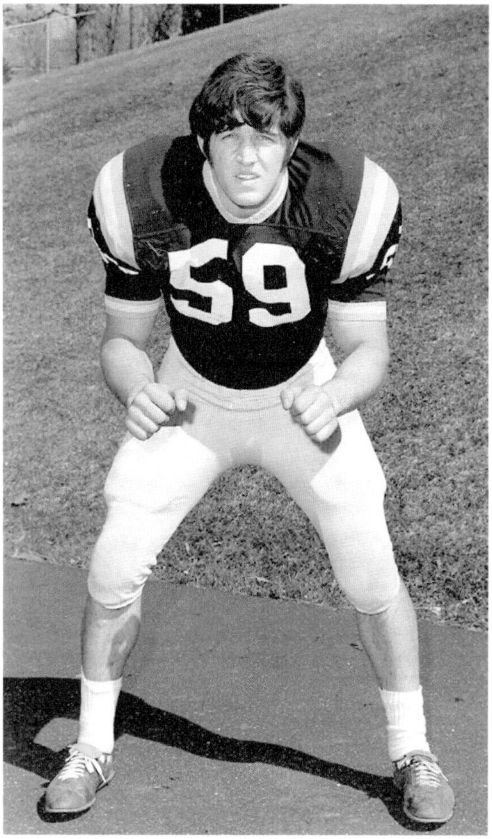

THERE WAS SIMPLY NO BETTER DEFENSIVE player in the MAC in the early 1970s than Dominic Riggio. He was voted the league's Defensive Player of the Year in 1972. The next season, he recorded 18 tackles for loss that year, including 5 in one game. He was twice named the team's MVP.

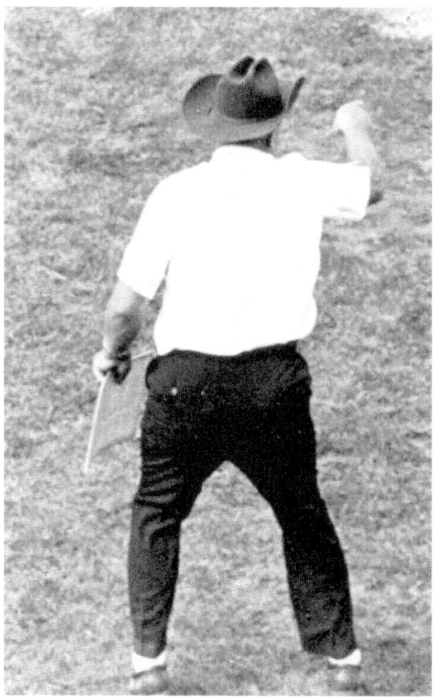

COACH BILL DOOLITTLE'S BRONCOS WERE FINDING success a bit frustrating to achieve. They won a respectable seven games in 1972 and six games in 1973 but could not finish higher than third in the conference. Things fells off in 1974 when the team went winless in the MAC.

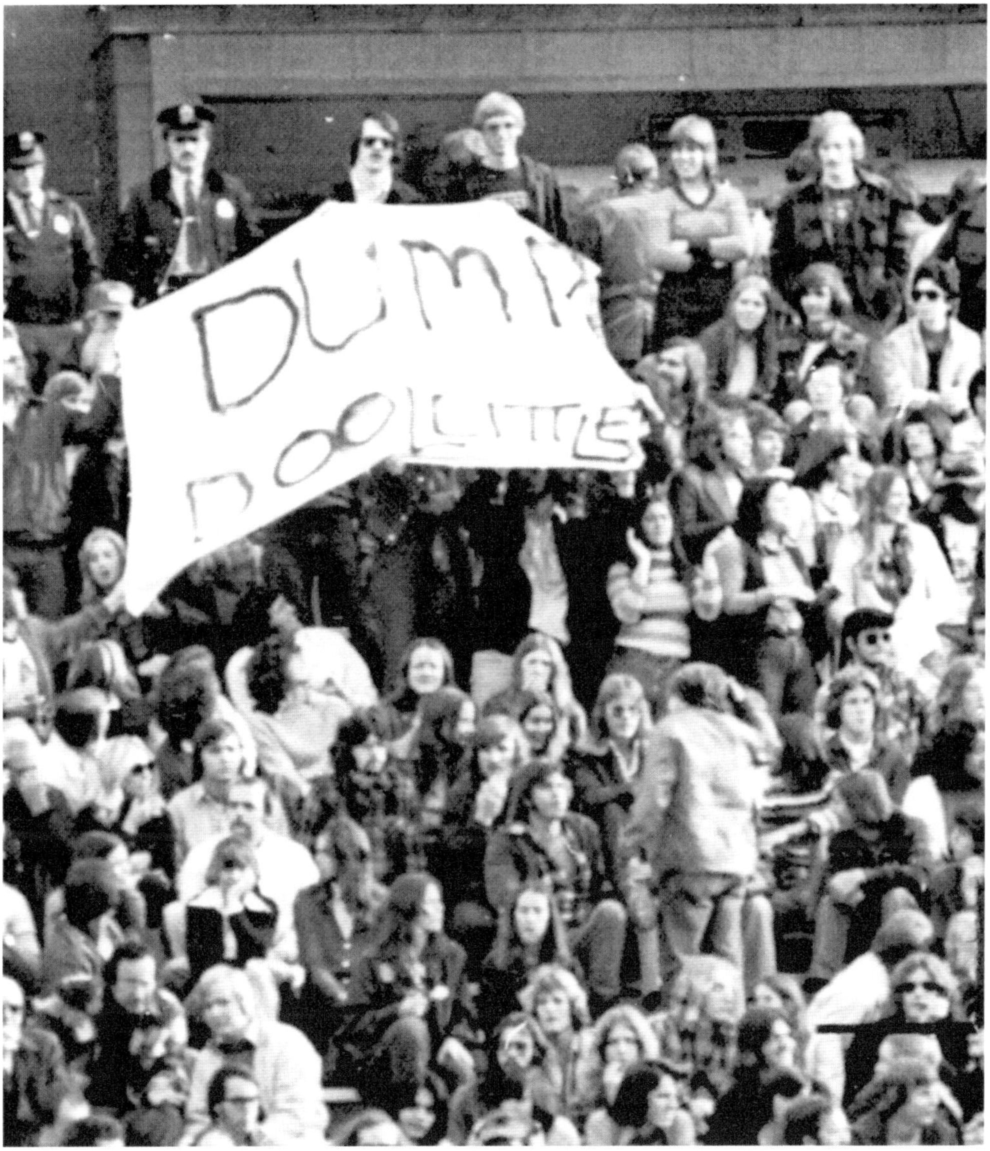

AS QUICKLY AS BRONCO FANS RALLIED BEHIND Doolittle in the mid-1960s, they turned on him when things got rough in the mid-1970s. The impressive list of talented individual players and stellar squad statistics on both sides of the ball were not reflected in the team's conference finishes. Although it won 65 percent of its games in the 1970s, WMU never finished higher than third in the final MAC standings. Impatient for better results, catcalls came out of the stands for changes at the top. Doolittle stepped aside in 1974 following a disastrous 3-8 season.

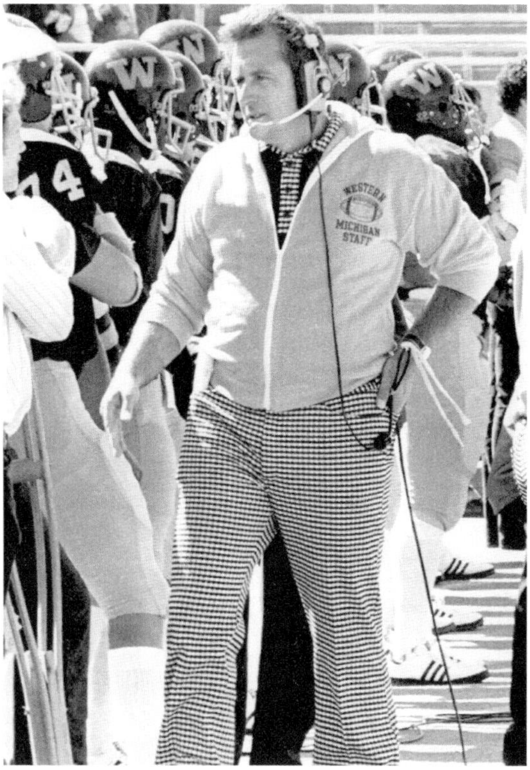

THE ARRIVAL OF ELLIOT UZELAK TO GUIDE the Broncos did little to change their fortunes immediately. The team lost its first 10 games of 1975 to extend its worst losing streak ever to 14 games. The Broncos finished 1975 on a high note by defeating Eastern Michigan University 24-14 to avoid a winless season.

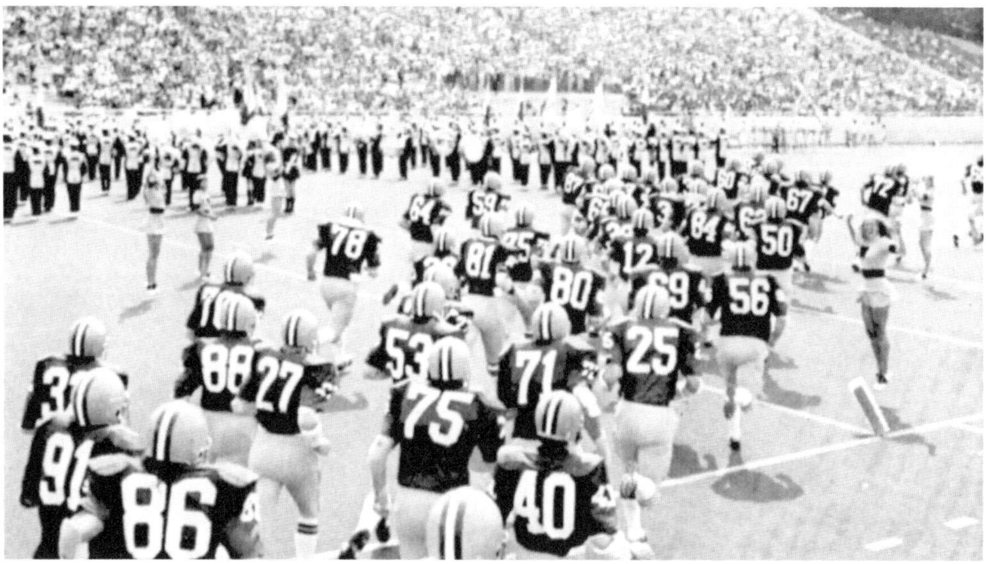

THINGS STARTED SHAKY FOR THE BRONCOS in 1976 as they began the season with a 2-3 record, but then coach Uzelak got things clicking. They won five of their next six games and finished up with a 7-4 record. For his marshaling efforts, Uzelak was named the MAC Coach of the Year.

WMU GOT BACK TO WHAT it did best by assembling a stingy defense that crushed any opponent charge. In 1976, the team ranked first in the nation in team pass defense by allowing only 78.5 yards per game and ninth in the nation in rushing defense with 285 yards per game.

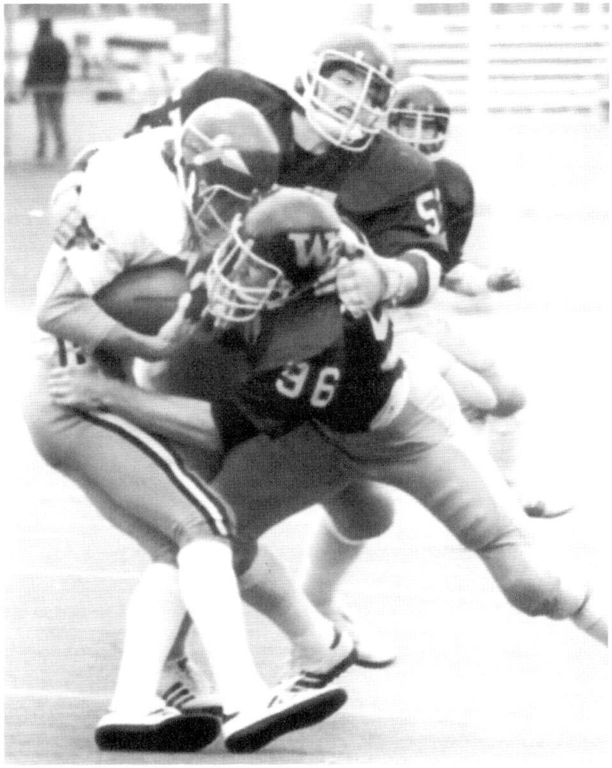

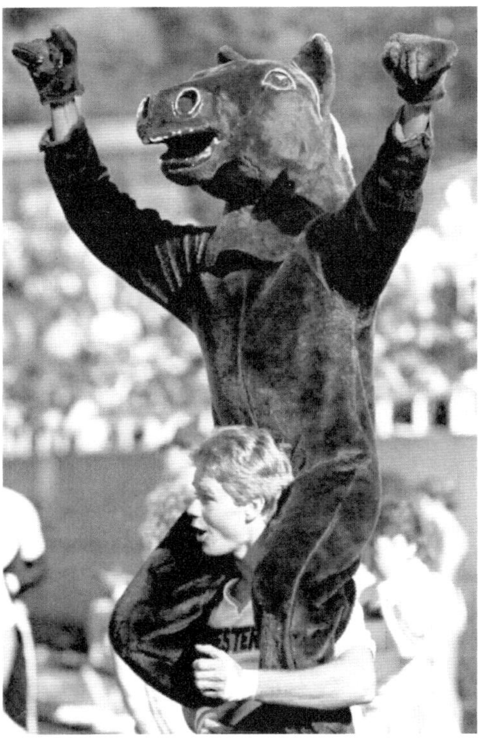

THE RANKING WAS NOT ACHIEVED THROUGH easy opponents either. WMU faced off against foes such as the University of Minnesota, playing the Gophers close in both 1976 and 1977. A pair of fourth-quarter Gopher touchdowns broke open a tight battle in 1976 that the University of Minnesota won 20-10, while the Gophers relied on a last-second field goal to pull out a 10-7 victory in 1977.

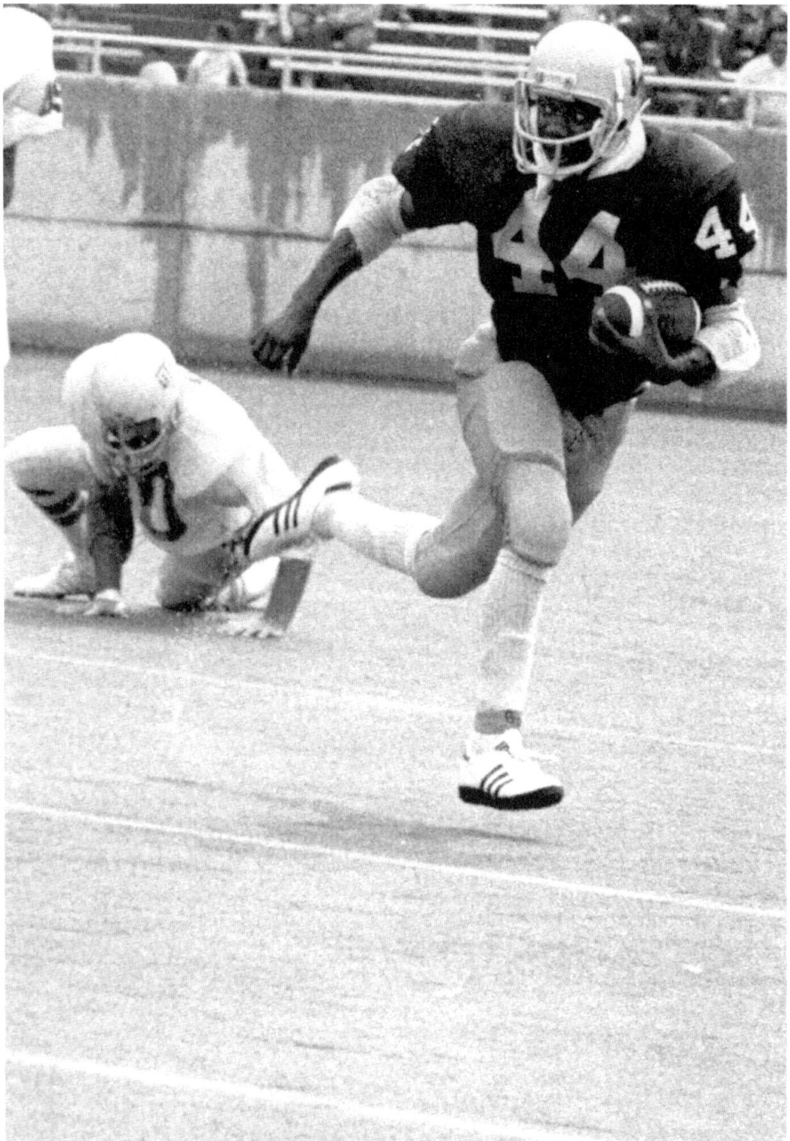

JEROME PERSELL JUMPED RIGHT OUT OF the blocks, rushing for 241 yards in his sophomore season opener against Eastern Michigan University. From there, he became the Broncos' most potent offensive weapon in decades. By the time 1976 was completed, Persell had amassed 1,505 yards, second only to the University of Pittsburgh's Heisman Trophy winner Tony Dorsett. His 19 touchdowns tied a school record that had stood for 60 years. The following year, he did it again. He ranked third in the nation in rushing behind Heisman Trophy winner Earl Campbell and Oklahoma State University's Terry Miller. When his career at WMU was over, Persell become the third runner in NCAA Division 1-A history to rush for over 4,000 yards in just three years; he had three MAC Offensive Player of the Year awards, Bronco MVP trophies, and two All-America honors filling his trophy case.

ERIC MANNS WAS WMU'S DIFFERENCE maker on defense in 1978. He set a new standard for tackles with 186 that season. In one game against Ball State University, Manns totaled 100 interception return yards. He earned what would be the second of his three All-MAC awards that season as the Broncos had a strong seven-win season.

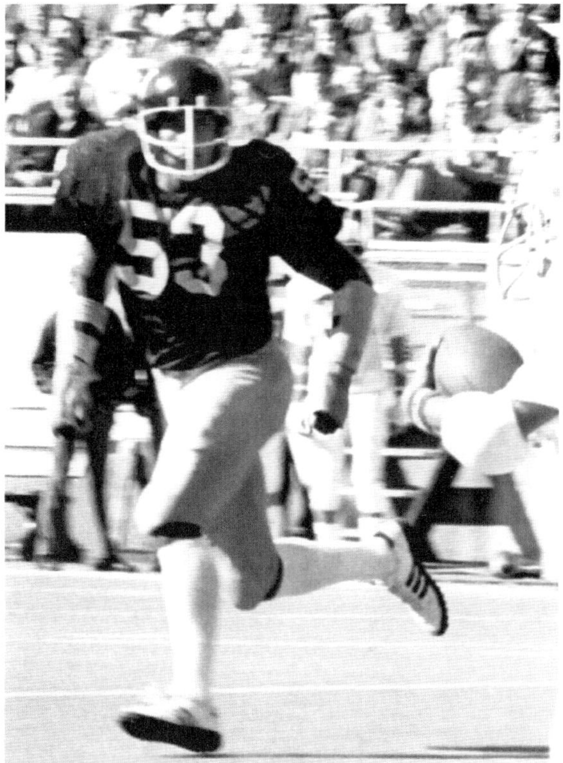

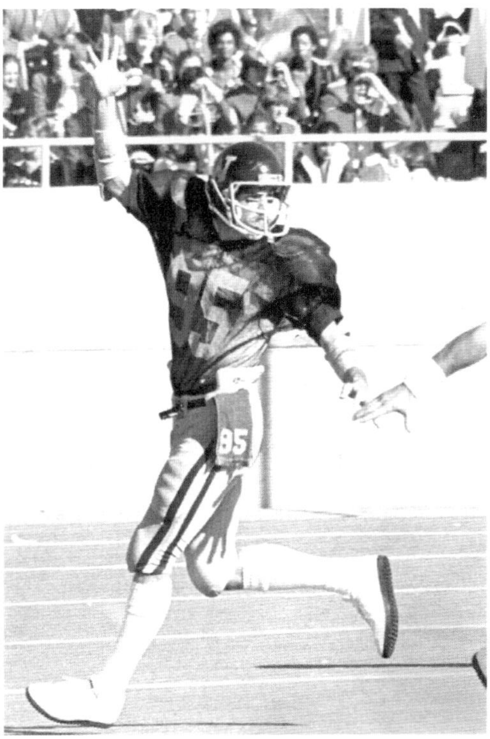

END BOB PHILLIPS WON TWO ALL-MAC first-team honors in 1981 and 1982, but his biggest day came against Ball State in the 1981 contest at Waldo Stadium. In that game, Phillips set a new team record with 203 yards in receptions as the Broncos defeated the Cardinals 14-3.

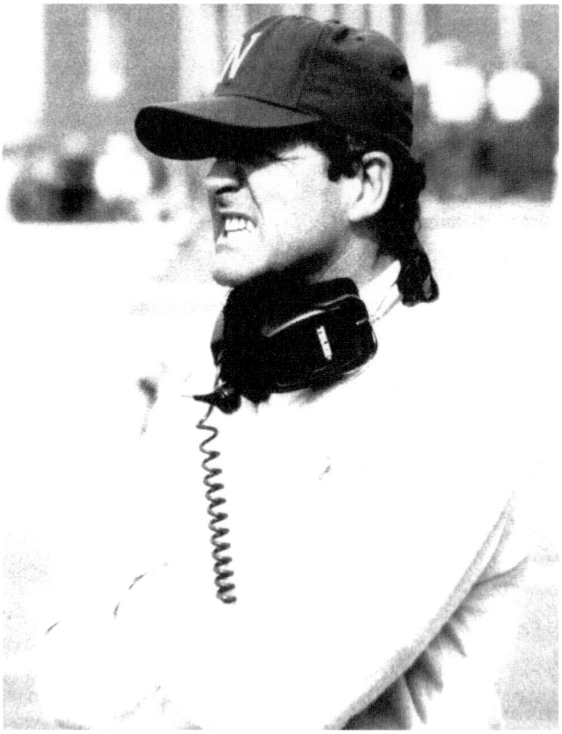

THE YEAR 1982 WAS A STANDOUT year for WMU. Under first-year head coach Jack Harbaugh, the Broncos completed a 7-2-2 record, their best record in 40 years, and nearly claimed the MAC title, finishing second. Their two ties came against their biggest in-state foes, Central Michigan University and Eastern Michigan University.

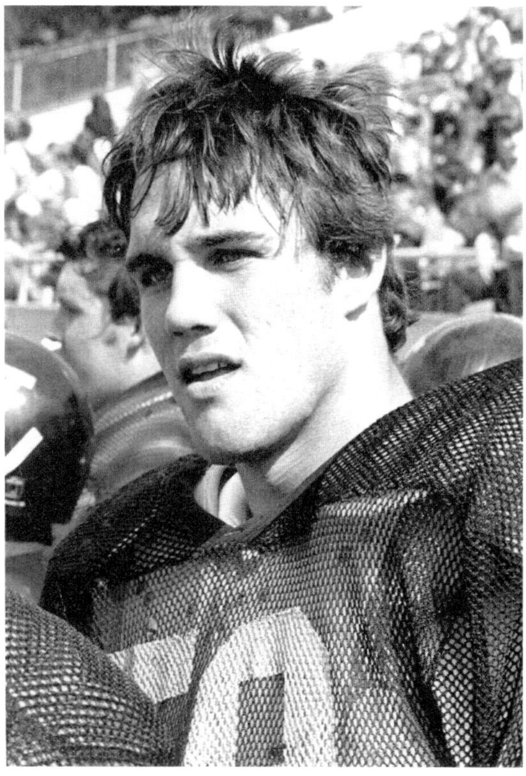

WMU'S 1982 OFFENSIVE LINE WAS anchored by center Matt Meares. The hole maker was named to the Football Coaches All-NCAA 1-AA team and led the Broncos to a second-place finish in their conference.

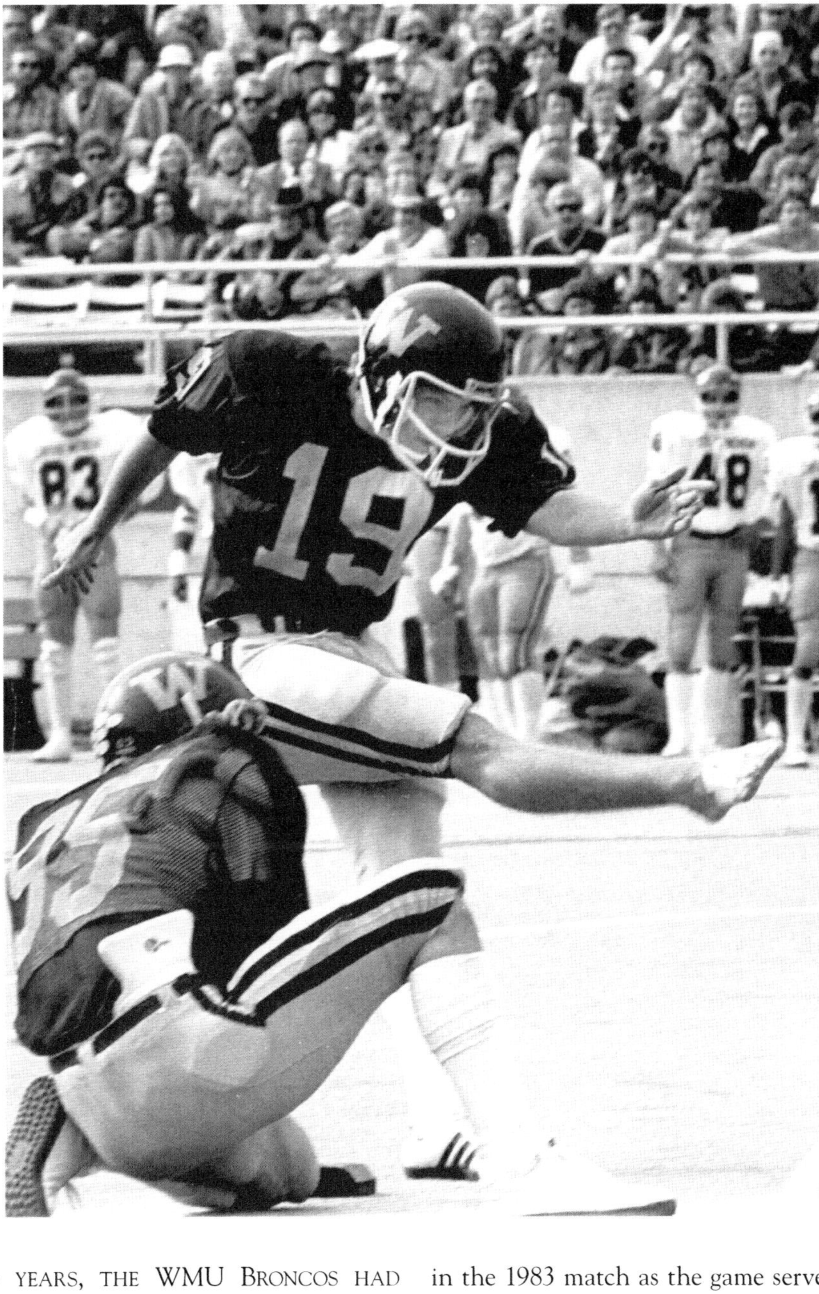

FOR 43 YEARS, THE WMU BRONCOS HAD learned to dread any trip down to Oxford, Ohio, to play Miami University. Although the Broncos had been able to claim victories over Miami during those years, not once in any of their 19 visits were the Broncos able to play on Miami's home turf and return home with a victory. Miami had extra motivation in the 1983 match as the game served as the dedication match for its new Yager Stadium. It was a tight battle all afternoon with Miami holding an 18-17 lead in the game's final seconds. On the final play, kicker Mike Prindle connected on a 47-yard field goal to give the long-suffering Broncos a party-crashing 20-18 win.

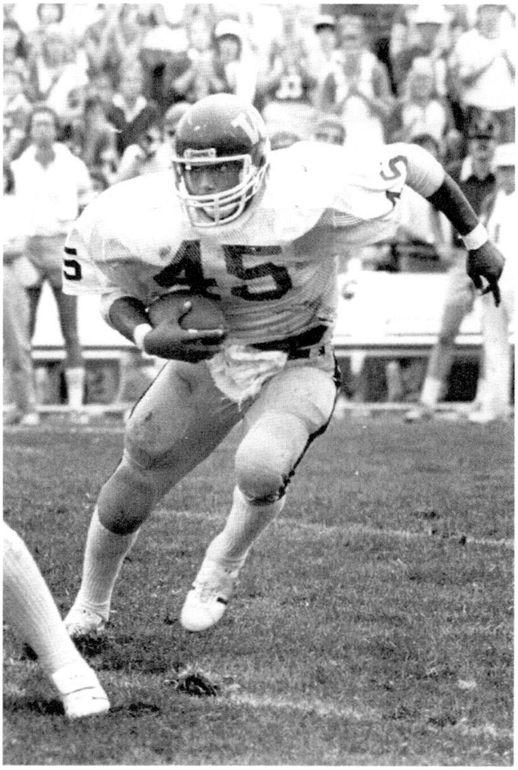

SHAWN FAULKNER GAVE WMU ONE OF its best rushing attacks ever. In 1983, he averaged 151.6 yards per game, good for the second-best average in the nation. He also ranked third in the country in all-purpose yards and was easily named the team's MVP that year.

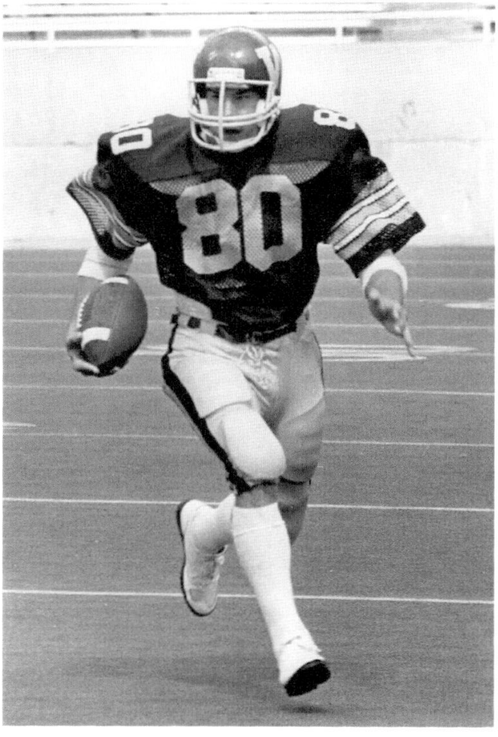

WMU'S HOPES FOR THE FUTURE WERE confirmed with the 1983 performance of tight end Kelly Spielmaker. In a key conference game against the University of Toledo, he hauled in 12 passes for 186 yards. He was named the MAC Freshman of the Year that season. He finished his career with 140 catches for 1,747 yards.

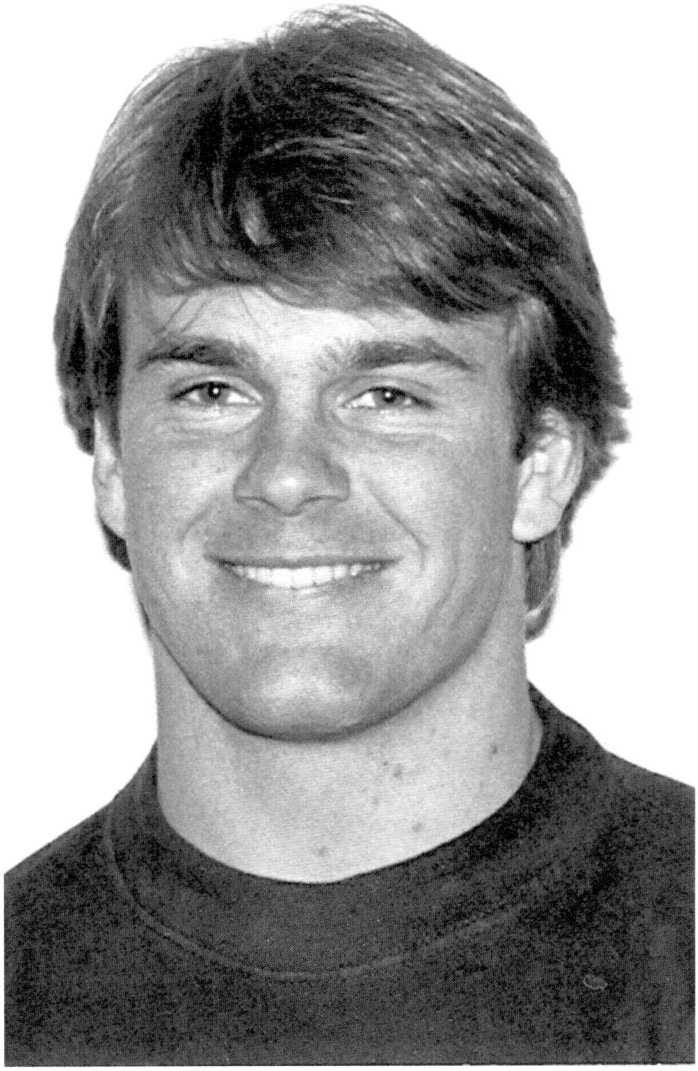

JOHN OFFERDAHL DID NOT DRAW MUCH attention when he first arrived on campus. As an undersized walk-on linebacker, he impressed coaches enough during fall camp to earn a full scholarship and elevate himself to a starting role in the season opener. By the time his career at WMU was over, Offerdahl had set a MAC career record for tackles with 694 and was tabbed as the MAC Player of the Year in 1985. He also established team records for forced fumbles and recorded over 23 tackles in a game three times. Twice he was selected to an All-America team. But Offerdahl's heroics did not stop when he left Kalamazoo. His dramatic goal line stop of Heisman Trophy winner Bo Jackson was the highlight of the Senior Bowl, and he went on to an eight-year career in the NFL, earning five Pro Bowl nods.

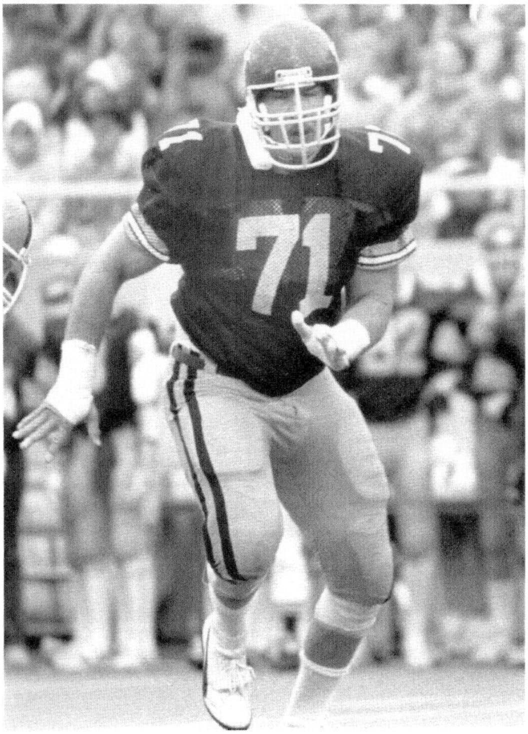

THE BRONCO DEFENSE WAS A POWERFUL force in 1986 thanks to the talents of defensive tackle Mike Garalczyk. He established a new record with 45 tackles for loss that season. His talents were recognized by the conference when he was named MAC Defensive Player of the Year. He set a new team career-position standard with 302 tackles in his career.

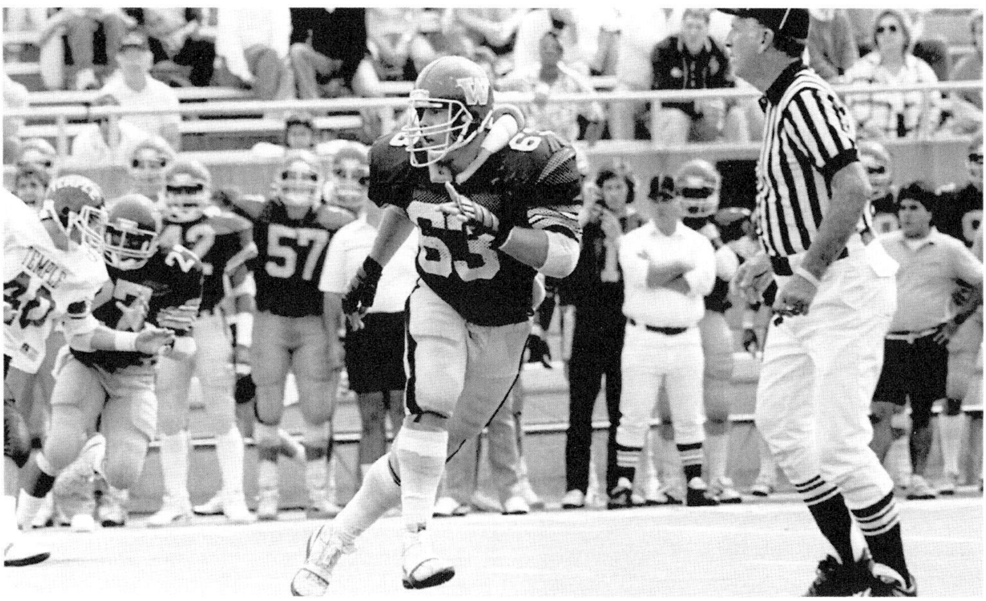

WMU HOSTED TEMPLE UNIVERSITY IN 1986, and despite a valiant effort, the Broncos were crushed 49-17. The record books will not show the loss, however. An NCAA investigation revealed Temple had used an illegal player, and the Owls were forced to forfeit the game. It is the only forfeited game in Bronco history.

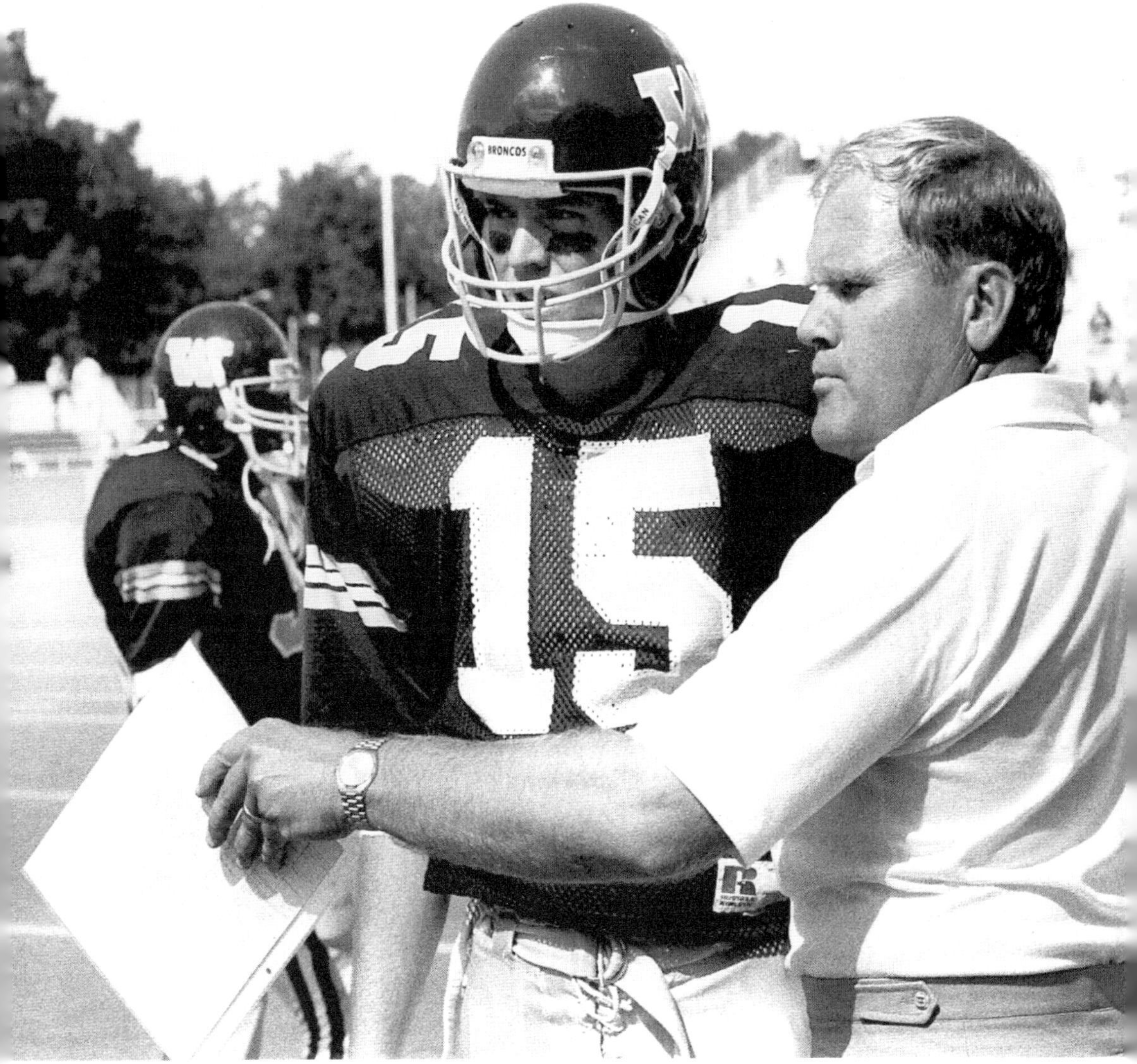

EAGER TO RETURN WMU TO THE TOP OF THE MAC, the university undertook a search for a new coach before the 1987 season. Its search took it to Al Molde, a stocky mentor with 16 years of experience behind him. His previous stints had taken him from Sioux Falls College to Central Missouri State University and Eastern Illinois University, and he brought along a staff that boasted a combined 100 years of working together. At Eastern Illinois, Molde had earned Coach of the Year honors. Molde oversaw one of the most dynamic periods in WMU football history. He installed a new professional-set offensive formation that relied on a one–running back set and emphasized the passing game. The new wide-open format allowed the school to put the spotlight on its talented quarterbacks and receivers and put many of WMU's passing records at risk.

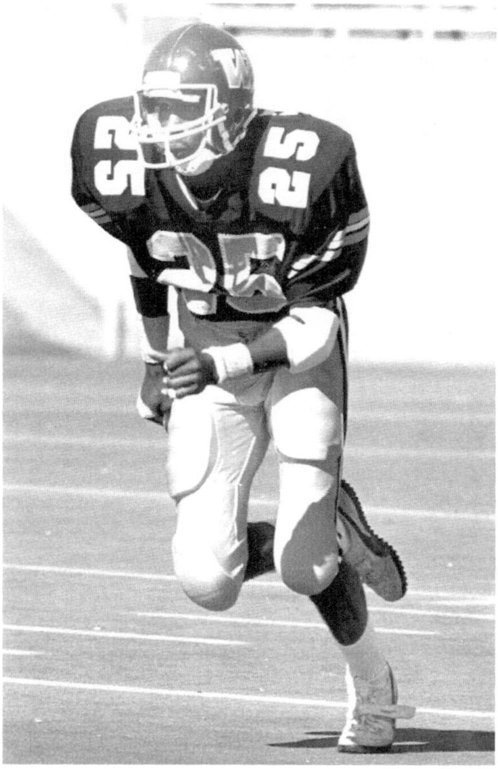

THE NEW AERIAL ATTACK ALLOWED TRACK star Jamie Hence to become a vital part of WMU's offensive attack. In 1987, he established new records by catching 50 passes for 828 yards. He also led the MAC with six touchdown passes. In the season finale against Ohio University, Hence caught a league-record 16 passes.

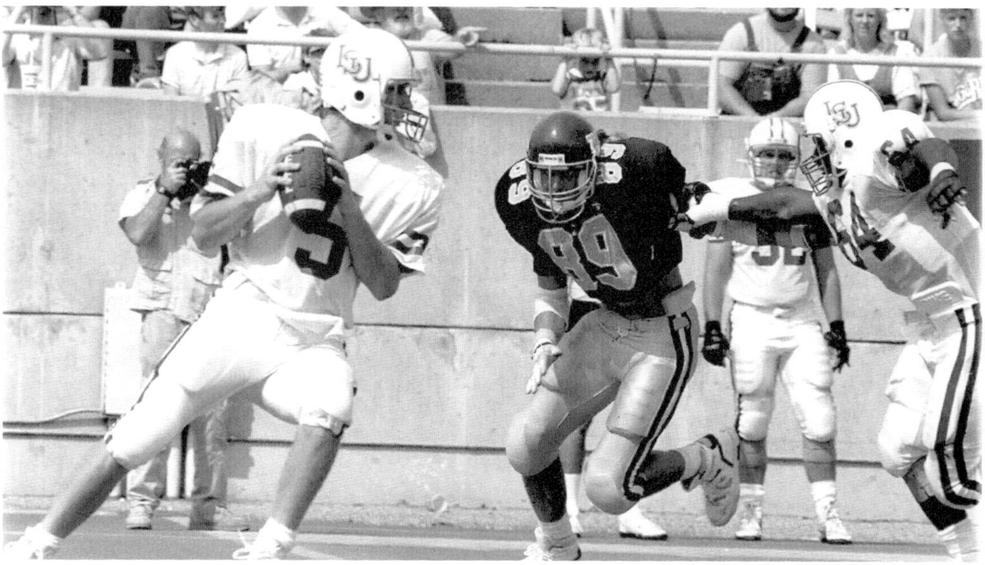

LINEBACKER JOEL SMEENGE MADE SURE THE 1987 WMU offense did not steal all the headlines. As a sophomore, he recorded 80 tackles, including 15 tackles for loss, sending the opposition back 76 yards for his efforts. He was named to the All-MAC first team, the first of three such honors bestowed on him.

3

Over One, Over All, We Will Reign

1988-2006

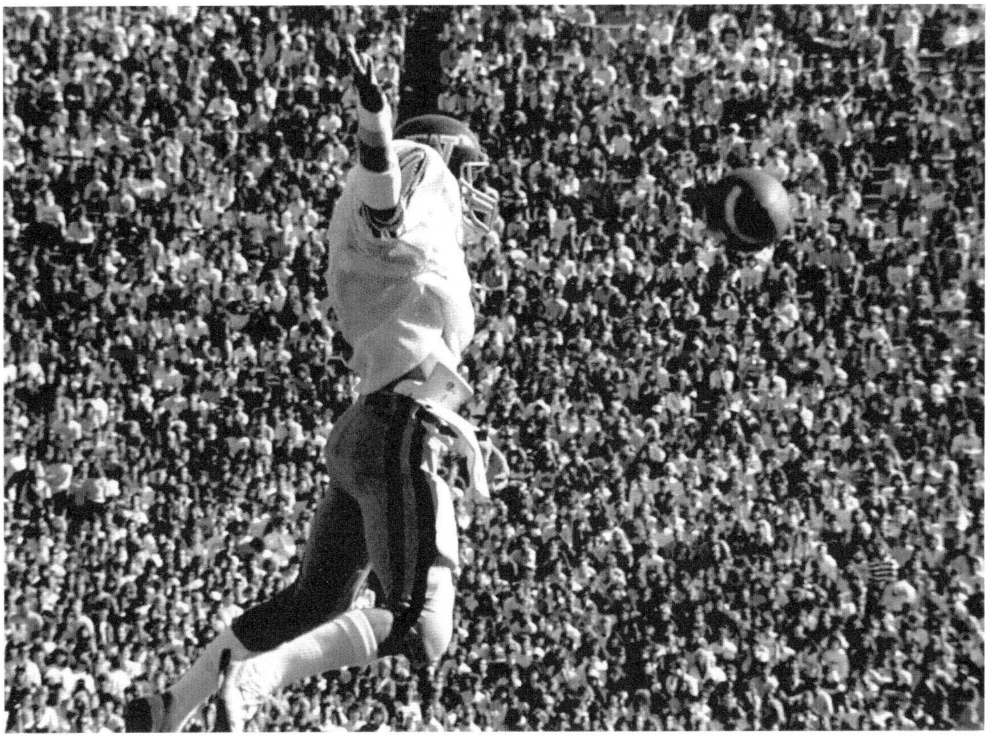

College football reached its greatest stage starting in the late 1980s. As televised games, bowl games, and championships became the hottest items on the menu, WMU football grew right along with the rest of the sport. The team achieved its first outright conference title. When the MAC grew and separated into two divisions, WMU rose to the top then as well. The fans responded in the largest numbers ever seen in the league's history. And once again, the Broncos achieved the prize of postseason play. Many players who prowled the Waldo Stadium turf went on to achieve accolades within the league, across the nation, and, in several cases, professional glory.

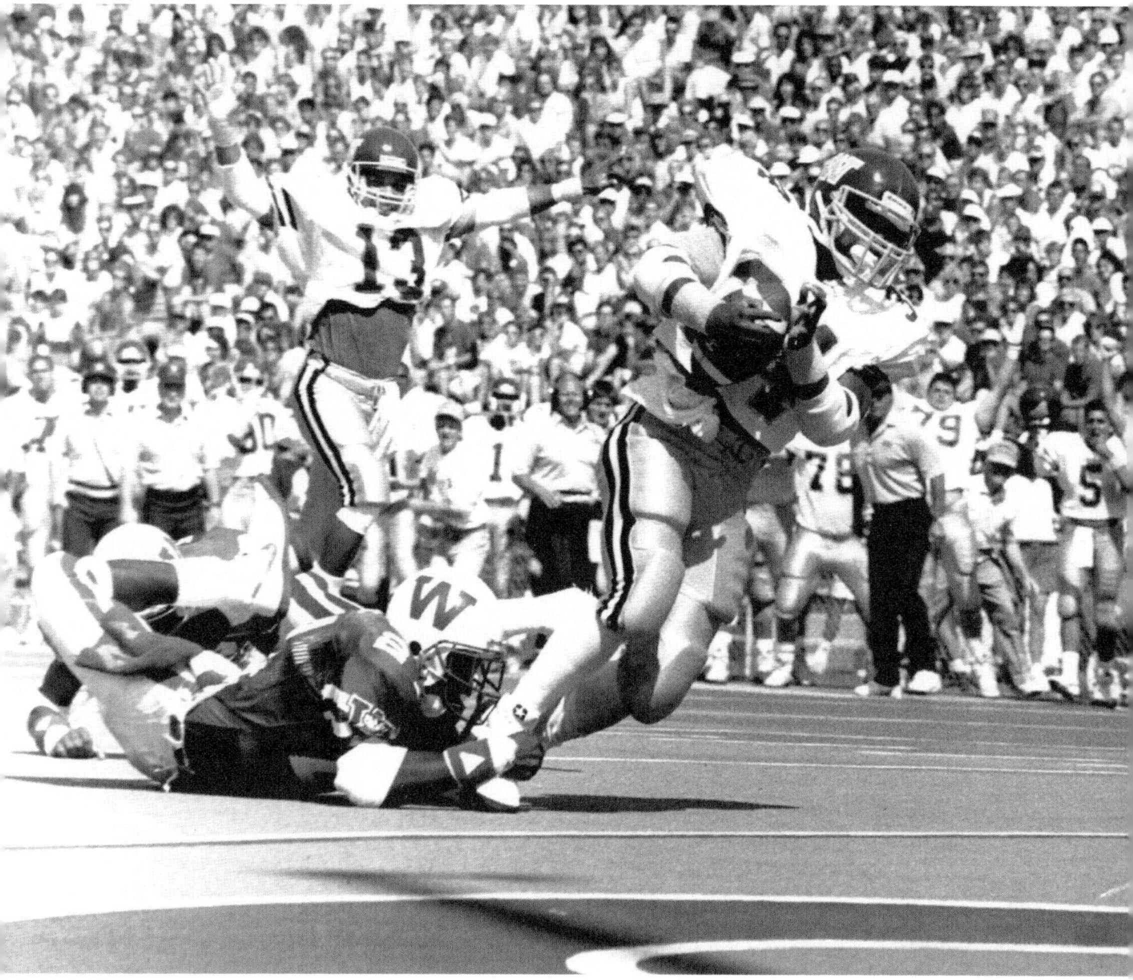

THE 1988 SEASON STARTED OFF WITH ONE OF the biggest bangs in WMU football history. The Broncos traveled to Madison, Wisconsin, to face the University of Wisconsin Badgers on their home turf. WMU had never defeated a modern Big Ten opponent in 12 tries and had not enjoyed a winning season since 1983. Little was expected to be different on this day. The odds were even more against them when it was learned that starting quarterback Tony Kimbrough would be out of the game with a leg injury. That meant backup quarterback David Kruse would need to carry the load. The game started off as expected, with Wisconsin jumping out to an 11-0 lead in the opening quarter. Miscues and penalties held the Broncos down. But then the Broncos started to click. Kruse was completing passes to Bruce Boyko, and running back Rob Davis was finding holes. WMU chipped away at the Badger lead and finally pulled ahead. When the gun sounded, the Broncos had a 24-14 upset win. Kruse completed 22 of 40 passes for 247 yards and 1 touchdown pass. Davis rushed for a career-high 136 yards and scored two touchdowns.

PAUL AGEMA WAS A BACKUP FULLBACK WHO always seemed to deliver big plays when the team needed it, come rain or shine. Coach Al Molde referred to Agema as a "great mudder" who could run no matter what the turf or what field condition he faced. Agema was a workhorse when the Broncos faced Ball State University with the MAC championship on the line.

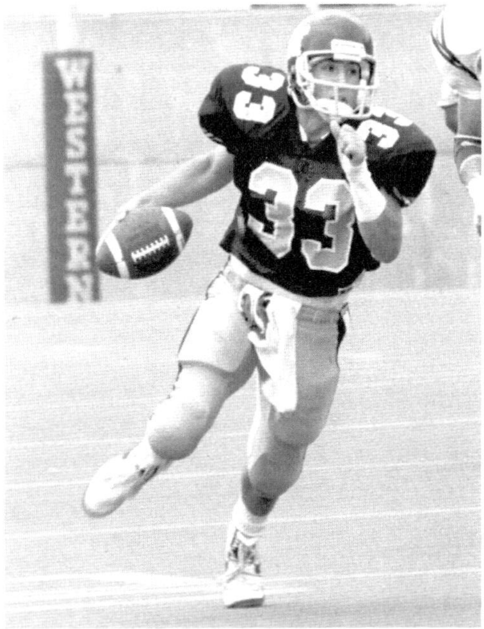

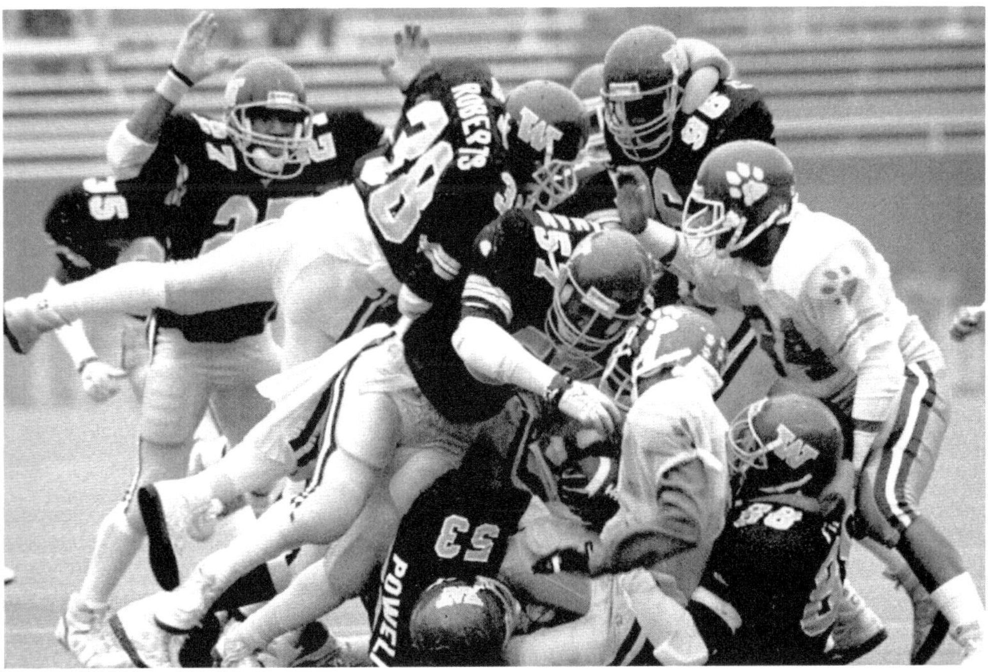

WMU'S DREAM SEASON HAD AS MUCH TO DO with its punishing defense as its opportunistic offense. "Every time we needed a big stop, we got it," said head coach Al Molde. Linebacker Eric Hoffman recorded 20 tackles in a game twice during the season to earn the team's Defensive MVP honor. Strong safety Willie Berrios recorded 114 tackles. "The team has risen to every challenge and adversity this season," Molde said.

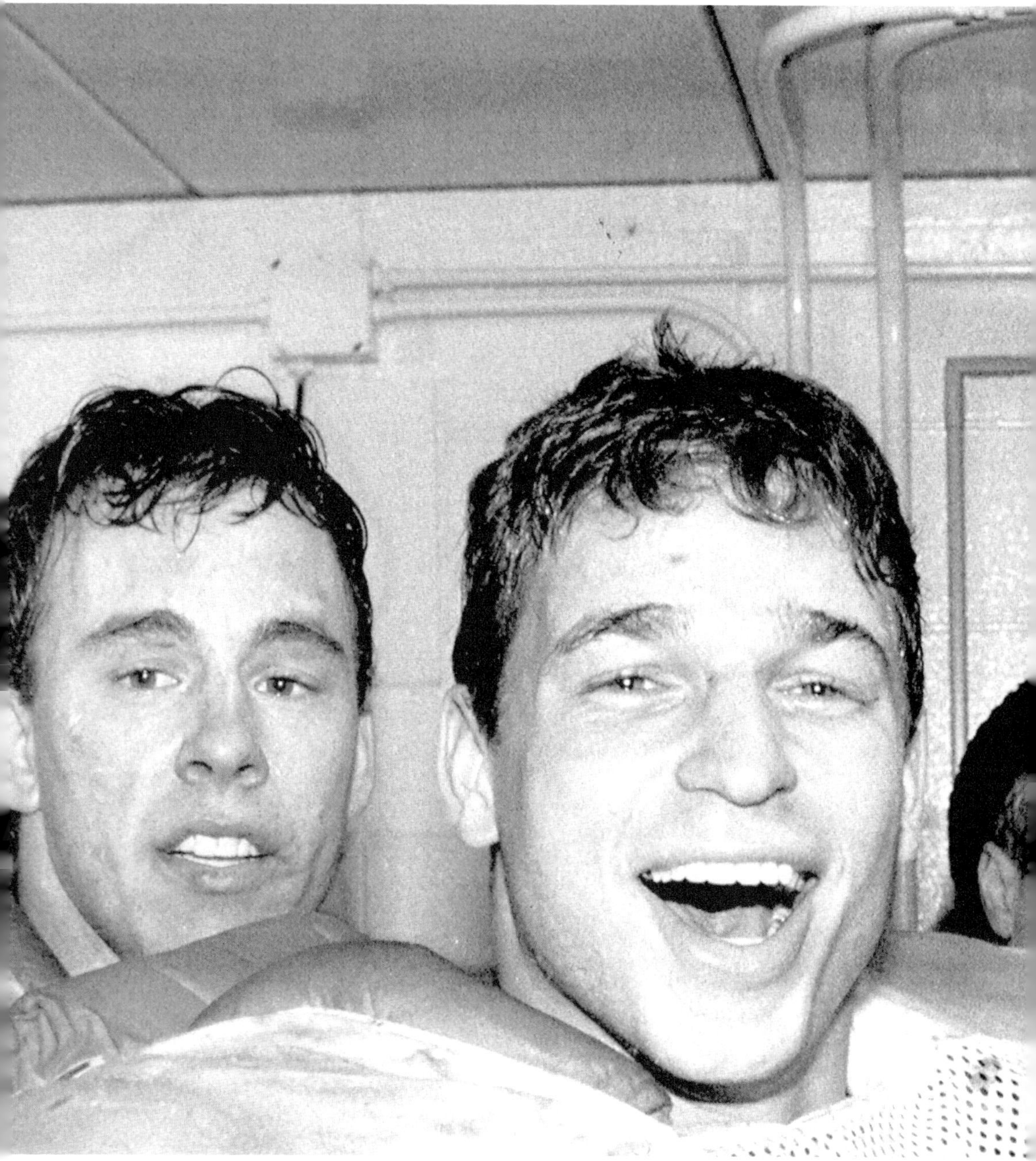

WHEN WMU FACED BALL STATE UNIVERSITY late in the 1988 season, there were still two weeks left in the regular season, but a win over the Cardinals would clinch the first ever outright MAC championship for WMU, and the Broncos showed they had no patience. Despite freezing and rainy conditions, the Broncos battled through and claimed a 16-13 win. Senior kicker John Cook booted field goals of 21, 22, and 28 yards, and quarterback Tony Kimbrough hooked up with Bruce Boyko for a 10-yard touchdown pass late in the first half.

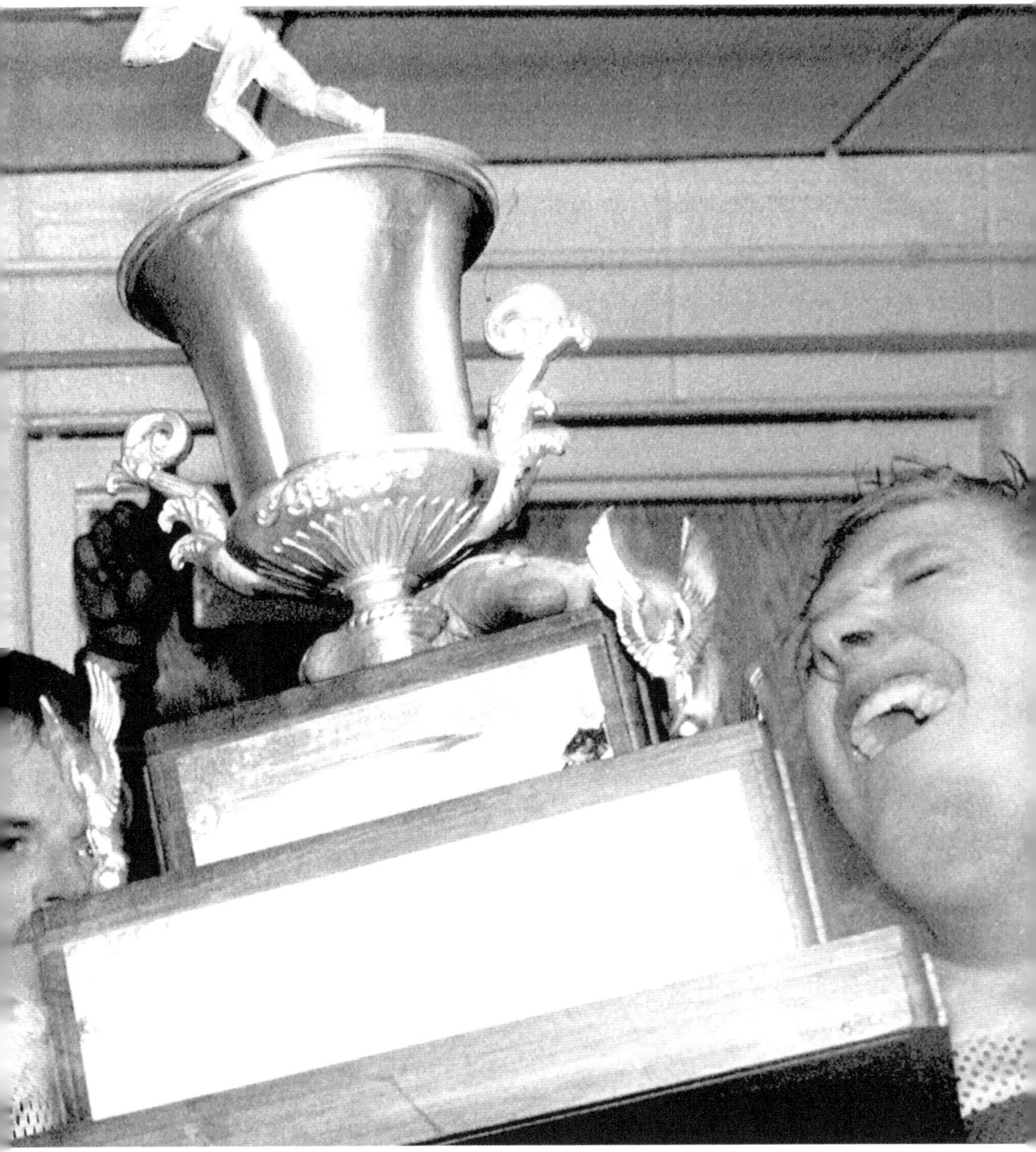

When passing became difficult, the Broncos turned to a running game of Paul Agema and the scrambling skills of Kimbrough. He finished the day with a game-high 97 yards rushing, despite facing a Ball State defense that was ranked eighth in the nation. When the gun sounded, the Bronco players lifted coach Molde on to their shoulders and carried him into the visitors' locker room where the biggest celebration in Bronco history got underway.

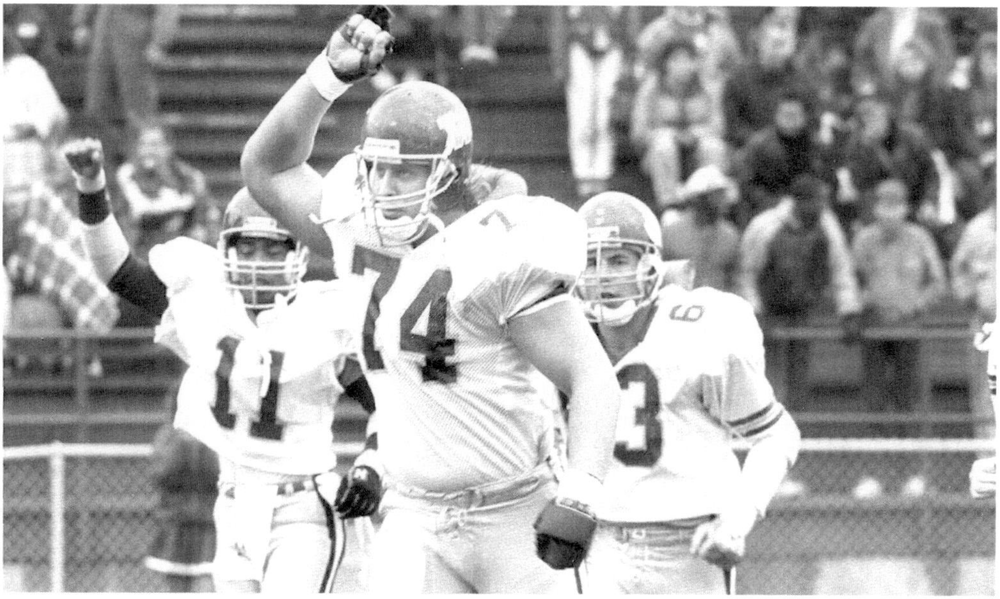

KEVIN HAVERDINK HAD ALL THE TOOLS TO HELP WMU in its bid for its first MAC championship. He was six foot seven and 275 pounds with good agility. But he overcame a big obstacle when he was forced to play the final portion of the 1988 season with a broken leg. His offensive-line play helped spring the Bronco running game when it needed it the most, and he was named a first-team All-MAC player and a third-team All-American.

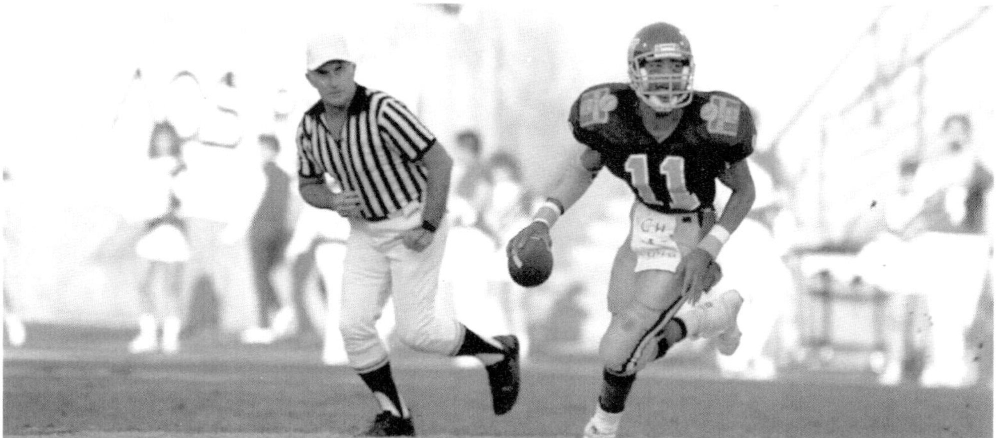

A JUNIOR COLLEGE TRANSFER, TONY KIMBROUGH proved to be one of the most versatile quarterbacks WMU has ever suited up. In his short 14-game career, Kimbrough managed to impact the MAC record books by twice passing for four touchdowns in a game. He also put his name at or near the top of WMU's record books for total yards, completions, passing yards, and touchdown passes. He was the MAC MVP in 1988 and ranked 19th in the nation in pass efficiency.

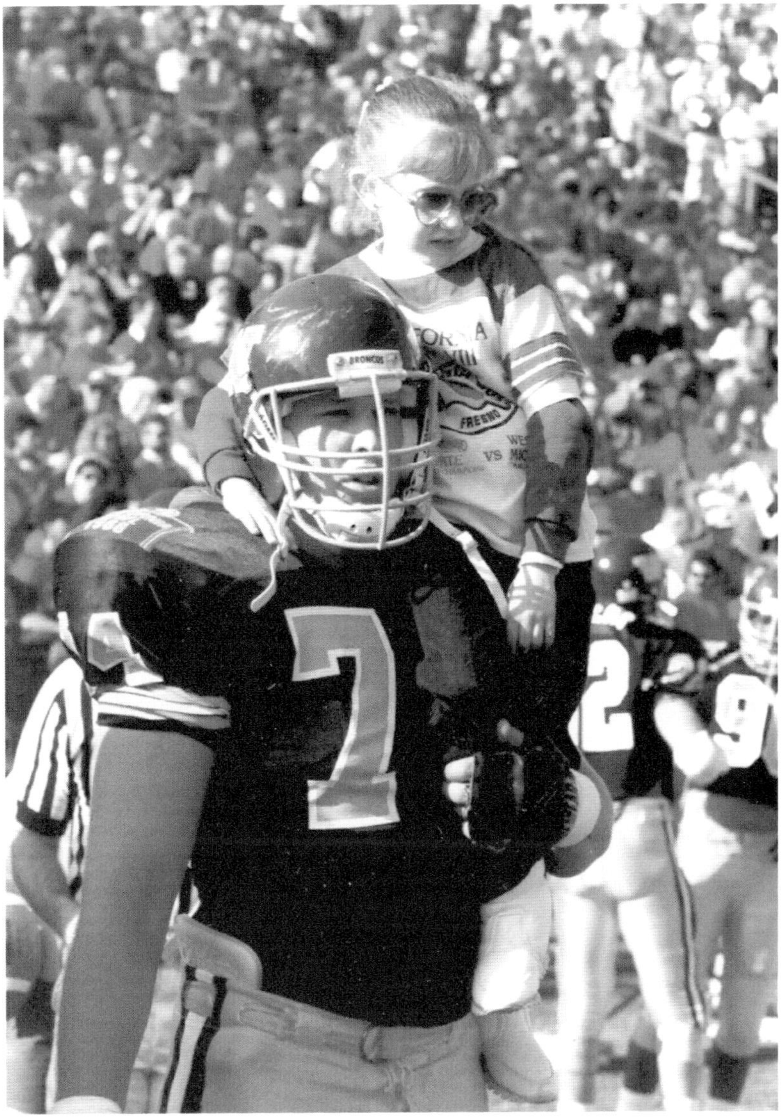

THE CALIFORNIA BOWL WAS THE BIGGEST event to hit WMU football in quite some time. As MAC champions, the Broncos were invited to Fresno, California, to play the Fresno State Bulldogs on their home turf. Thousands of Bronco fans accepted the hospitality and traveled en masse to show their support for the team. They knew the challenge would be tough. The Bulldogs had a top-ranked defense, and it would take a mistake-free effort by the Broncos. Things started out well enough. After falling behind, the Broncos took a 17-14 halftime lead with a touchdown pass to Robert Oliver, a short plunge by Robert Davis, and a John Cook field goal all in the last 9:32 of the second quarter. But turnovers plagued the second half. The teams traded touchdowns in the third quarter before Fresno State took control the rest of the way. WMU managed a final touchdown in the game's final minute. The marathon game lasted over four hours and ended with WMU on the losing end 35-30.

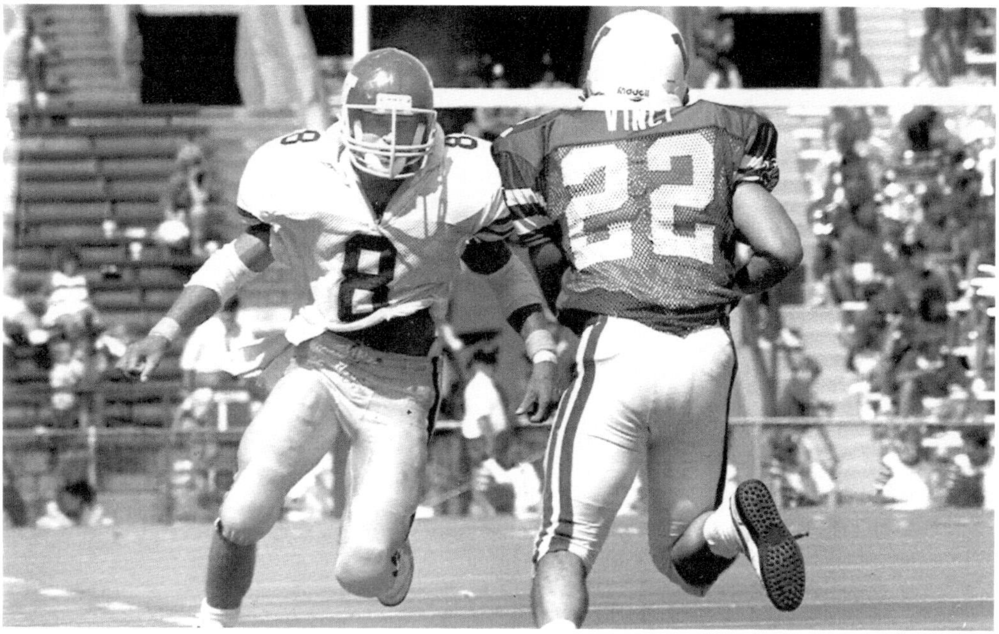

WMU FOOTBALL COACH AL MOLDE CALLED Willie Berrios "the greatest success story in Western football history." The strong safety arrived as a walk-on and soon worked his way up to the status of a three-year starter. In 1987, he set a school record for tackles in a game with 27 against Central Michigan University and ranked second on the team in tackles the next year.

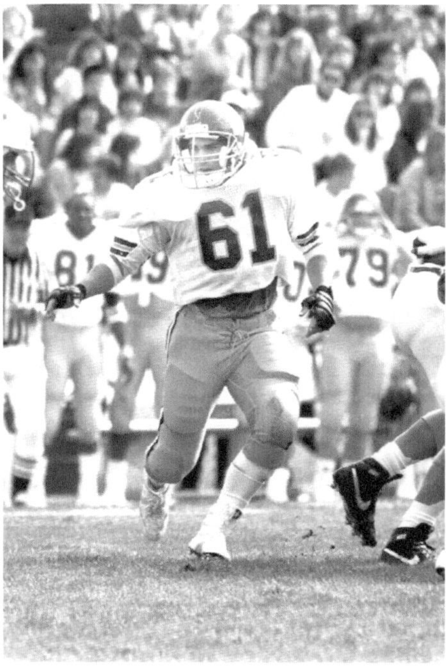

SEAN MULHEARN STARTED OFF ON A PARTIAL scholarship but quickly earned a full ride by turning in a key goal line tackle against Eastern Michigan University in 1988, averaging almost 11 tackles a game in 1989, and being named the Defensive Player of the Year in 1990.

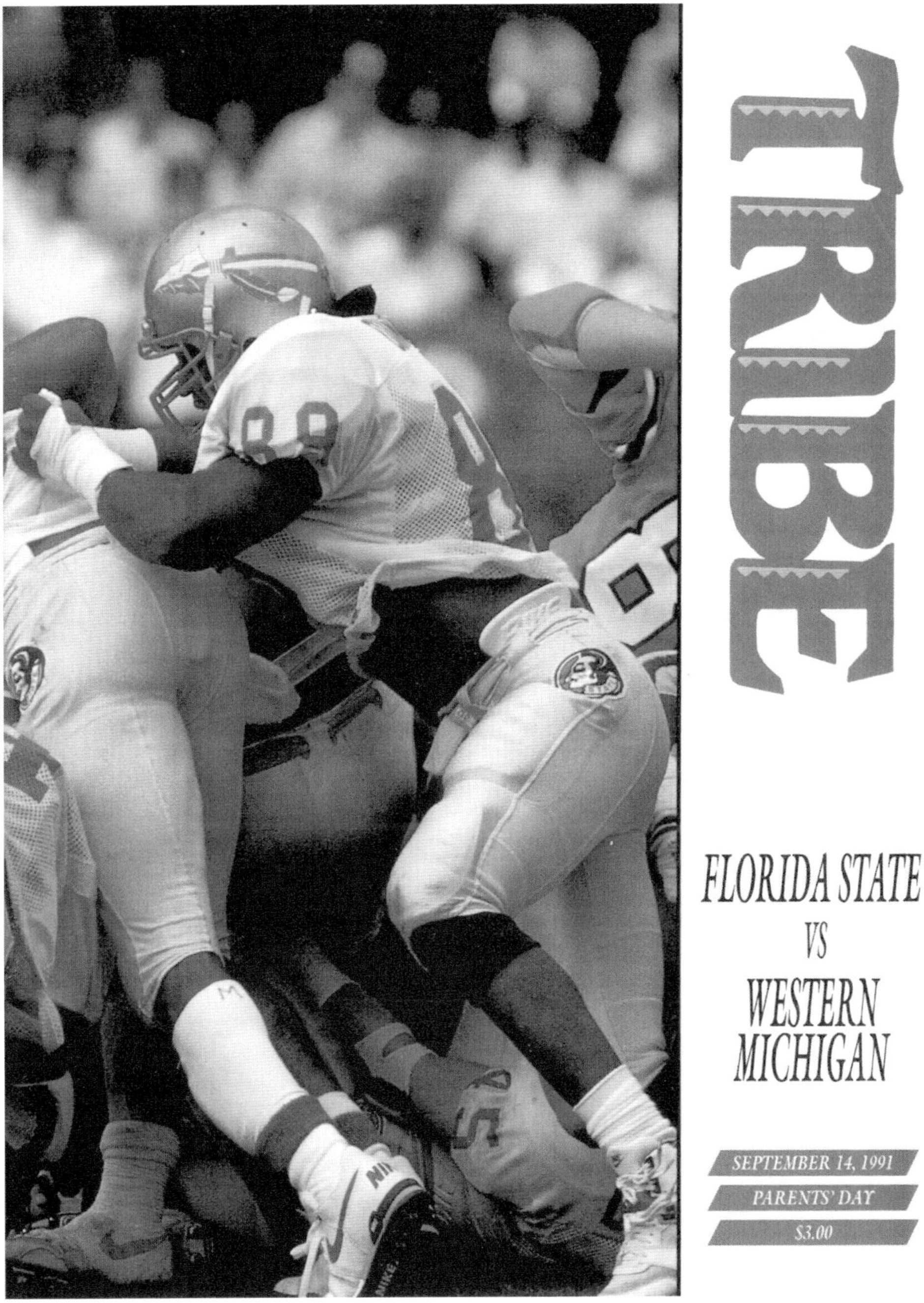

WMU GOT ITS BIGGEST CHALLENGE IN HISTORY in September 1991 as the team traveled down to Tallahassee, Florida, to play the top-ranked Florida State University Seminoles. It was the first time a Bronco team has played a squad ranked No. 1. There would be no upsets, however, as the Seminoles rolled 58-0.

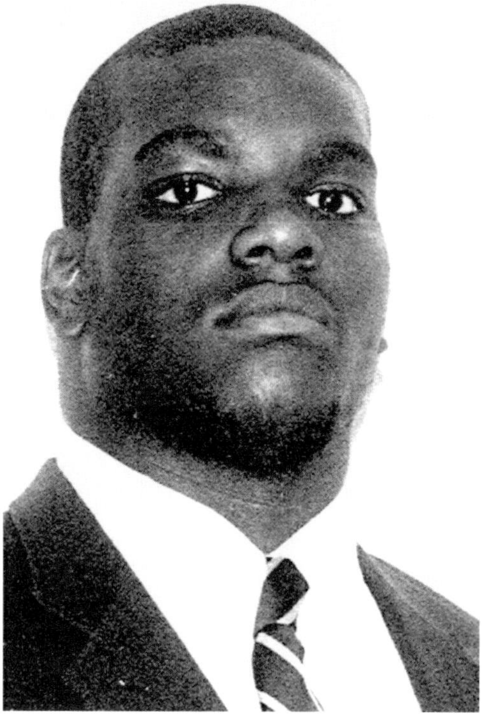

For the second year in a row, Paul Hutchins was named to the All-MAC first team, making him the first Bronco offensive tackle to win that back-to-back honor. He was a runner-up for the MAC MVP Award. Standing six foot six and weighing 340 pounds, Hutchins was one of the Broncos' biggest players.

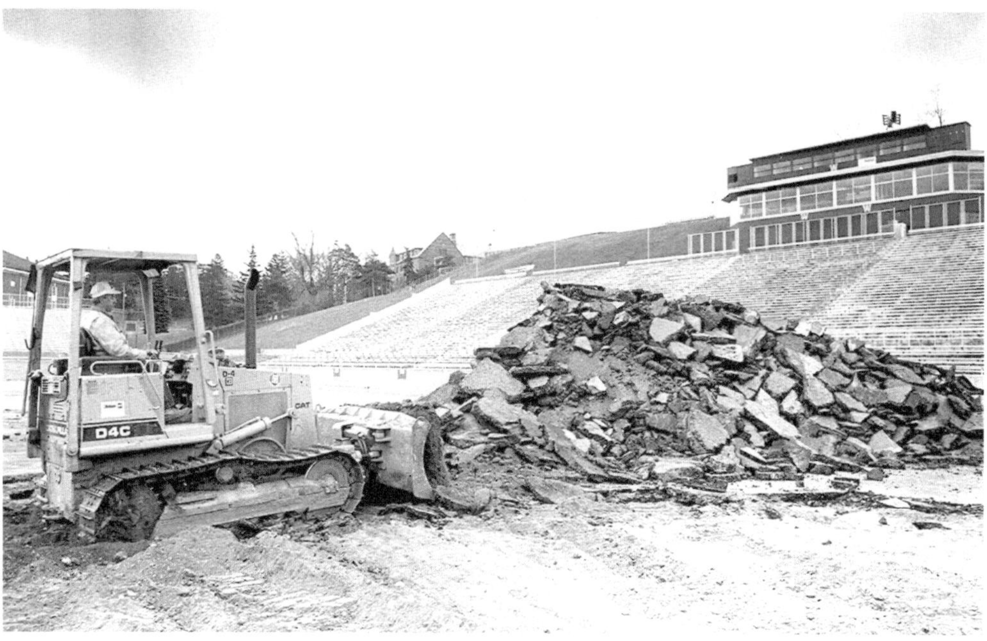

Waldo Stadium underwent a face-lift of sorts in 1992 when bulldozers dug up the old sod and replaced it with a new drainage system and artificial turf called Prescription Athletic Turf. It was one of many renovations to the stadium and the field that WMU undertook.

PETER TUFFO WAS ONE OF THE Broncos' best linebackers in 1992 and 1993. In 1992, he led the squad with 114 tackles, including 10 for loss. The next year, against Ohio, he recorded 17 tackles, including 3 for loss. He finished with 131 tackles and earned an All-MAC first-team designation.

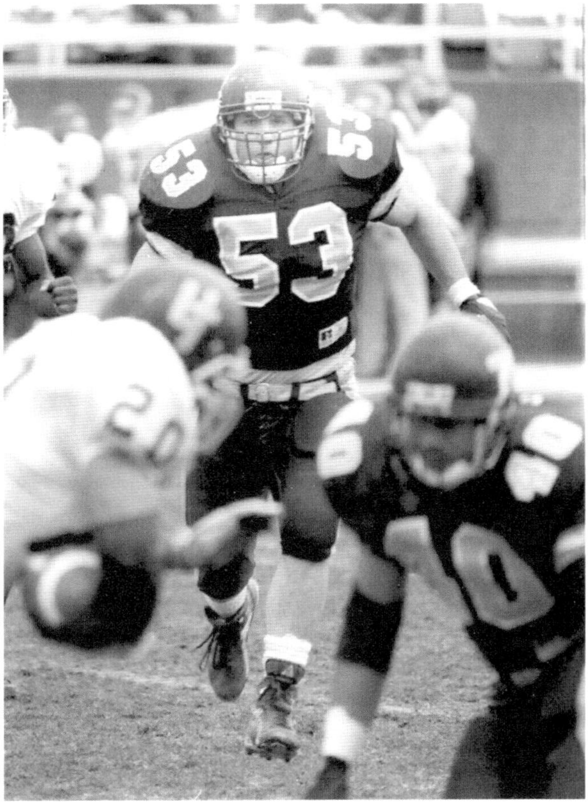

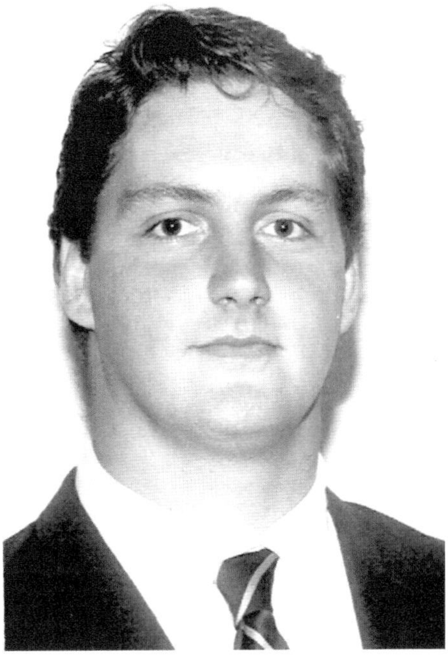

TOM NÜTTEN WAS THE ONLY TRUE FRESHMAN to letter in 1991. Before his career was done at WMU, he spent time at center, tackle, and guard, earning an All-America designation along the way. The Quebec native was drafted No. 1 by Hamilton in the Canadian Football League and in the seventh round of the NFL draft by Buffalo.

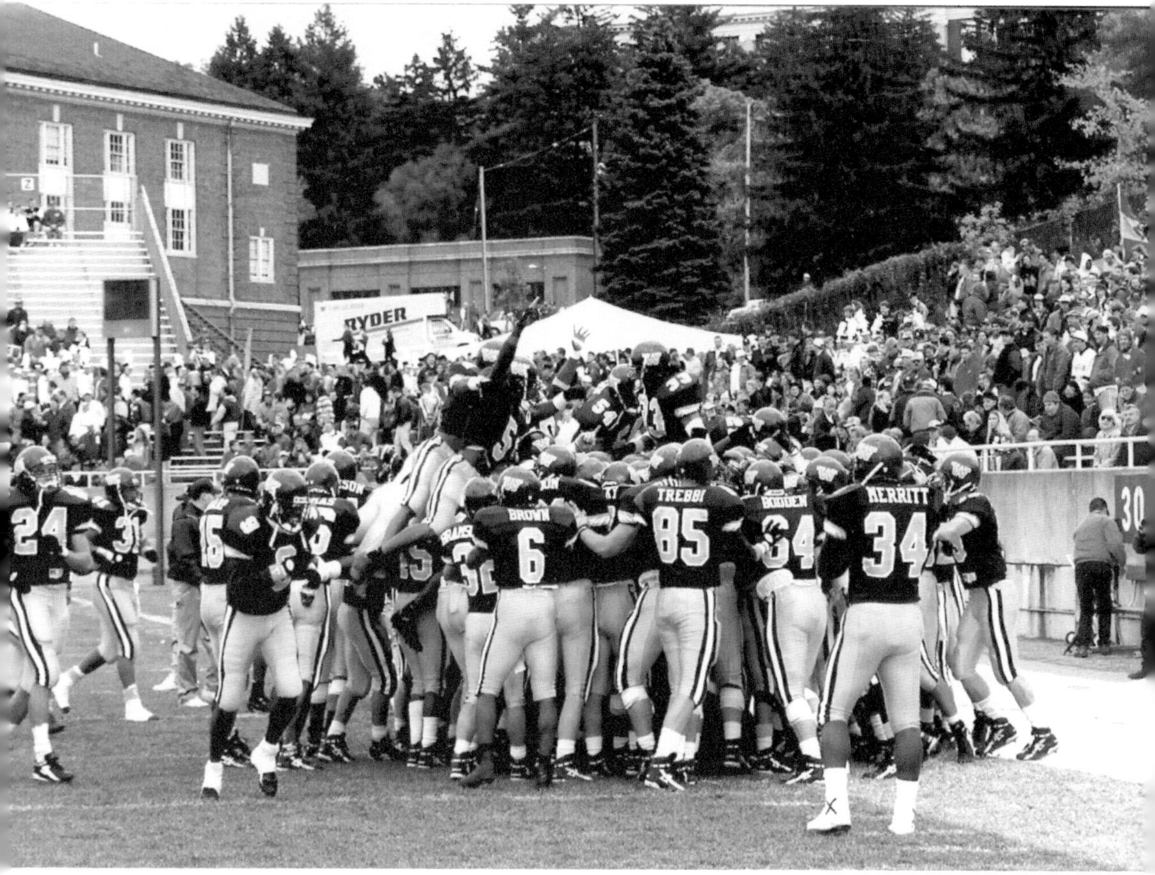

THE BRONCOS CONTINUED TO BE A FACTOR both inside and outside of the MAC in 1994. For the third straight year, they finished near the top of the league standings. The Broncos also claimed a rare win over a Big Eight school when they downed the Iowa State University Cyclones 23-19. They finished eighth in the nation in total defense and continued a streak of seven-win seasons. The Broncos were showing they were not afraid to schedule big-name opponents from outside the conference. University of Wisconsin, University of Maryland, and Florida State University had all been on the itinerary in recent years. In the coming years, Western would face University of Florida, Virginia Tech, and University of Michigan.

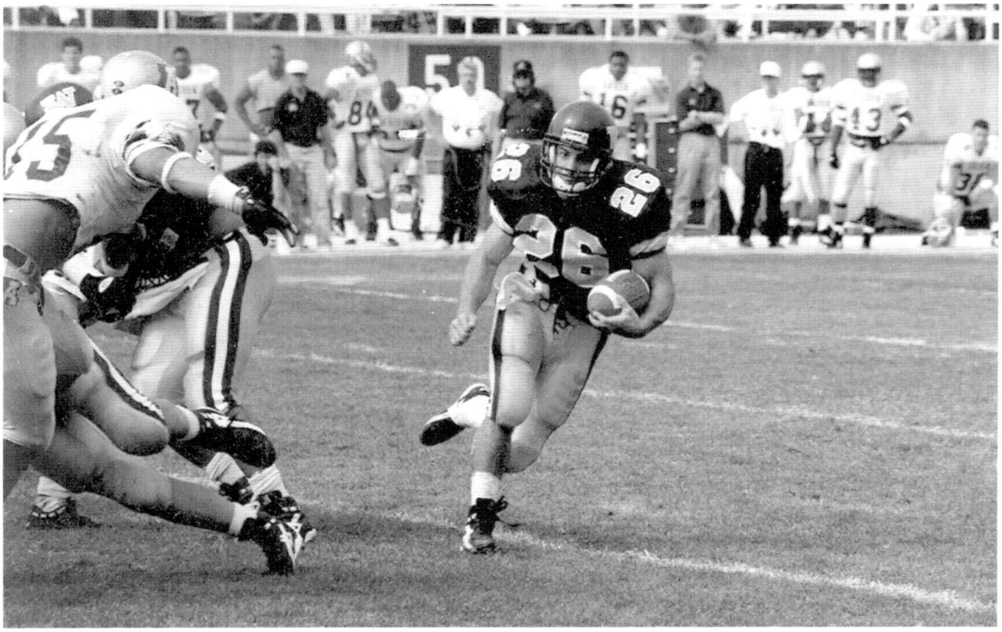

FORMER WALK-ON JIM VAKARO WAS A RARE breed. He was a star runner in a predominately passing offense. He showed his versatility in 1993 by finishing seventh in the MAC in rushing and ninth in the league in receptions.

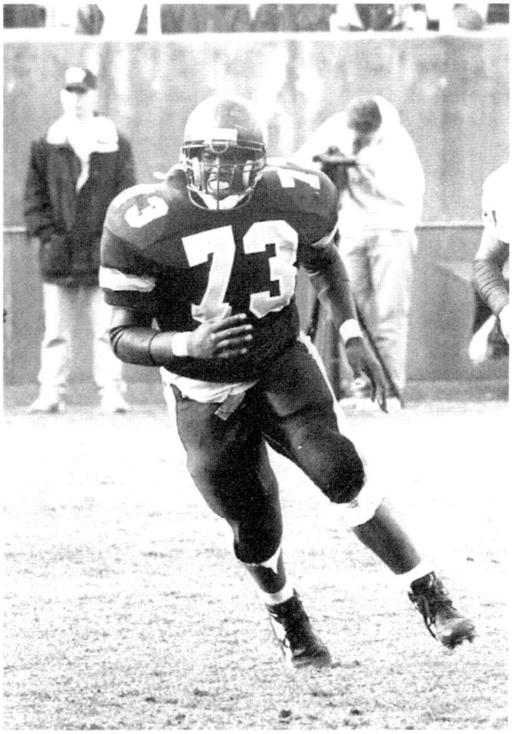

ONE OF JUST TWO BRONCO DEFENSIVE linemen to win All-MAC honors three times, Dion Powell was a true talent for the Broncos. As a senior, he was selected as the runner-up for the MAC Defensive Player of the Year award.

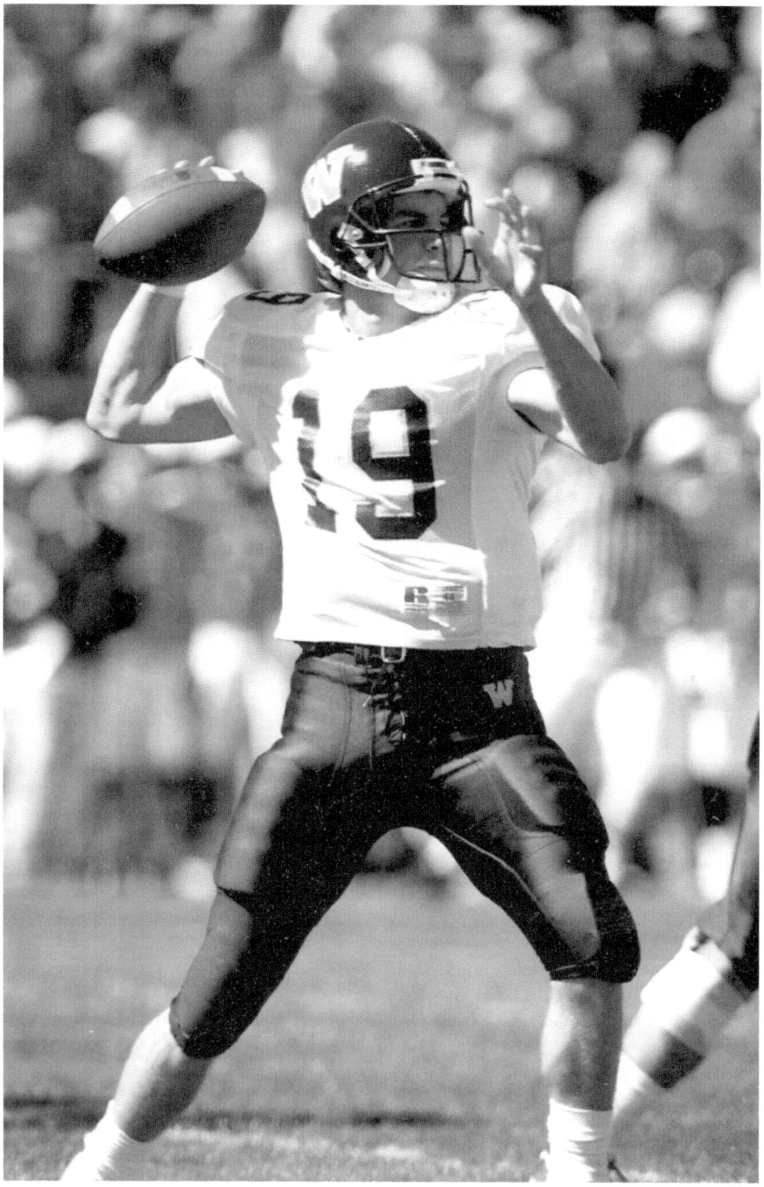

QUARTERBACK JAY MCDONAGH LEARNED HIS trade as an option quarterback in his Chicago high school. He was recruited by Iowa State University as a defensive end but ended up at WMU, despite the fact that the Broncos featured a passing offense. McDonagh had no trouble adjusting, however. He became only the third sophomore in Bronco history to earn the team's MVP award, after Hap Coleman in 1940 and Jerome Persell in 1976. But he did not stop there. He went on to win that honor two more times. As a junior, McDonagh ranked 14th in the nation in total offense. Behind his leadership, the Broncos never failed to win at least seven games in a season. The running quarterback ended his career as one of WMU's top passers with 6,148 yards and connected on 59 percent of his throws.

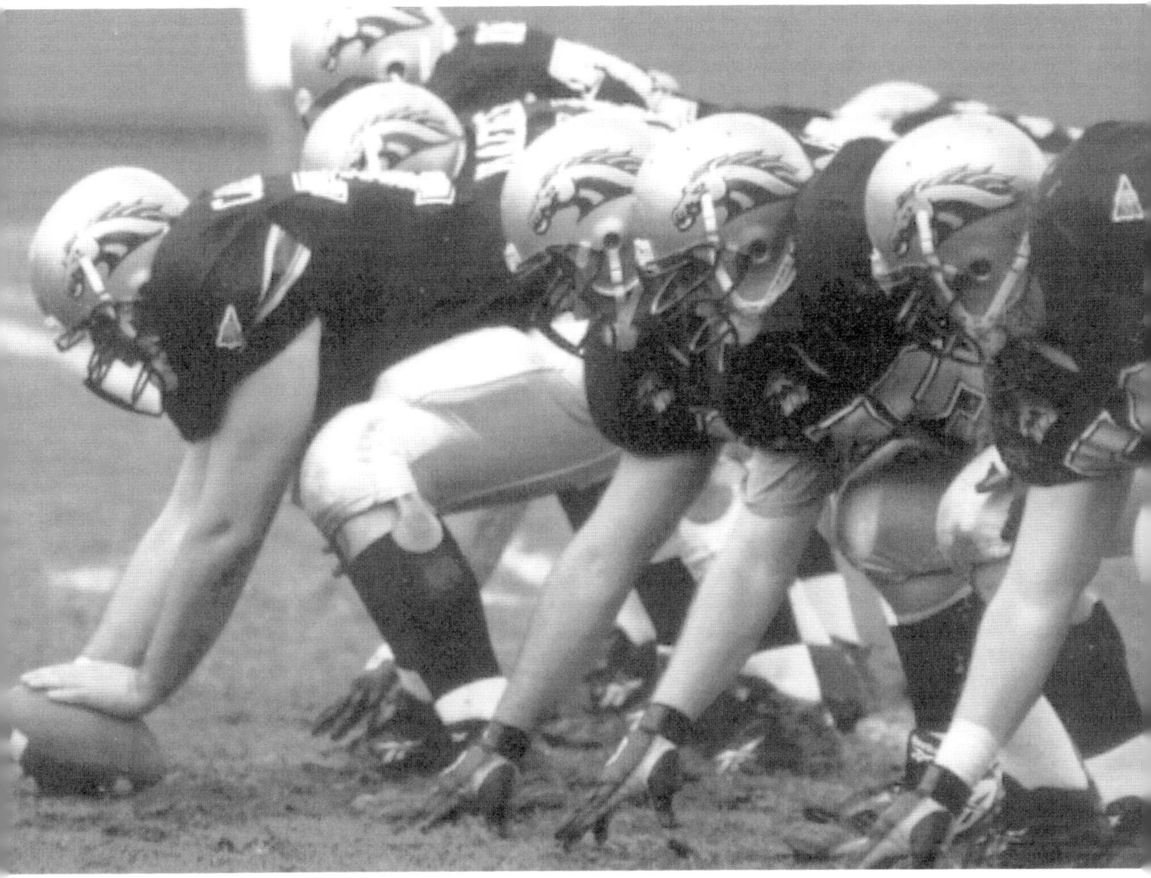

WMU HAS HAD ITS FAIR SHARE OF GOOD seasons throughout its history, and several times, they have been able to put together streaks of successive winning campaigns, but nothing compares to the success the Broncos achieved in the 1990s. As the "me" decade of the 1980s ended, the team decade of the 1990s began for WMU. The Broncos won seven games and tied for third in the conference in 1990. They won seven games again the next year and followed that up with identical 7-3-1 records in 1992 and 1993. They finished second in the conference both years with their only conference loss in 1993 coming at the hands of Central Michigan University. The Broncos kept the consistency up for the next two years, once again recording identical 7-4 records in 1994 and 1995.

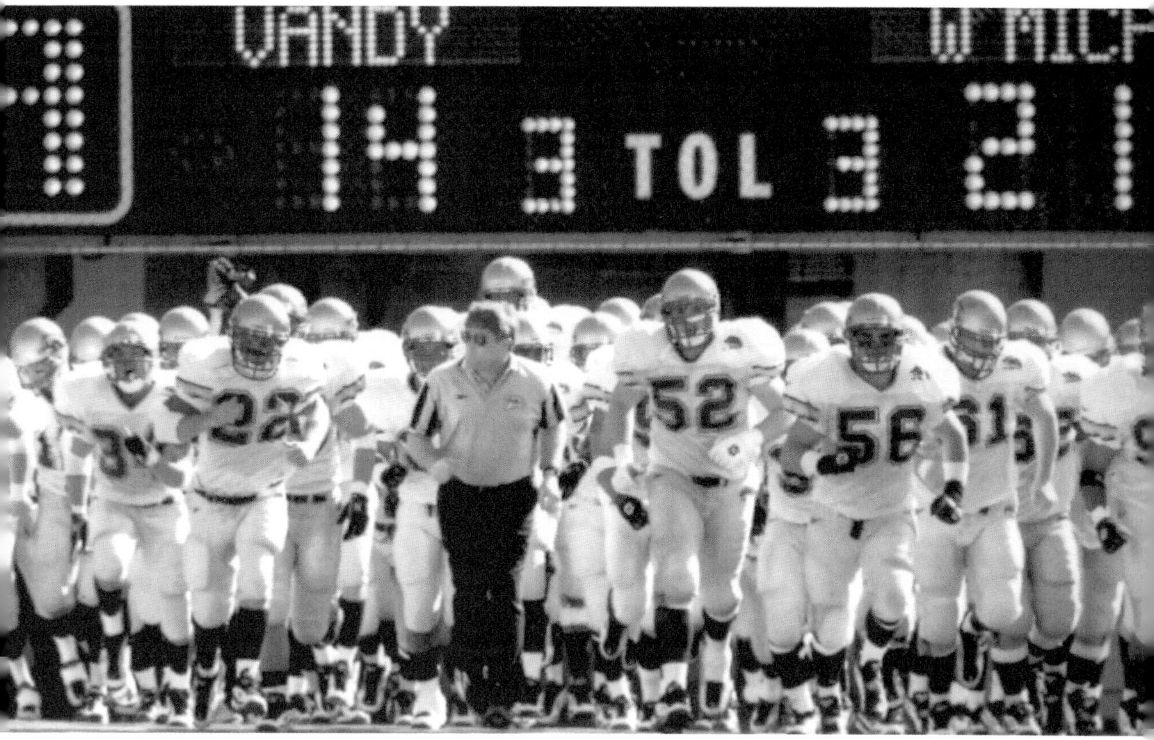

NEW WMU FOOTBALL COACHES SEEMED TO always be a shot in the arm whenever the team was ailing, and Gary Darnell was no exception. The Broncos suffered through a 2-9 record in 1996 before selecting former University of Florida interim head coach Darnell to change the course. Darnell took over the helm for the Gators for the final seven games of 1989. His resume also boasted stints as the defensive coordinator at Notre Dame (1990–1991), Florida (1988–1989), Wake Forest (1986–1987), as well as Kansas State (1978–1982). As WMU's head coach, he succeeded almost immediately. The team won eight games in 1997, posting the nation's most-improved record for Division 1-A teams. Making the turnaround even more impressive, Darnell's team accomplished the feat with 10 true freshmen seeing playing time. Proving there would be no sophomore slump for either him or his players, the Broncos followed that up with a 7-4 mark in 1998.

ONE OF THE ROOKIE STARS IN COACH Darnell's resurgent squad was running back Robert Sanford. The dazzling newcomer was named the 1997 MAC Freshman of the Year and a second-team freshman All-American by the *Sporting News* when he rushed for 1,033 yards in his first year as a Bronco. (Courtesy of GS Photo.)

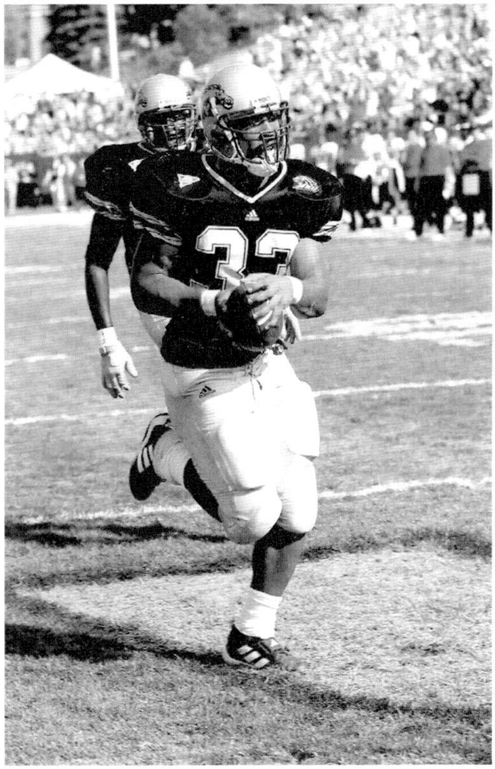

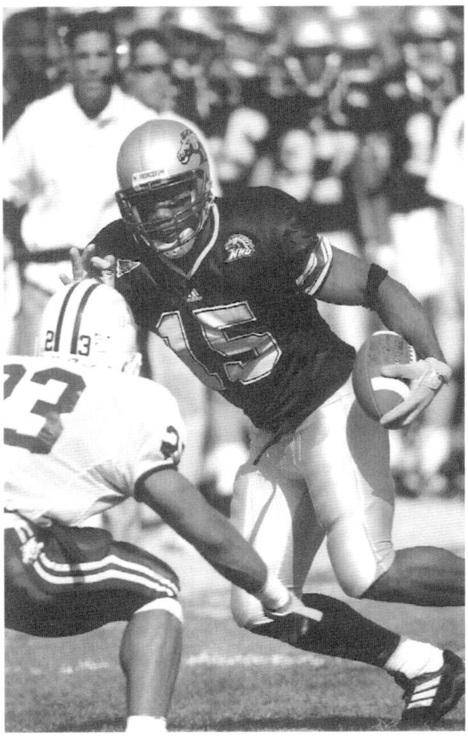

BIG RIVALRIES CALL FOR BIG GAMES, AND Bronco wide receiver Corey Alston delivered. Against Eastern Michigan University in 1997, he set the NCAA record for most receiving yards by a freshman when he caught 263 yards. The Broncos needed those yards as they squeaked out a 41-38 win over the Eagles. (Courtesy of GS Photo.)

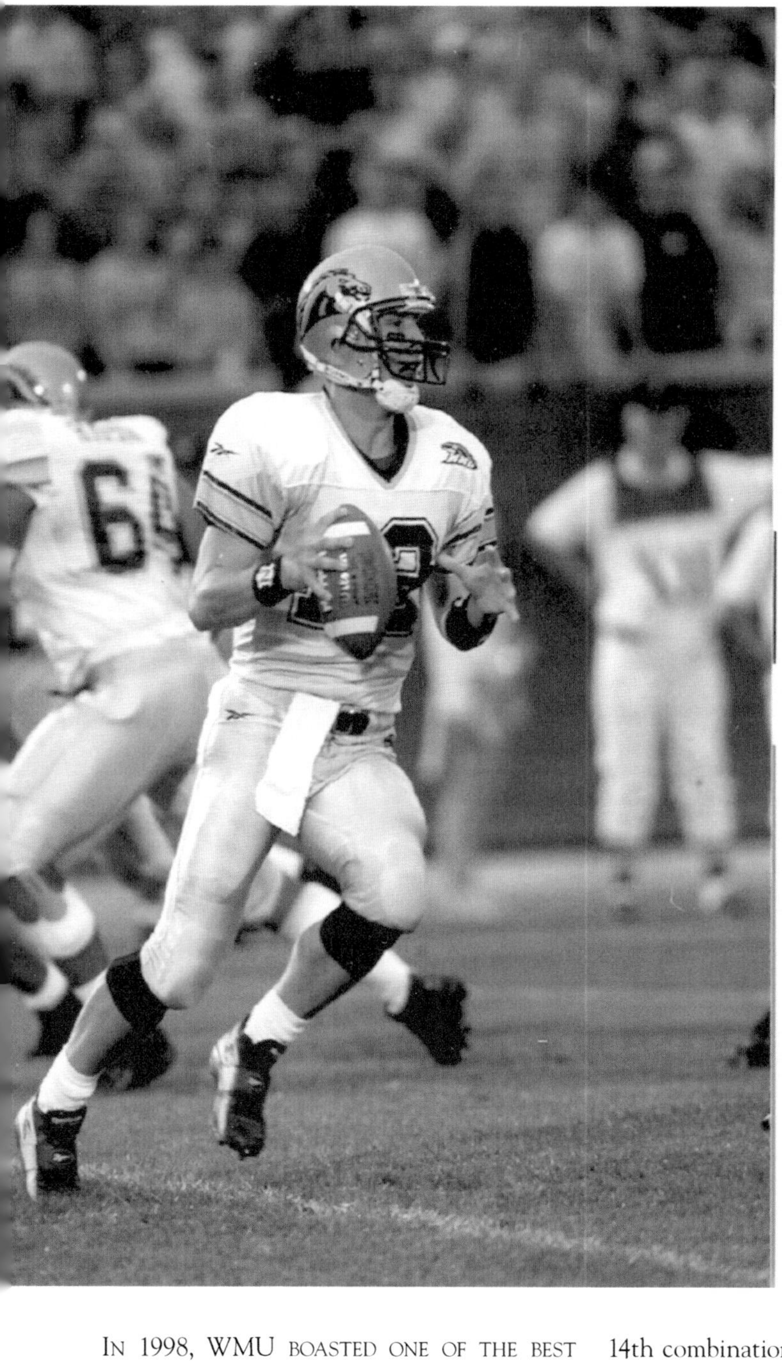

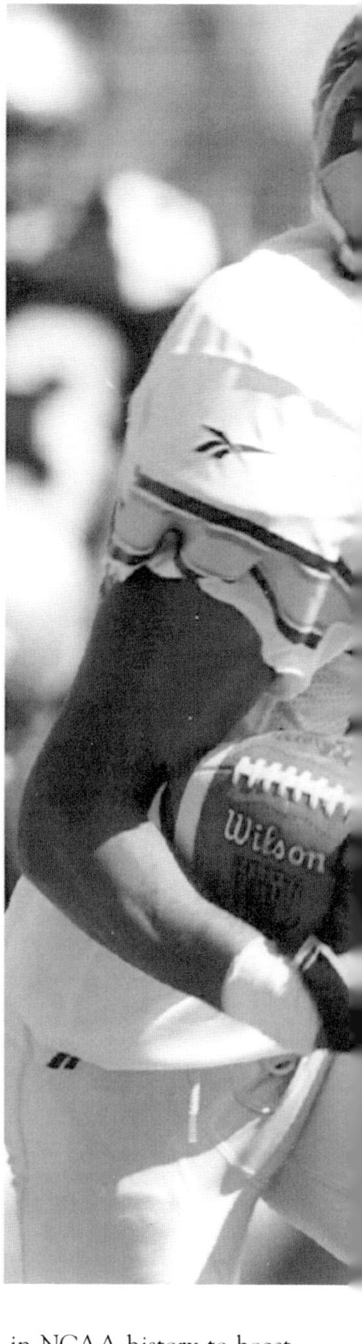

In 1998, WMU boasted one of the best trios in college football history in quarterback Tim Lester (left), running back Darnell Fields (middle), and wide receiver Steve Neal (right). The threesome teamed up to become only the 14th combination in NCAA history to boast a 3,000-yard passer, a 1,000-yard rusher, and a 1,000-yard receiver in the same season. The powerful Bronco offense averaged over 300 yards per game and produced the ninth-best passing

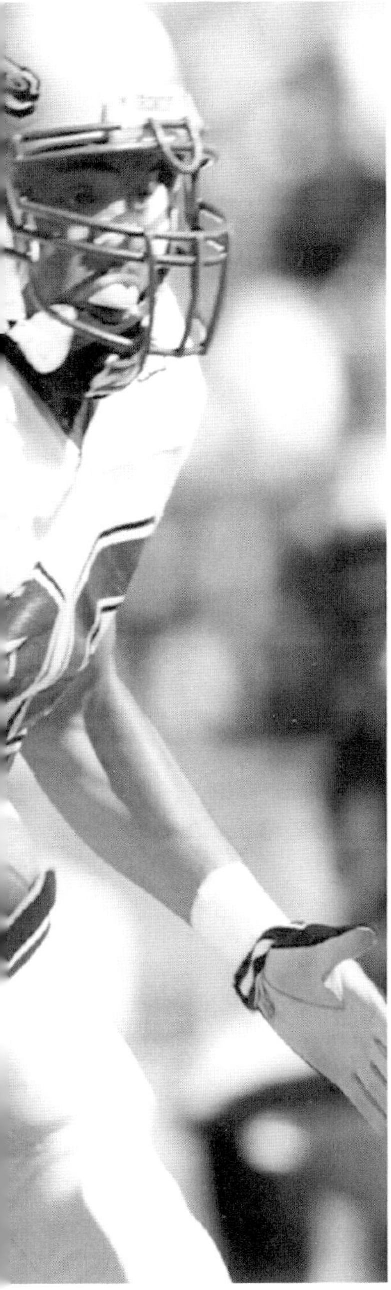

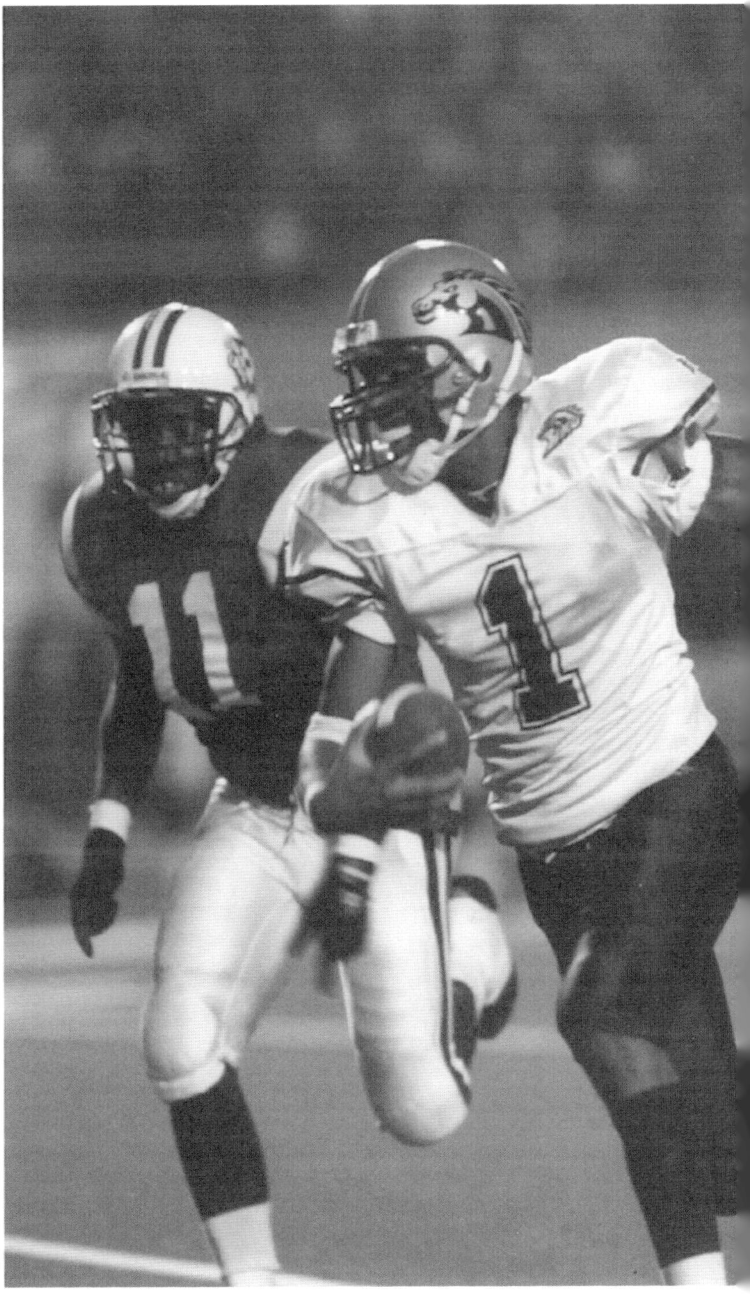

attack in the nation. Lester ended up rewriting the WMU record book and finished his career as the NCAA Division-I fourth-best passer of all time. The big play threat of Fields kept defenses on their toes while earning first-team All-MAC accolades three times. All three earned All-MAC honors in 1998.

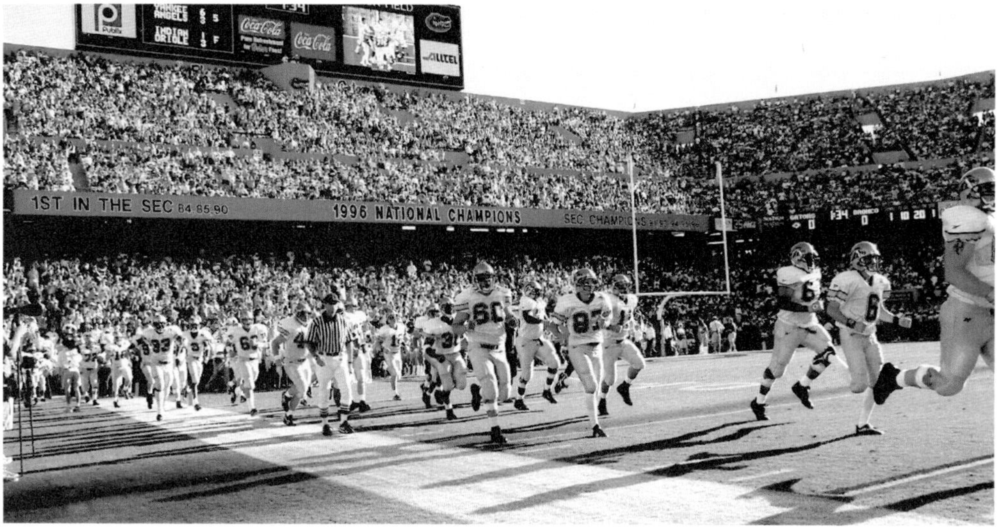

WMU'S 1999 SQUAD TOUGHENED ITSELF EARLY in the season with gut-checking games against the University of Florida and the University of Missouri. Despite hard fought losses to the Gators and Tigers, the squad took the experience back into league play and promptly crushed 41 different school records the rest of the way. The unstoppable Broncos claimed their second straight MAC West title before the month of October was over. (Courtesy of GS Photo.)

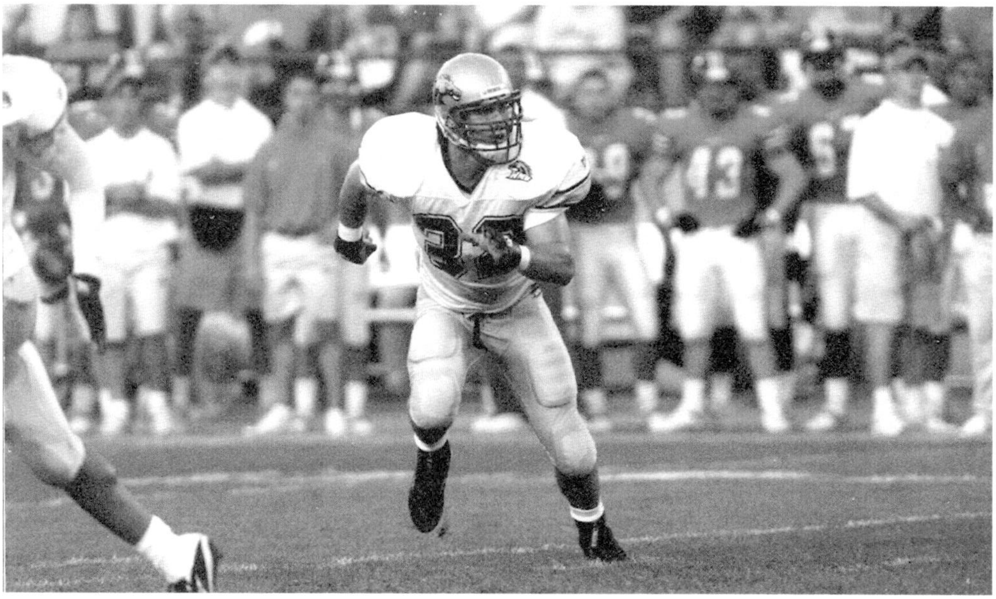

SCOTT NILES CAME OUT OF NOWHERE TO become one of the Broncos' most productive defenders. The unheralded inside linebacker recorded 35 tackles in his first five games of 1999 and added 107 tackles in his last seven games.

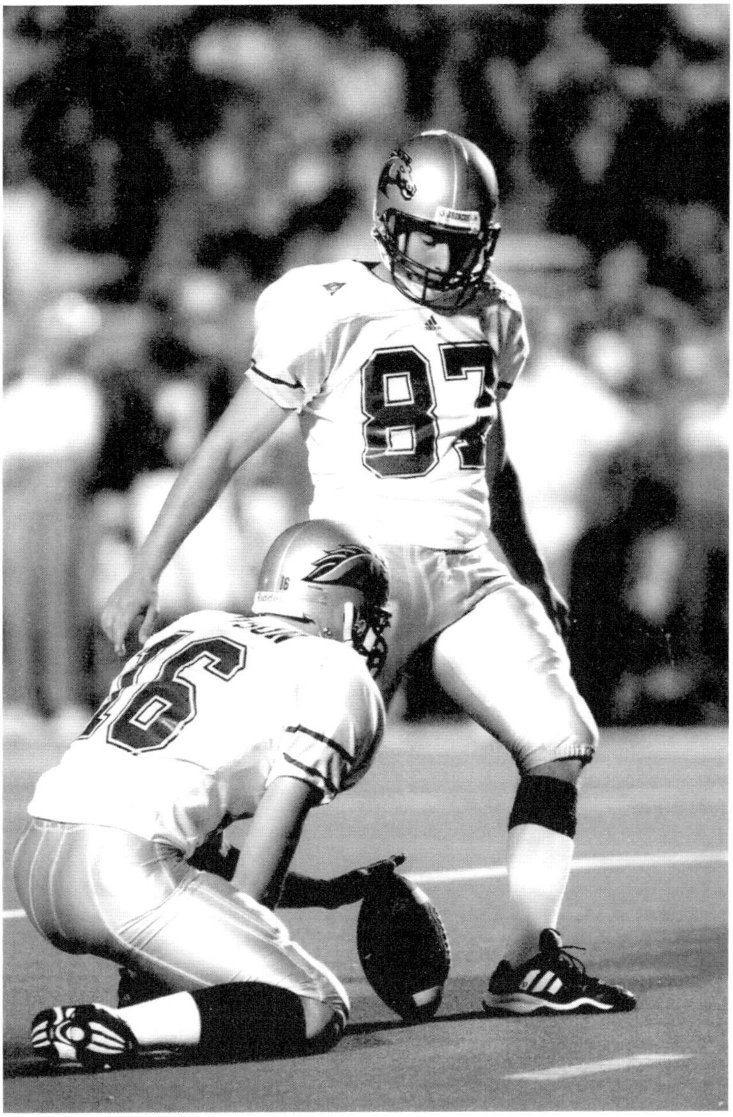

IN ONE OF THE MOST EXCITING GAMES WMU ever played in, the Broncos gave No. 10–ranked Marshall University a scare until the game's final seconds in the 1999 MAC championship game. WMU quarterback Tim Lester had given his team a 23-0 third-quarter lead before Marshall stormed back. The Broncos' Robert Sanford set a championship game record with 163 rushing yards. Lester completed 27 of 41 passes for 282 yards and two touchdowns. The Broncos' huge lead came courtesy of Brad Selent field goals from 31, 32, and 36 yards, a Lester to Corey Alston 16-yard pass, and a 1-yard scoring run by Sanford. Marshall stormed back with 27 unanswered points to overcome the deficit. Lester's four-yard scoring pass to Jake Moreland with 7:30 left gave WMU the lead at 30-27 until the final seconds. Marshall quarterback Chad Pennington tossed a one-yard touchdown pass to Eric Pinkerton with four seconds left for the victory.

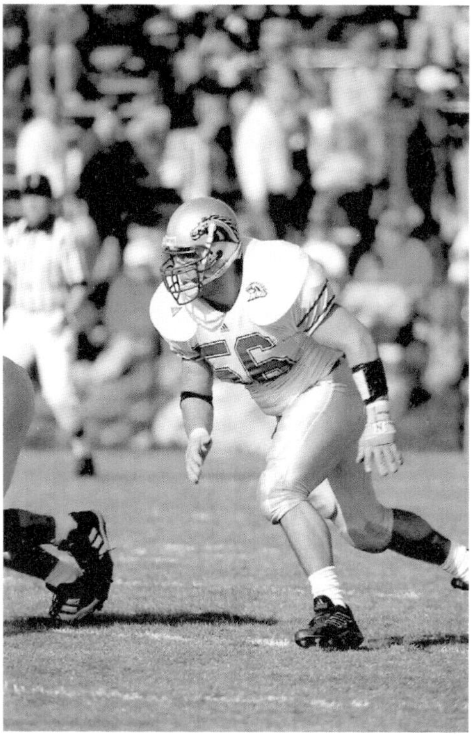

GARRETT SOLDANO WAS WMU'S TEAM MVP in 2000 when he compiled 309 tackles, the ninth best in WMU history. He finished 12th in the MAC in tackles and led all Broncos with 115 stops in 2000. (Courtesy of GS Photo.)

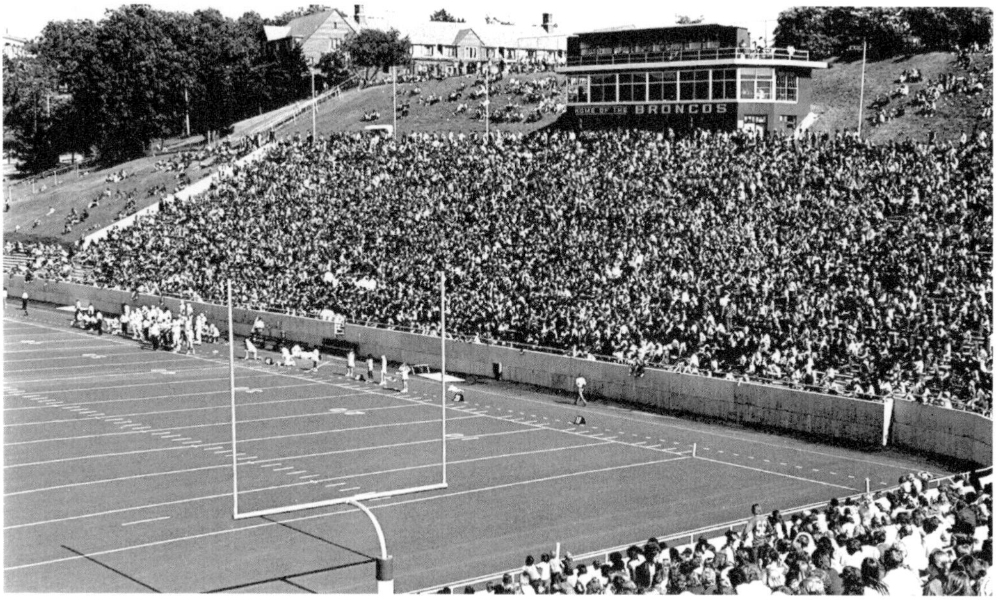

BRONCO FANS RESPONDED EN MASSE TO THE Broncos' success. Between 1998 and 2000, Waldo Stadium played host to four of the six largest crowds to witness a MAC regular-season game. Their 2000 game against Indiana State University brought 36,361 fans to the game, the second-largest total in league history. WMU responded with a 56-0 victory.

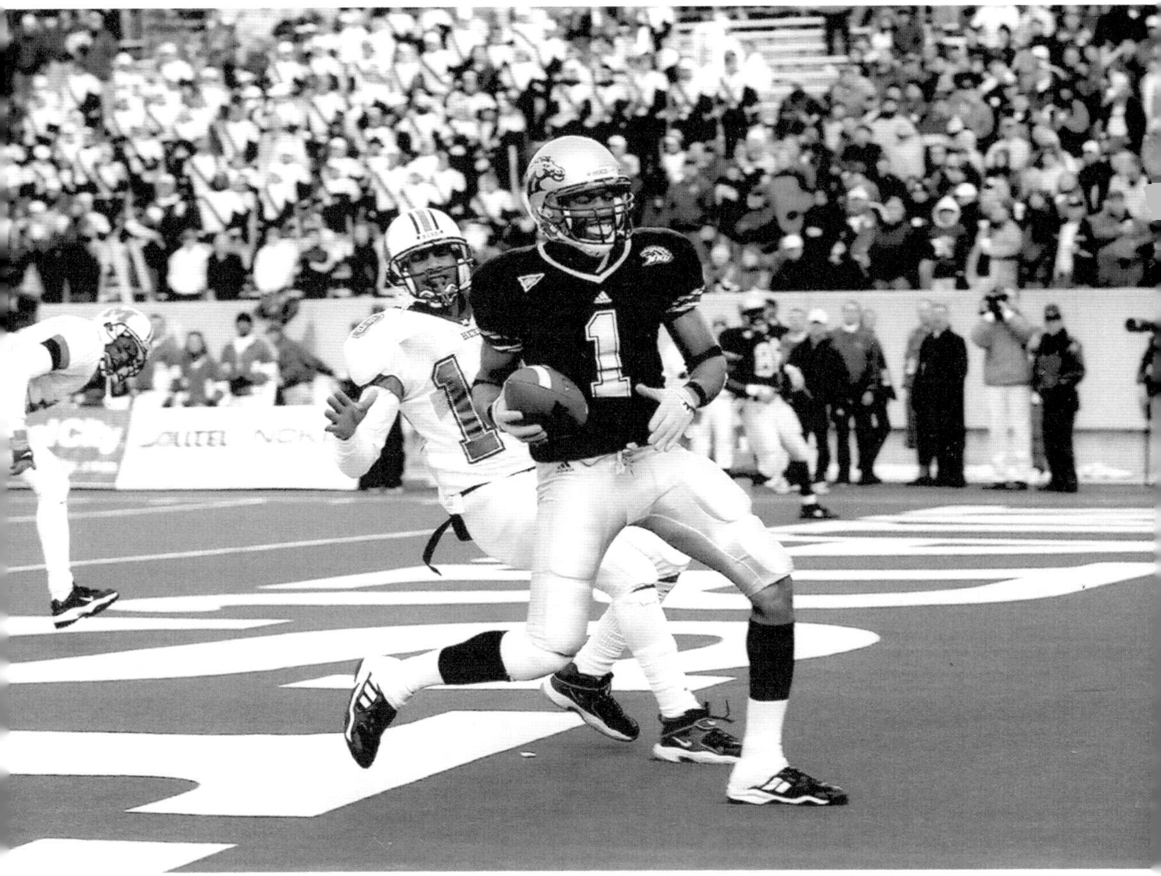

WMU'S SECOND TRIP TO THE MAC championship game against Marshall University in 2000 ended with fourth-quarter heartbreak just like the year before. After falling behind 13-0 at the half, Western rallied back behind first-year starting quarterback Jeff Welsh. WMU scored with 47 seconds left in the third quarter when Welsh connected with Steve Neal on a 22-yard touchdown pass. On the next Bronco possession, they grabbed a 14-13 lead on a 41-yard strike from Welsh to Josh Bush and Brad Selent's point after touchdown. Star Marshall quarterback Byron Leftwich fought back with a 29-yard touchdown pass to John Cooper with 6:14 on the clock to reclaim the lead for Marshall. Two last-gasp Broncos rallies fell short, allowing Marshall its fourth-straight MAC title.

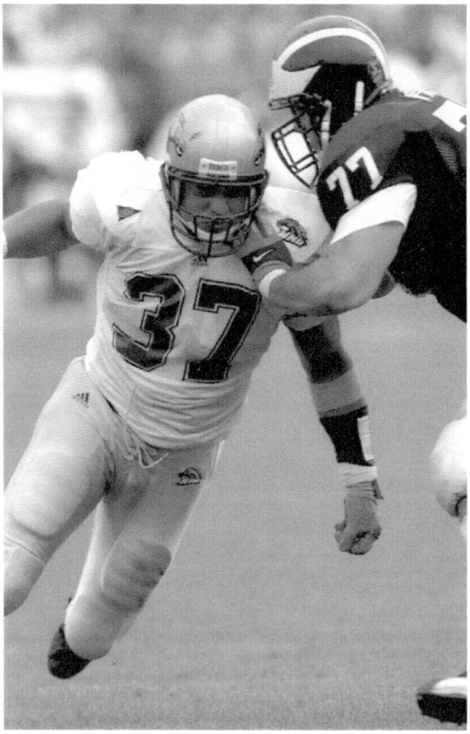

ALTHOUGH WMU REGULARLY FACED OFF against Central Michigan University, Eastern Michigan University, and sometimes even Michigan State University, playing the University of Michigan Wolverines in Ann Arbor was a rare occurrence. The teams met once in Michigan Stadium during the war years, but it was not until 2001 that the Broncos got a real taste of the "big house." The Wolverines were not gracious guests as they knocked off Western 38-21. (Courtesy of GS Photo.)

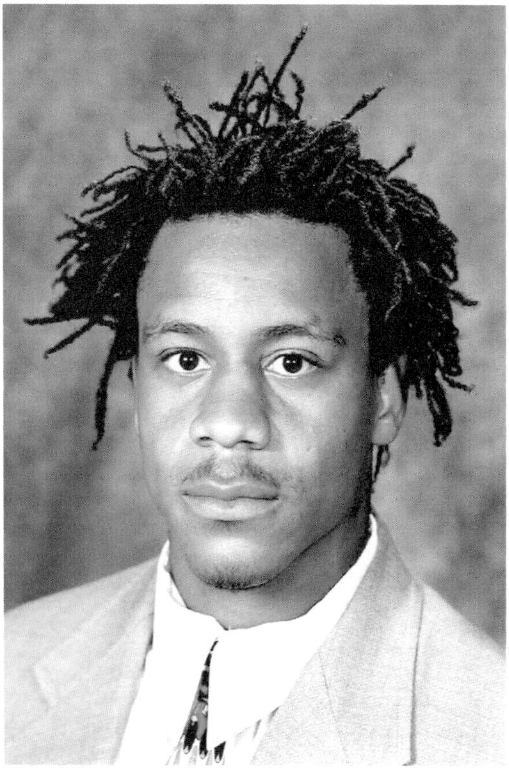

THE FLAMBOYANT RONALD ROGERS WAS a dynamic cornerback for the Broncos. The Miami native set school records for pass breakups (38) and started in 46 consecutive games. He was an All-MAC selection in 2001 when he ranked second in the league in kickoff return yards (23.2) and second in forced fumbles with four. (Courtesy of GS Photo.)

WIDE RECEIVER JOSH BUSH WAS WMU's Offensive MVP in 2001 by virtue of his team-leading receptions (48), receiving yards (617), and all-purpose yards (809). He finished his career in the top 10 for Broncos in receptions, receiving yards, and touchdowns. (Courtesy of GS Photo.)

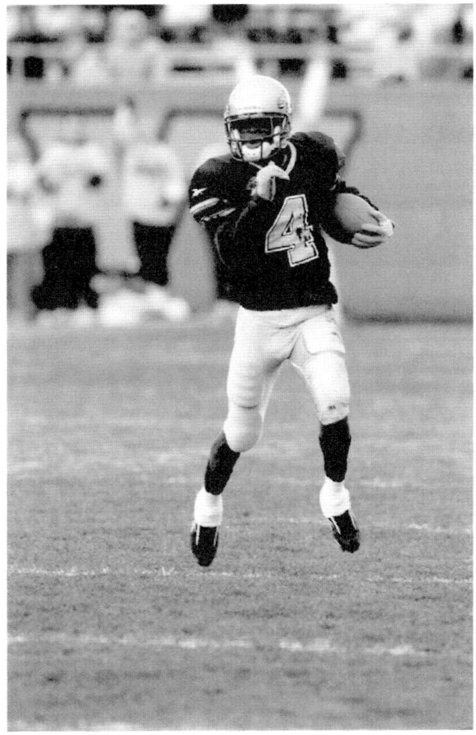

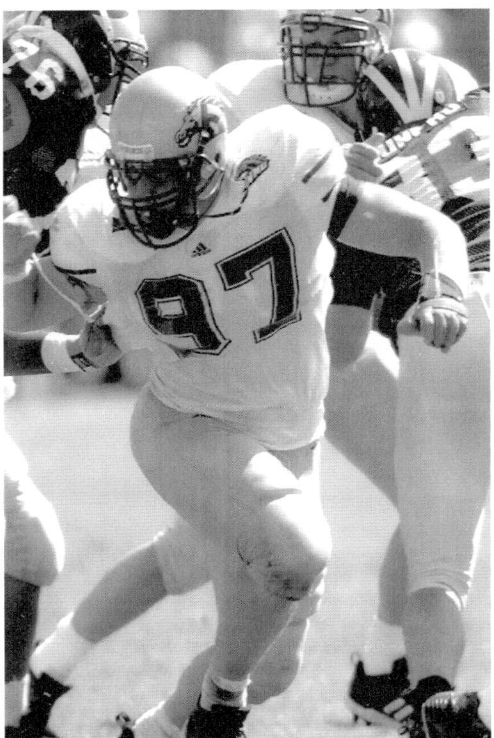

CHRIS BROWNING WAS A WELL-DESERVING All-MAC first-team selection in 2002 due to his on-field skills, but he was a true force in the WMU weight room. Browning was a fiend at workouts and was dubbed the winner of the team's "Hard Hat" award. (Courtesy of GS Photo.)

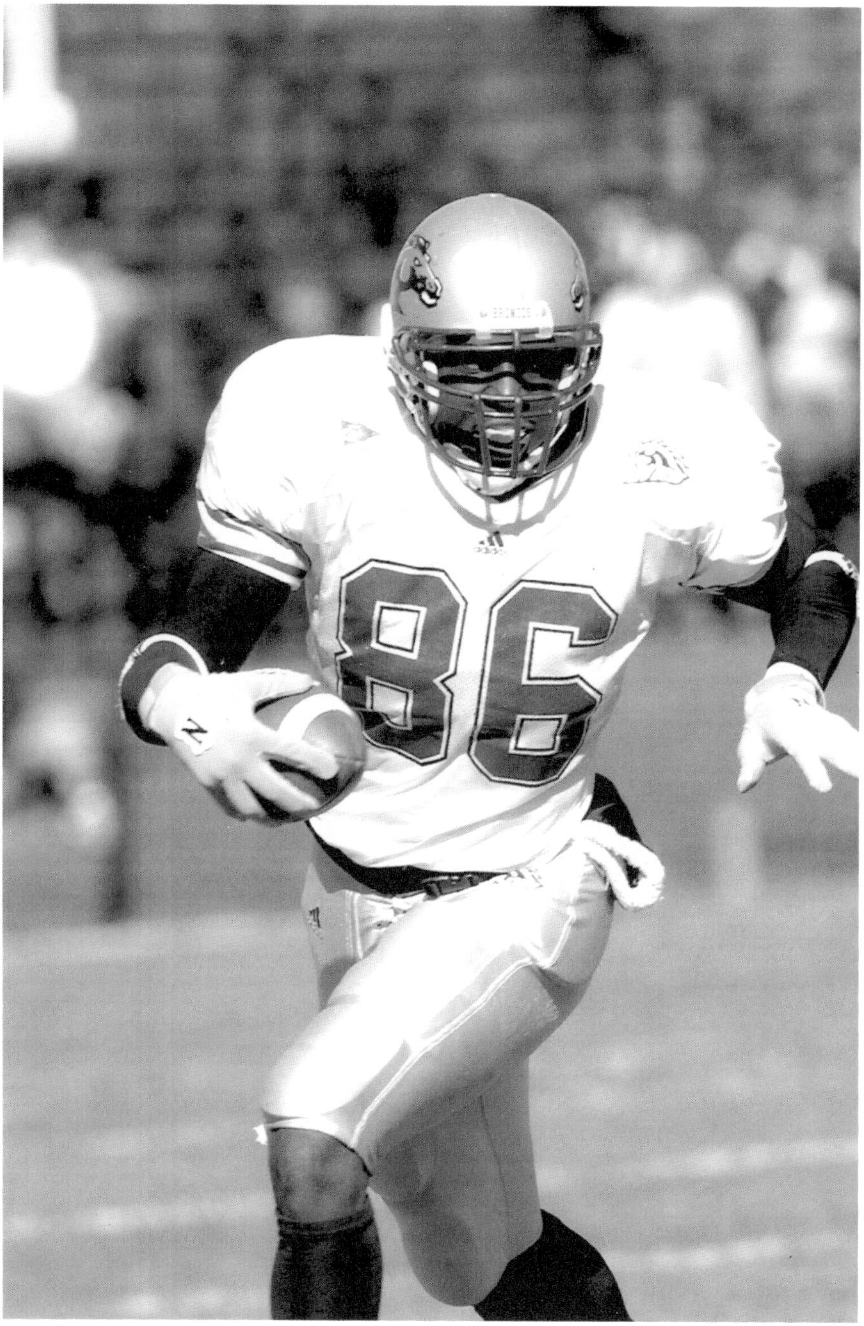

MOBOLAGI AFARIOGUN IS THE MOST DECORATED tight end in Bronco history. The Detroit native was named to three All-MAC teams; twice he was a first-team selection. He produced an impressive 105 catches for 1,079 yards and 11 touchdowns in his career. Afariogun was the receiver the Broncos could always count on when they needed that critical third-down yardage. (Courtesy of GS Photo.)

KENDRICK MOSELY'S SPEED WAS ONE OF THE Broncos' biggest weapons in 2003. He ended his career ranked second in career catches, third in receiving yards, and first in punt return yardage. He turned a streak of 42 games in which he caught a pass. (Courtesy of GS Photo.)

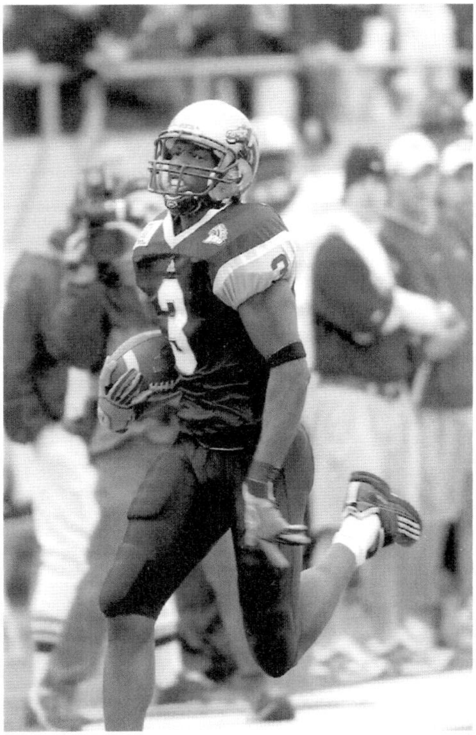

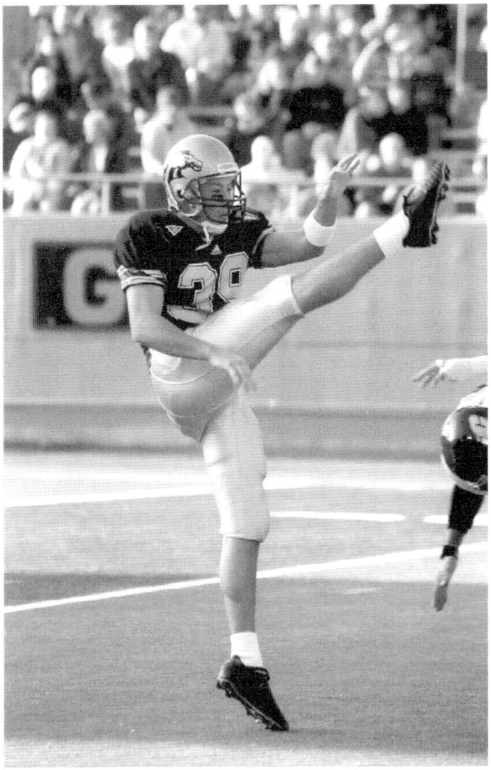

THE PINPOINT ACCURACY OF ADAM Anderson's punting was a critical weapon for Western. Against Central Michigan in 2002, he produced three punts over 50 yards; five of those ended up inside the 20-yard line and four of those inside the 4-yard line. Pinning the Chips back helped the Broncos to a 44-21 win. (Courtesy of GS Photo.)

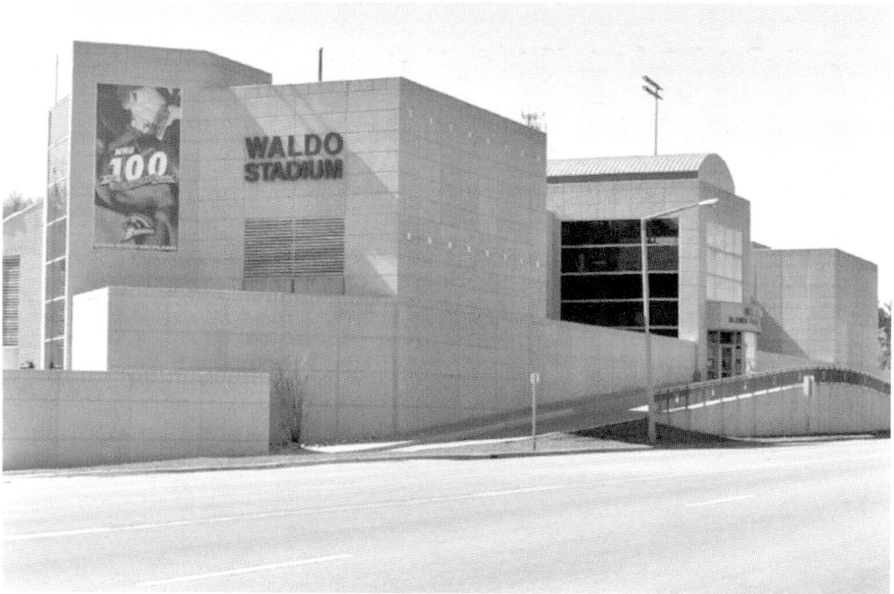

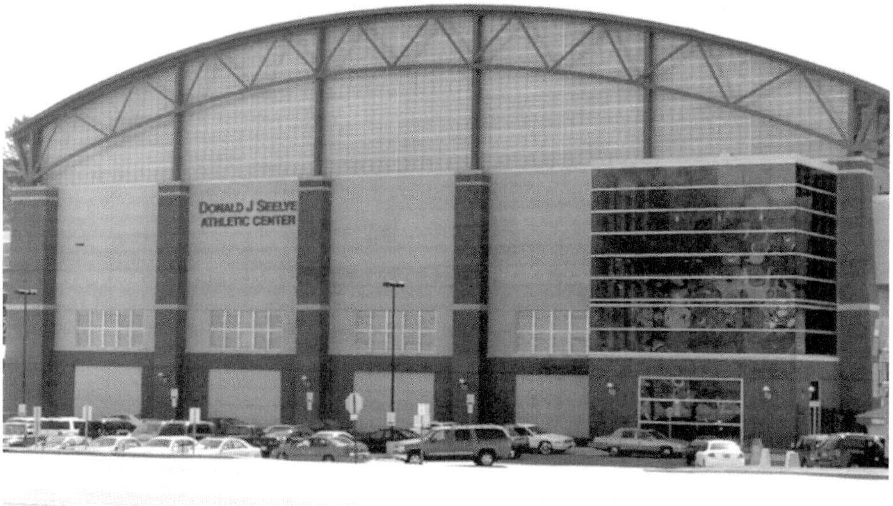

WALDO STADIUM HAS SEEN MANY FACE-LIFTS since opening in 1939, but the boldest occurred in 1998 and 2003. The entire facade of the old stadium got a face-lift with the construction of the Bill Brown Alumni Football Center. The center features home and visitor locker rooms, a 6,400-square-foot weight room, and new medical and equipment rooms, along with an auditorium. Upper levels brought new club seating, lounges, and coaching rooms. The new Donald J. Seelye Indoor Athletic Center gave WMU a new look both inside and out. The facility provides an eight-story-high indoor practice field as well as a location for a new state-of-the-art video board. Other updates at Waldo Stadium include the installation of a new NeXturf playing surface in 2001.

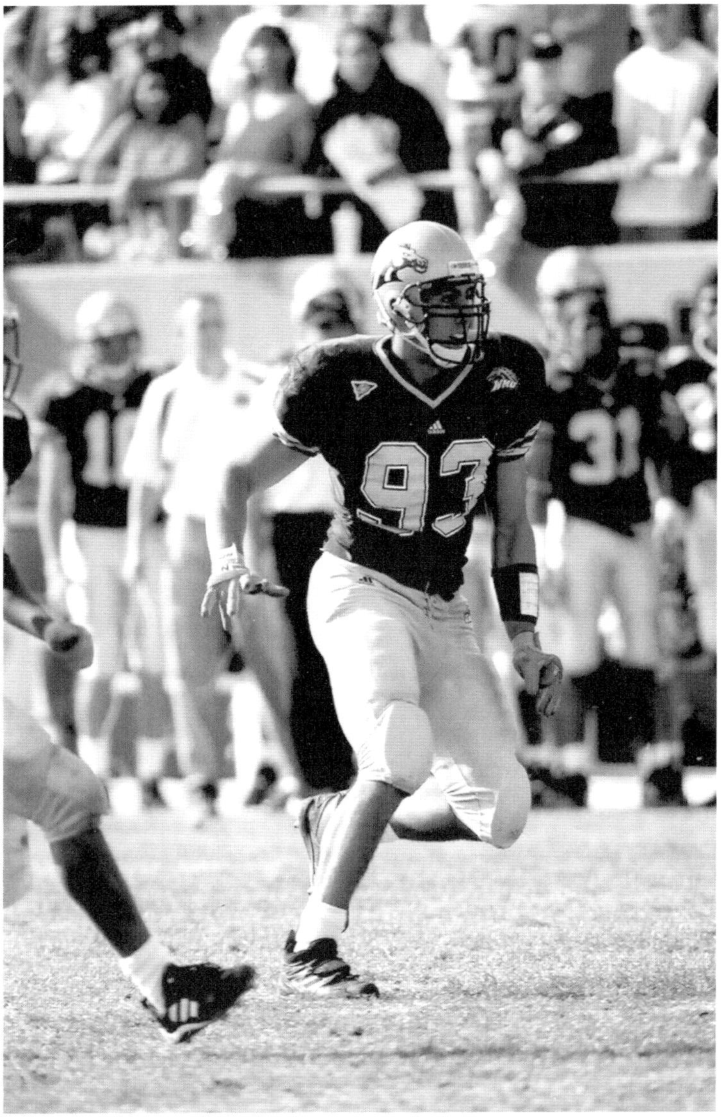

JASON BABIN BECAME THE FIRST BRONCO player ever to be selected in the first round of the NFL draft. The Houston Texans selected the outstanding defensive end in 2004 as the 27th overall pick that year, following one of the most celebrated defensive careers WMU had ever seen. He was named as an All-American on several lists, grabbed back-to-back MAC Defensive Player of the Year honors, and was the Broncos' team MVP. Babin set Broncos career marks in sacks (38) and tackles for loss (75), breaking Joel Smeenge's marks in both categories. He also had 299 career tackles, eight forced fumbles, two fumble recoveries, and even recorded three receptions as well, playing blocking back in WMU's power-I formation. Babin saw action in every one of the team's 112 games during his four-year career. He made an immediate impact in the NFL by starting all 16 games and recorded 54 tackles and four sacks for the Texans in his rookie year. (Courtesy of GS Photo.)

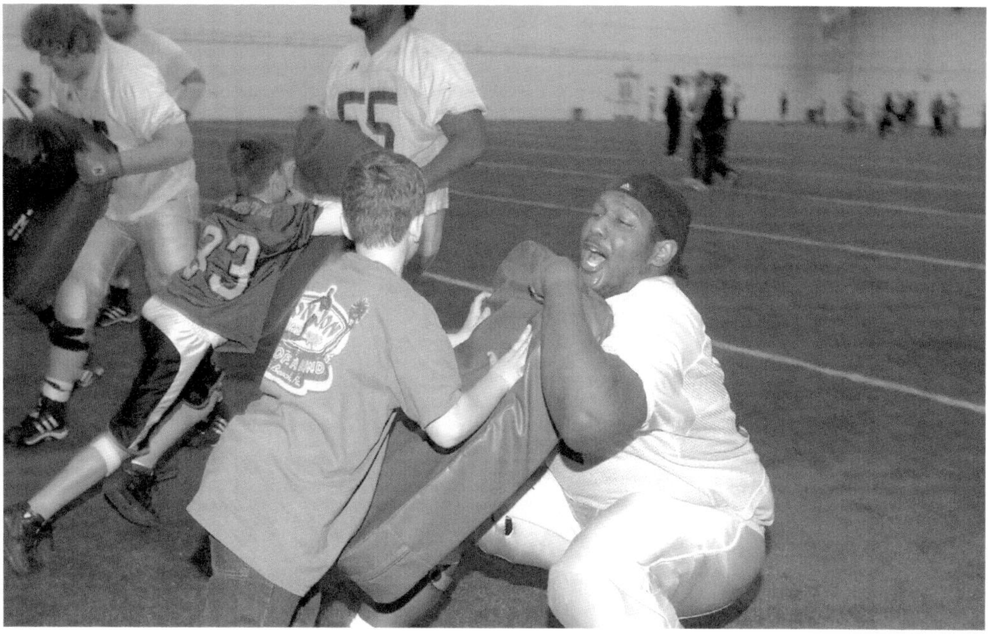

ONE OF THE MOST IMPORTANT TENETS OF BEING a WMU student-athlete is the call for the players to give their time and talents back to the community. Whether it is through delivering donated food to a local food bank, visiting area schools to speak and read with youth, or volunteering at local shelters, Bronco football players have always been eager to support the communities of southwest Michigan that have supported the Broncos throughout the years.

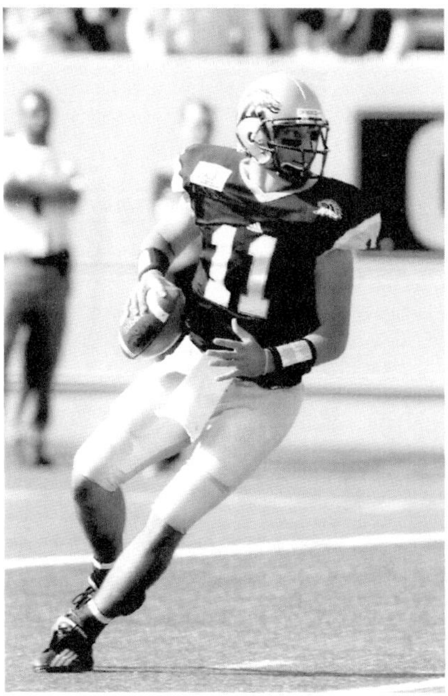

BRONCO QUARTERBACK CHAD MUNSON HAD A career-best game when WMU faced off against William and Mary in the home opener of the 2003 season. A senior, Munson threw a team-record six touchdown passes, including four in the first half as the Broncos overcame a 14-7 first-quarter deficit for the win 56-24. He completed 24 of 35 passes for a record-smashing 450 yards. (Courtesy of GS Photo.)

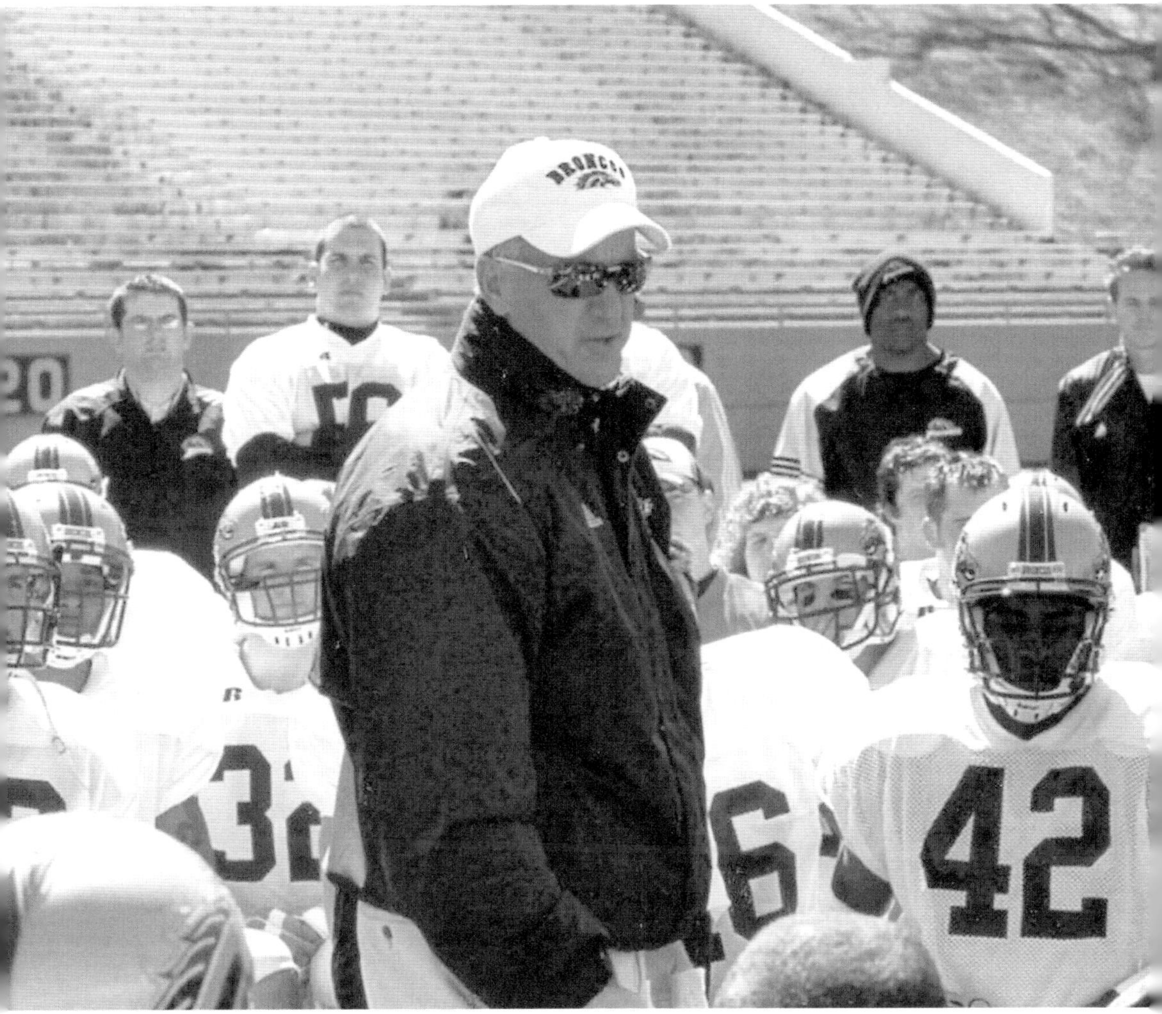

Bill Cubit became WMU's 14th head coach in 2005, inheriting a team that had gone 1-10 the year before. The former Stanford offensive coordinator took charge immediately and produced one of the Broncos' biggest turnarounds, finishing 7-4 overall and 5-3 in the MAC in his initial campaign. His team that had been projected to finish at the bottom of the MAC West Division standings instead was in the running for the title until the last week of the regular season. Cubit was named the MAC Coach of the Year for his tutelage. Cubit was familiar with WMU's surroundings, having served as the Broncos' offensive coordinator from 1997 to 1999. In his first stint with the Broncos, Cubit oversaw an offense that ranked in the NCAA Top 25 for passing offense, scoring offense, and total offense in back-to-back seasons.

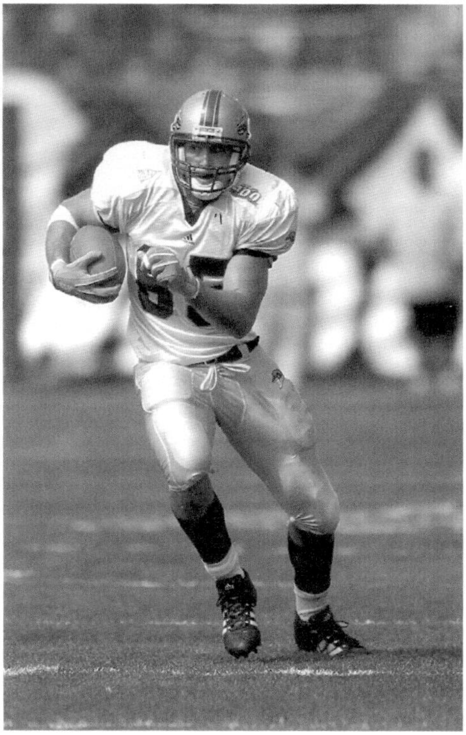

THE BRONCOS FOUND A BRUISING TIGHT END from Chelsea, Michigan, with Tony Scheffler's emergence on the team. Twice in his senior year, Scheffler was named a Mackey National Tight End of the Week, an honor given to the nation's best tight ends, and finished fourth in the final voting for the annual Mackey Award. In 2005, he was third in the nation among tight ends in receptions per game and fifth in the country in yards per game. He was drafted in the second round by the Denver Broncos in the 2006 NFL draft. (Courtesy of GS Photo.)

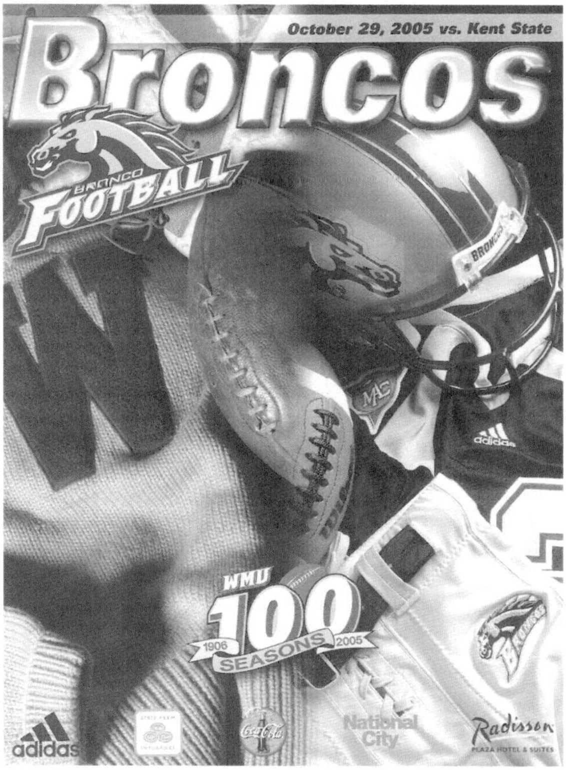

KICKOFF TIME FOR THE GAME BETWEEN the WMU Broncos and Ball State University was slated for seven o'clock, but the game did not end until four hours later when Ball State kicker Brian Jackson ended a five-overtime standoff between the schools. The longest game in WMU history produced gaudy numbers for both teams. They combined for 1,090 yards of total offense and 16 touchdowns while both quarterbacks—Ball State's Joey Lynch and WMU's Tim Hiller—threw for more than 300 yards. WMU's Nate Meyer had two chances to win it for the Broncos, but he missed a 49-yard field goal on the last play of regulation and missed a 32-yard kick on the final play of the fourth overtime.

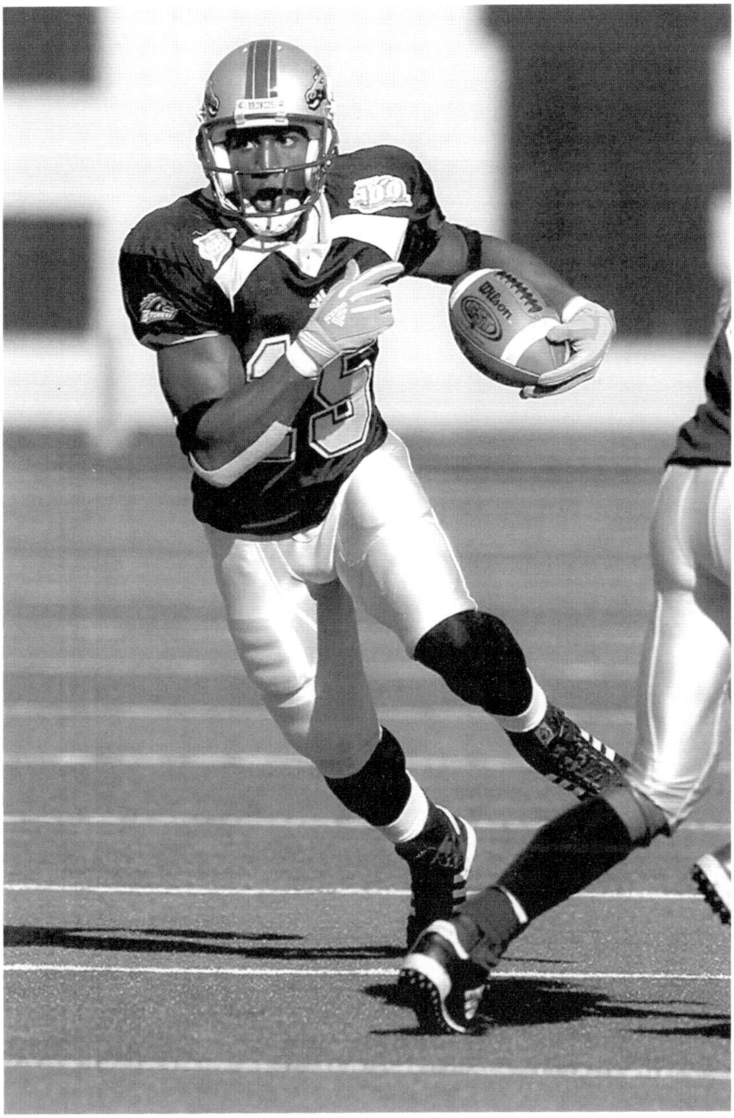

RECEIVER GREG JENNINGS SINGLE-HANDEDLY rewrote the Broncos record book during his time at WMU. By the time he graduated, Jennings held team career records for receptions (238), touchdowns (39), and all-purpose yards (5,050). He also holds single-season marks for receptions, touchdowns, and yards. In his senior year, he led the entire nation in total receptions and receptions per game, ranked second in yards per game and third among wide receivers in touchdowns. For his accomplishments, Jennings was named the MAC co-MVP in 2005. He became the 10th Bronco in history to be named an All-American and only the second WMU offensive-skill position to achieve the honor. He was recognized as an All-American by the Associated Press (third team), *Sports Illustrated* (second team), and *College Football News* (third team). He was drafted in the second round of the 2006 NFL draft by the Green Bay Packers. (Courtesy of GS Photo.)

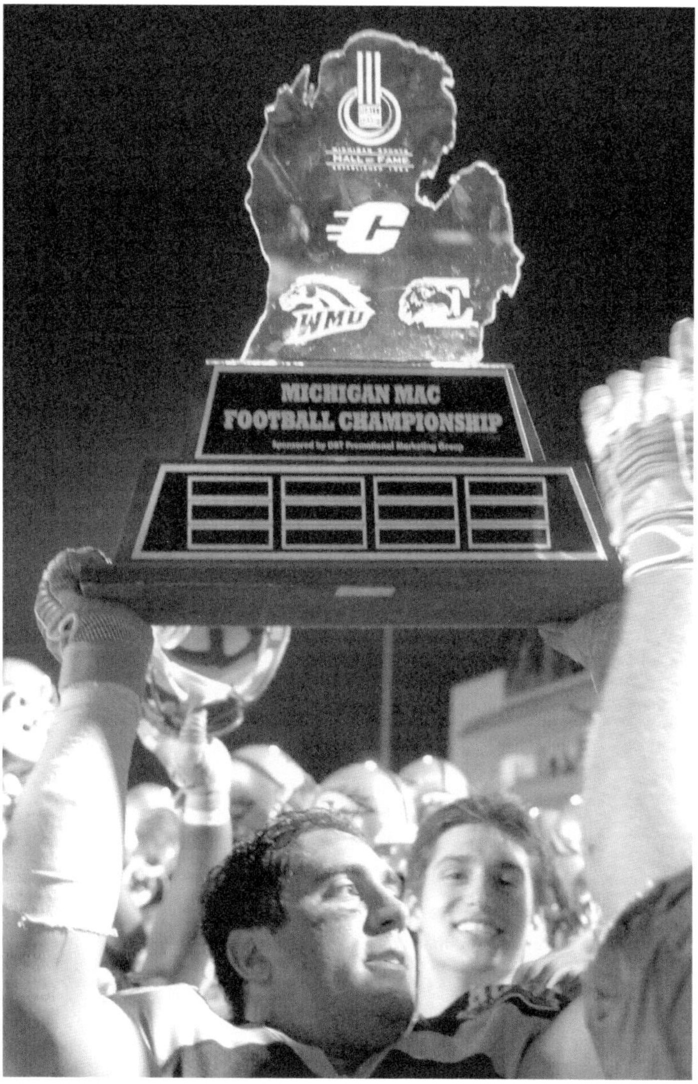

AS IF THE RIVALRY BETWEEN WMU, CENTRAL Michigan University, and Eastern Michigan University was not already deep-rooted, in 2005 the Michigan Sports Hall of Fame created the new Michigan MAC Football Championship trophy to go along with the bragging rights for the university that defeats the other two that year. The trophy remains in the possession of the winning school until one of the rivals claims the title. The three schools have played each other annually since 1978, but they have faced each other as far back as 1906 when WMU and Eastern Michigan first met. In the previous 27 years, WMU swept both the Chippewas and the Eagles eight times, including four times in the previous six years. The trophy got its inaugural home in Kalamazoo in 2005 when the Broncos claimed the title with a 31-24 win over Eastern Michigan in a game played at Detroit's Ford Field and a dramatic 44-36 win over Central Michigan. The Broncos held off a furious Central Michigan rally attempt in the game's final minute to claim the trophy.

4

Bring Us Fame

Western Michigan University's All-Century Team

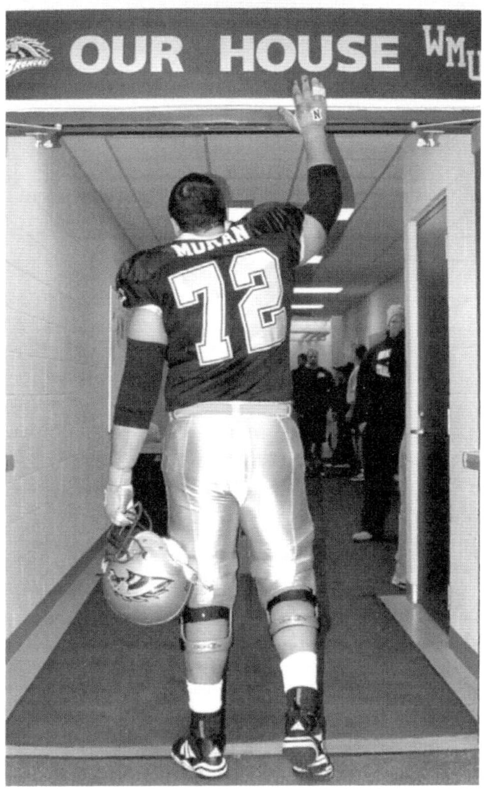

A group of students gathered together shortly after the beginning of the 20th century to play the new game of football, playing in front of no spectators save for a few girlfriends and curious passersby. The game itself was hardly noticed by any media scribes. At least the student yearbook recorded the team's accomplishments in that short three-game season, and later some mention in the local newspaper appeared. The players did not play for fame. They played for the love of the game. As the years progressed, it became impossible to avoid the scrutiny. But the players still played for the same reason: to support their fans, their community, and their school in "our house." Many of them achieved fame, most never did. To celebrate the school's 100th season, a group of noted Bronco football observers selected the 100 players whose achievements stood out among the thousands who have contributed to the team. The following pages feature those honored players.

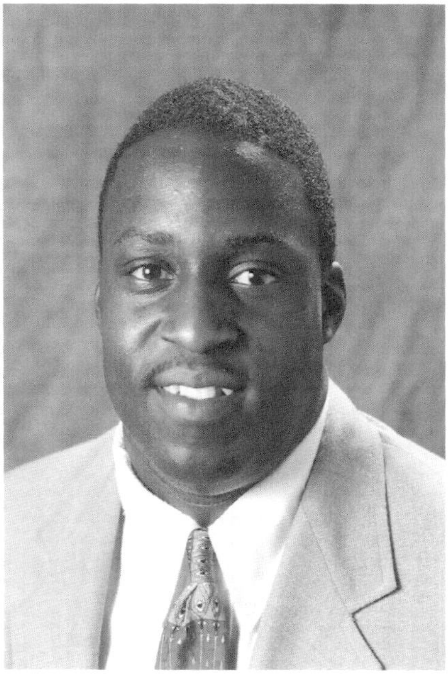

DETROIT NATIVE MOBOLAJI AFARIOGUN WAS named to All-Mac First team in 2000 and 2002. He finished his career with 105 catches for 1,075 yards and 11 touchdowns. He became one of the Broncos' best possession receivers with sure hands on critical plays.

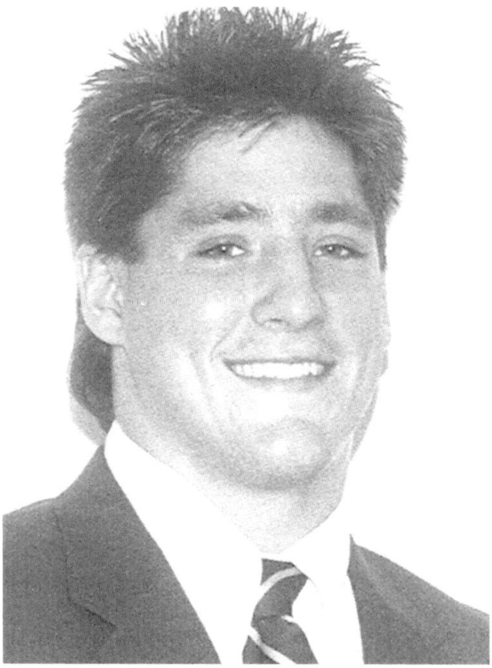

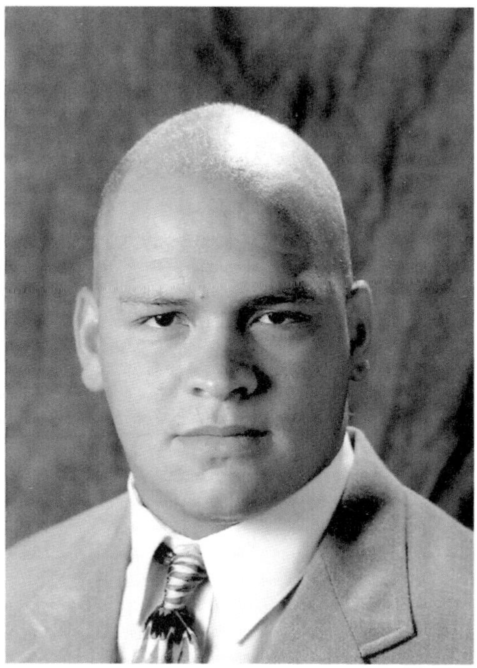

PAUL AGEMA (LEFT) WAS AN ALL-MAC second-team selection in 1988 and 1990 as a receiver. He recorded 276 all-purpose yards against Akron in 1990 and finished the season with 785 receiving yards. He set a school record with 57 catches in 1990. Anthony Allsbury (right) was an All-MAC first-team selection in 2000 and 2001. He compiled 93 tackles and 14 sacks during those All-MAC seasons.

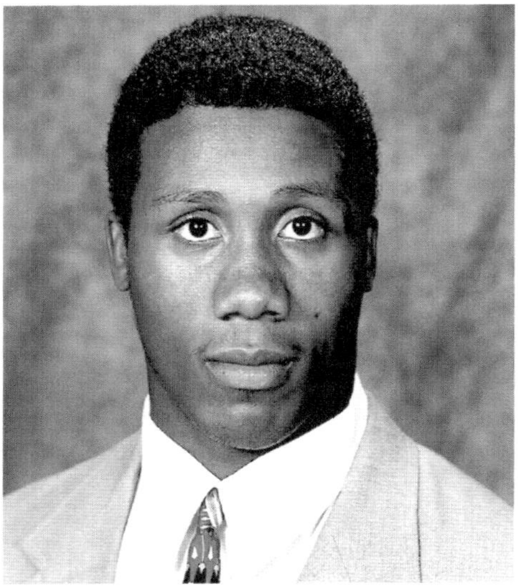

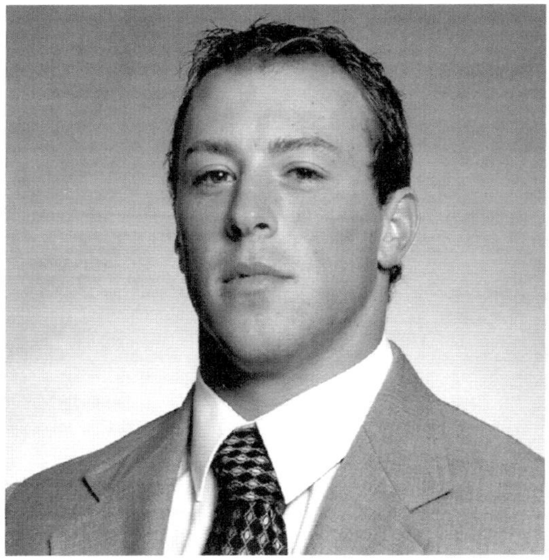

COREY ALSTON (LEFT) RANKS THIRD ON WMU'S all-time list in both receiving yards (2,456) and touchdown receptions (25). Adam Anderson (right) was one of WMU's best punters. He holds the WMU career record for punt average with 41.3 yards and season average at 43.9 yards. He was named to the All-MAC second team in 2004.

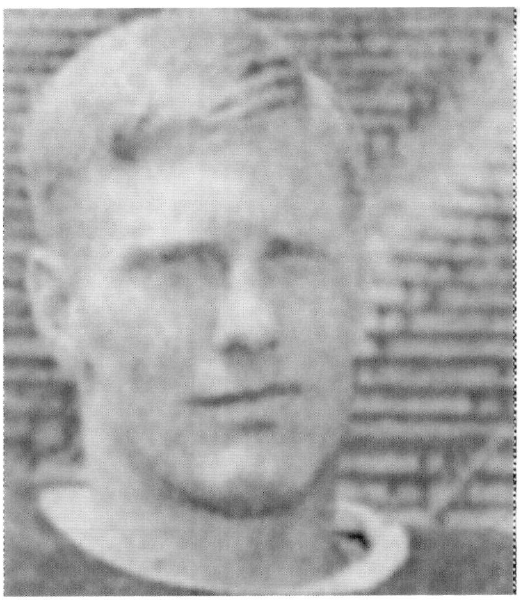

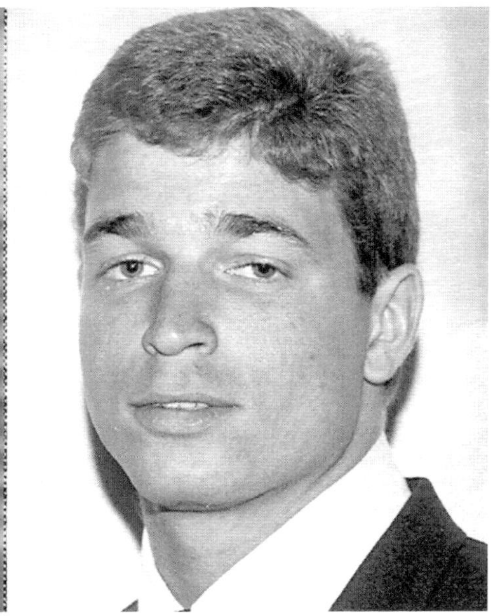

MARTY BARSKI (LEFT) WAS ONE OF WMU'S best defensive weapons in the mid-1960s. His 149 interception return yards ranks third all time for the Broncos. Willie Berrios (right) made his name known against Central Michigan University in 1987. In that game, he recorded 27 tackles, the most ever by a Bronco in a game. Not surprisingly, he led the team in tackles in 1988 with 114.

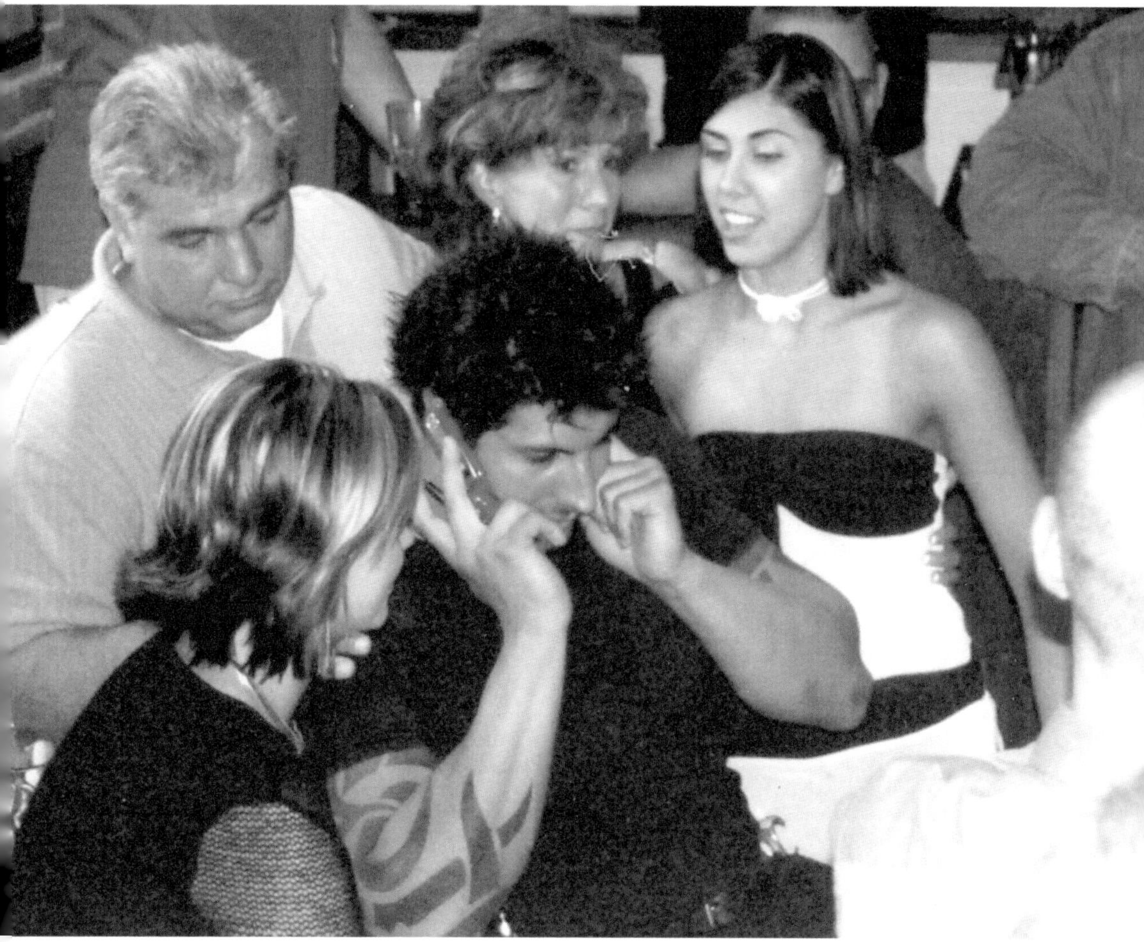

JASON BABIN TAKES A TELEPHONE CALL FROM the Houston Texans as he became the first Western player to be drafted in the first round of the NFL draft as the 27th overall pick in 2004. At WMU, he started 25 of 47 games, setting Broncos' career marks in sacks (38) and tackles for loss (75), breaking Joel Smeenge's marks in both categories (34 and 66, respectively). He also amassed 299 career tackles, eight forced fumbles, two fumble recoveries, and three receptions for 35 yards and blocked three punts. He earned first-team All-America honors from *The NFL Draft Report* and *College Sports Report* and added second-team honors from *Sports Illustrated*, the *Sporting News*, and *College Football News*. He was a first-team All-MAC selection and the league's Defensive Player of the Year for two consecutive seasons. Babin racked up a career-high 115 tackles, matched a career high with 15 sacks for 71 yards, and made 33 stops behind the line of scrimmage, breaking his own school record. (Courtesy of the Babin family.)

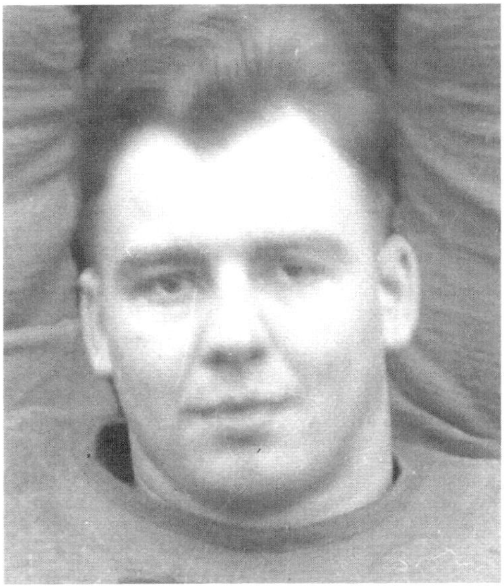

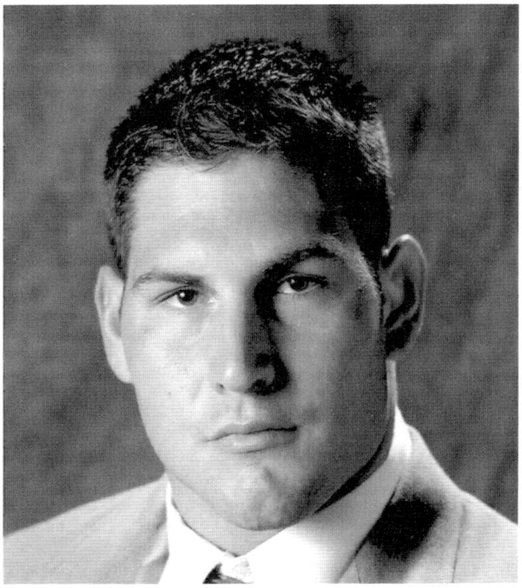

THE PROFESSIONALS RECOGNIZED THE TALENTS that Ray Bray (left) displayed as a Bronco and made him the first Bronco to be selected in the NFL draft. He played 10 seasons with the Chicago Bears and earned four All-Pro selections. Defensive end Chris Browning (right) was a one of the WMU defense's most disruptive forces. In his career, he recorded 167 tackles and 14.5 sacks.

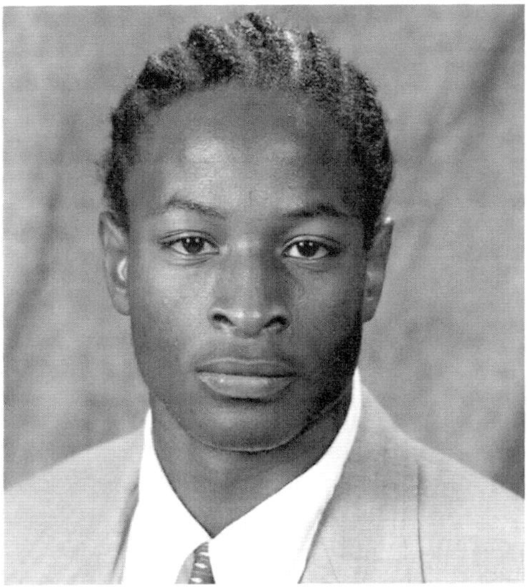

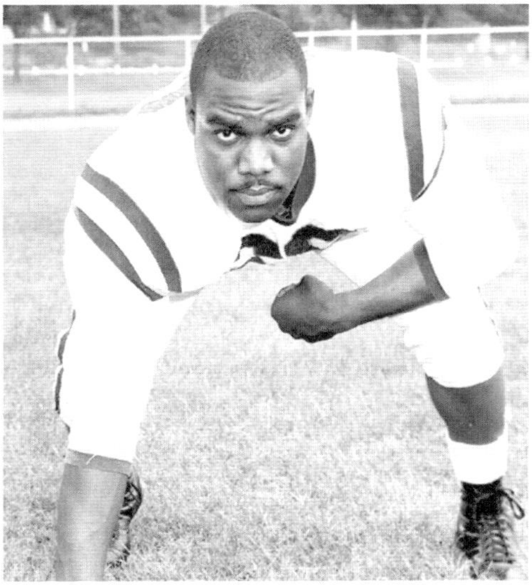

THE MULTIPLE TALENTS OF JOSH BUSH (LEFT) are evident with a look at the WMU record books. He ranks fifth all time in receptions, sixth in receiving yards, and he also holds the all-time single season record for punt return yards. Clarence Cheatham (right) became the first Bronco to ever receive All-America honors, being named to the Williamson All-America team in 1958 as a tackle. He was the Broncos' MVP in 1959.

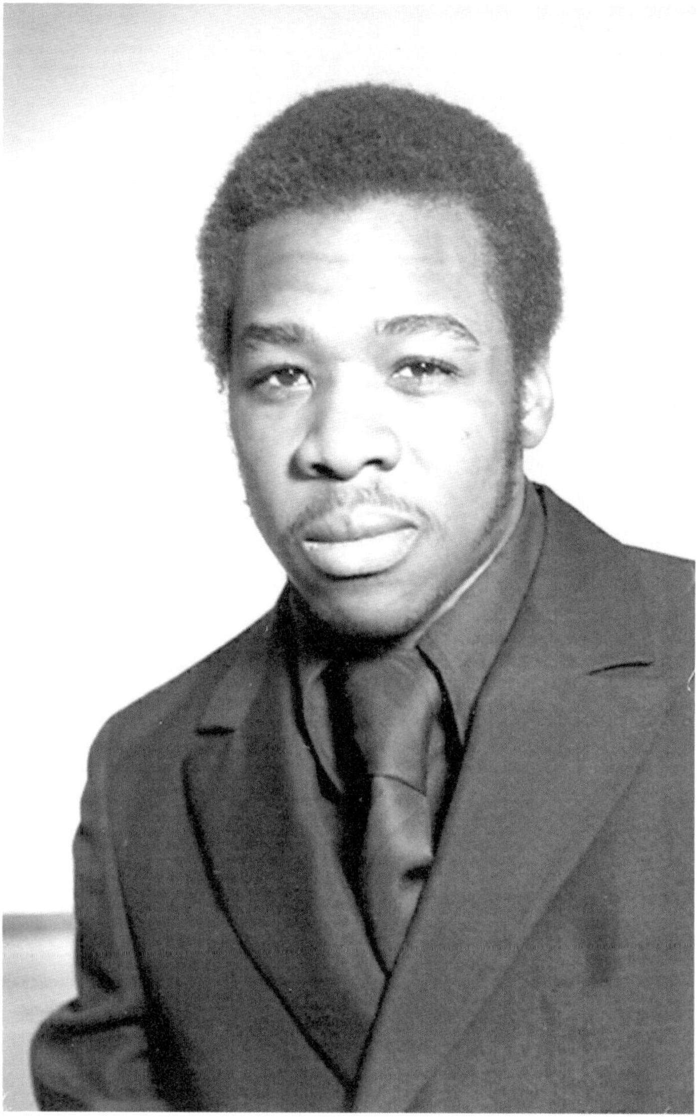

LARRY CATES WAS A HALFBACK WHO HAD many highlights in his WMU career in the early 1970s, but one win against Marshall University stands out to him. "In that game my brother Wesley returned a punt 89 yards for a touchdown and along the way faked the punter out of one of his cleats. I scored two touchdowns, and the papers wrote the next day that the Cates brothers had more tricks than the Barnum and Bailey circus, who just happened to be in town. Another game that stood out was against Kent State University. Their middle linebacker was the meanest-looking player I ever saw, with a face that only a mother could love. Every time I looked up he was in my face. He hit me so hard on one tackle that when I got up I didn't know which huddle to go to. As the battle went on, I was able to put a move on him that left him reaching for nothing but air as I went in to score with a grin on my face. We won that game 13-12."

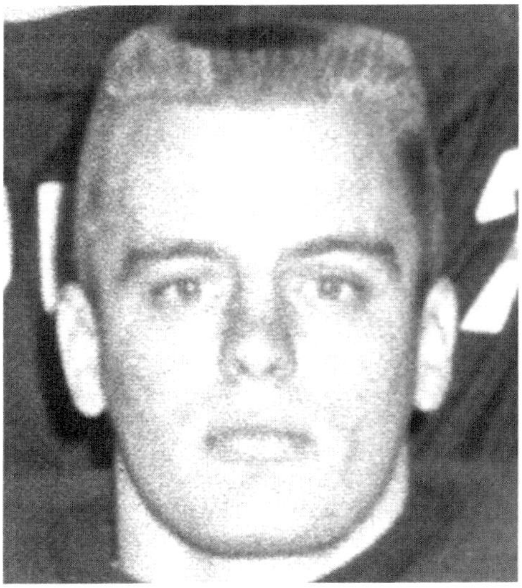

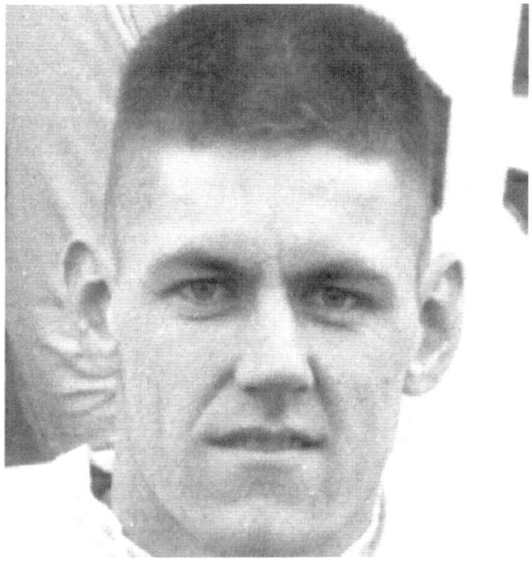

Quarterback Ed Chlebek (left) lead the Broncos to their first bowl appearance. He was selected to the All-MAC first team in 1961. He ranks fourth all time in completion percentage and threw for 2,290 career yards. Pat Clysdale (right) was a member of the 1949 All-MAC first team partly due to his recording of seven touchdown receptions that year to lead the entire conference. He returned to WMU to serve in several coaching and administrative duties.

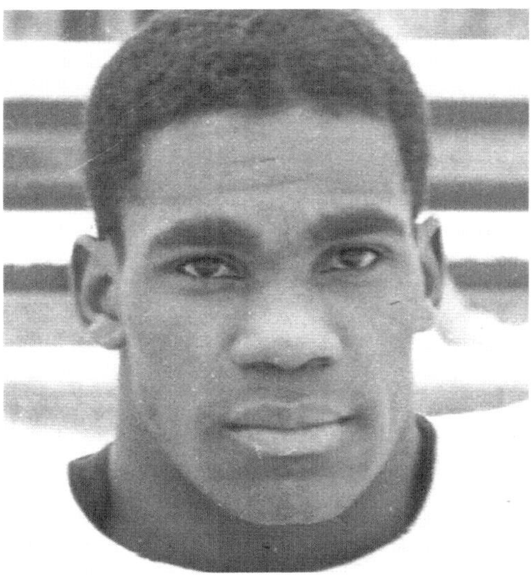

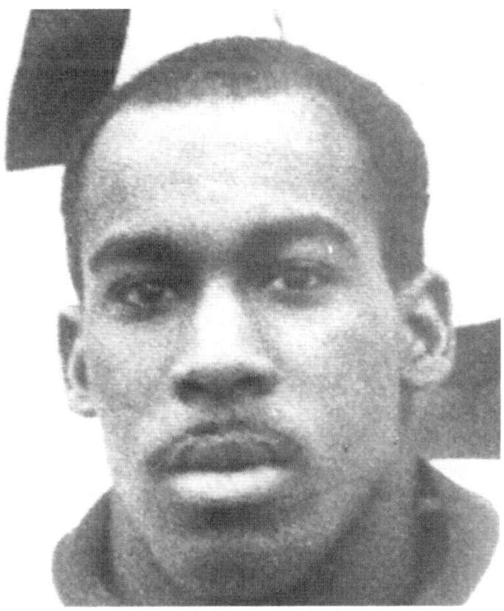

Horace "Hap" Coleman (left) was named to the Collier's Little All-America team in 1941 and ranked fifth in the entire nation in rushing. He once averaged 29 yards per carry in a single game. Lovell Coleman (right) was a 1959 selection to the Williamson All-America team as well as an All-MAC first-team honoree. He holds the WMU all-time record for career kickoff return and twice logged 100-yard kickoff returns for touchdowns.

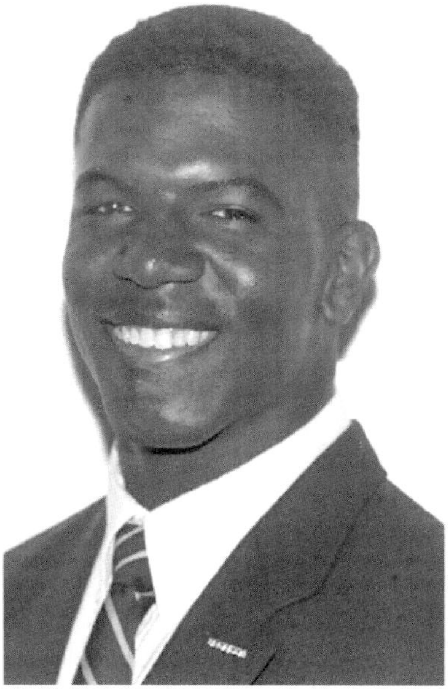

TERRY CREWS WAS AN ACCOMPLISHED FOOTBALL PLAYER both on the field and on the silver screen. He was an All-MAC second-team selection in 1989 and played for 10 years in the NFL. He later achieved fame in Hollywood by appearing in 19 movies, including *Soul Plane*, *Starsky and Hutch*, and *The Longest Yard*.

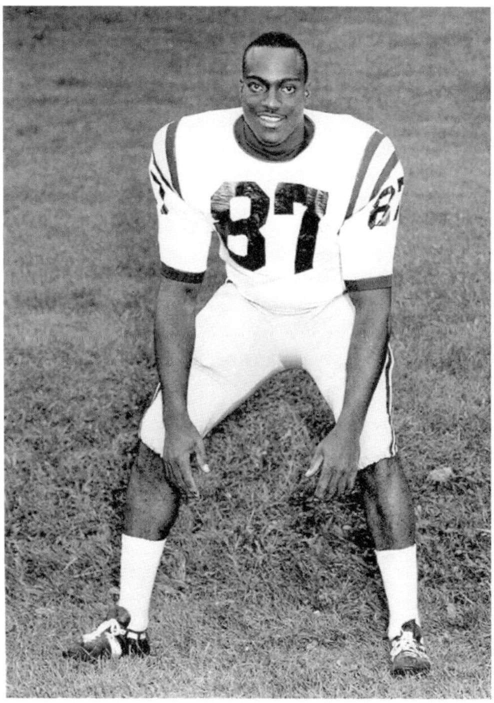

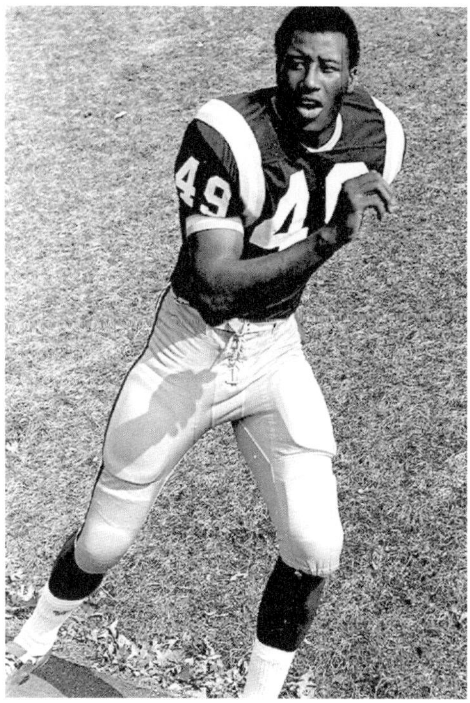

JERRY COLLINS (LEFT) WAS TWICE NAMED TO the All-MAC first team (1967 and 1968) as a defensive end. He went on to play professional football with the Buffalo Bills. Vern Davis (right) was WMU's biggest defensive weapon in 1970. His 13 pass breakups and five touchdown saves frustrated opponents all season long. He was selected to the All-MAC first team that year and later went on to play for the Philadelphia Eagles in the NFL.

SAM DUNLAP WAS A PURE SCORING MACHINE for the early Hilltoppers teams. He scored seven touchdowns in a single game in 1916, placing him second all time in that accomplishment. He also shares the record for most touchdowns in a season with 19. He was also one of school's best punters. Dunlap was one of the first African American athletic stars in the area.

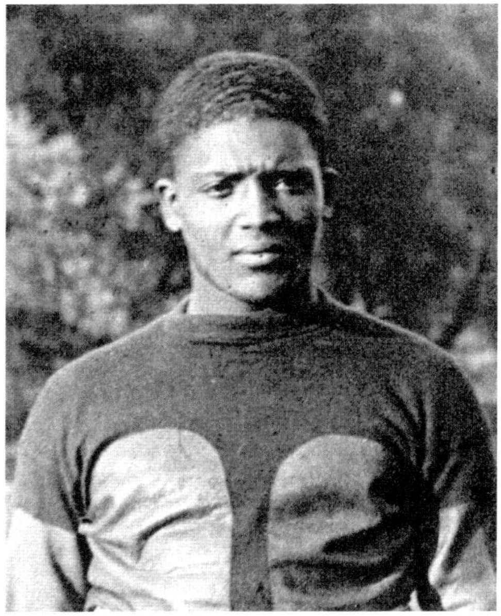

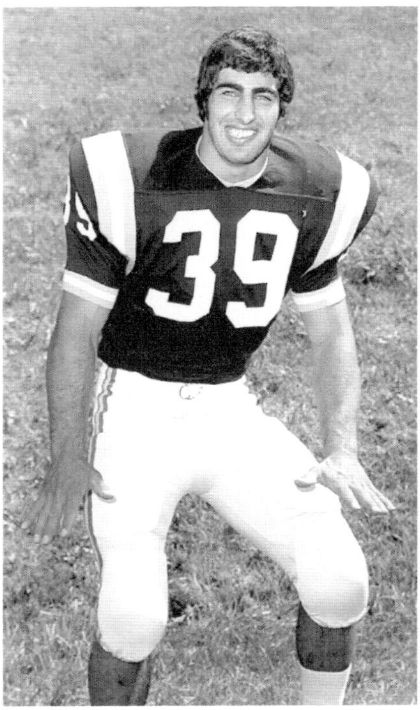

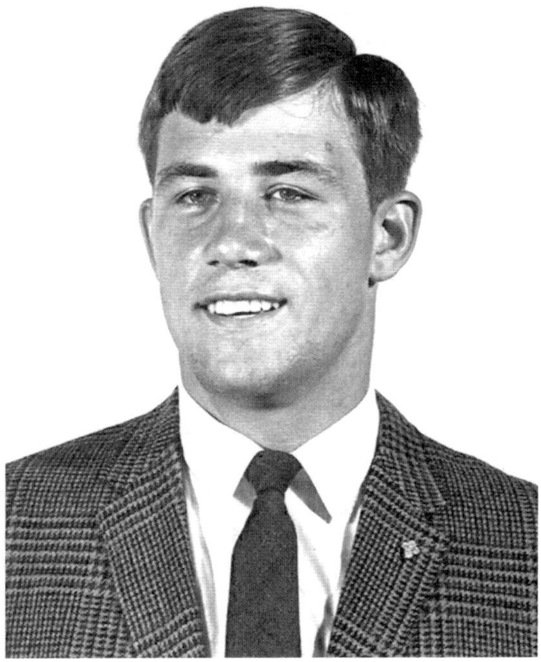

TOM ELIAS (LEFT) WAS A TWO TIME ALL-MAC first-team honoree in 1970 and 1971, the first Bronco linebacker to earn that designation. He is tied for 10th all time in tackles for the Broncos with 305. He was named the team's MVP in 1971. Greg Flaska (right) gave the Broncos a pair of sure hands from 1969 to 1970. He caught nine passes against Toledo in 1969 and was named to the All-MAC first team in 1970.

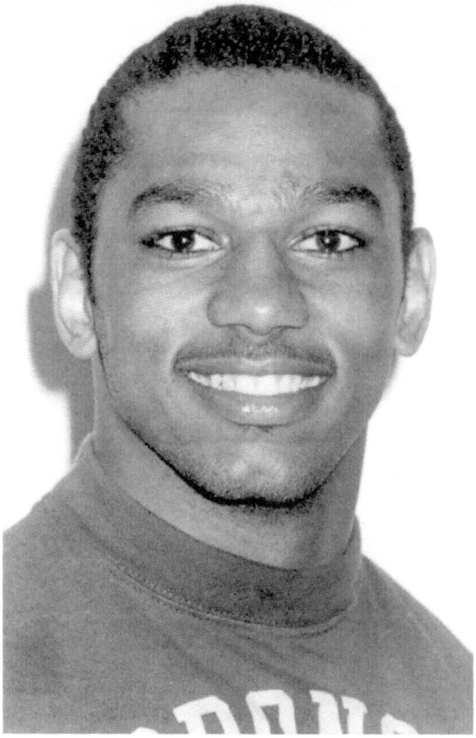

Shaun Faulkner was named to the 1983 All-MAC first team after ranking second in the nation in average rushing yards per game and third in all-purpose yards. He holds the WMU single-season record for rushing yards (1,668), attempts (394), and all-purpose yards (1,889). He was named the Broncos' MVP in 1983.

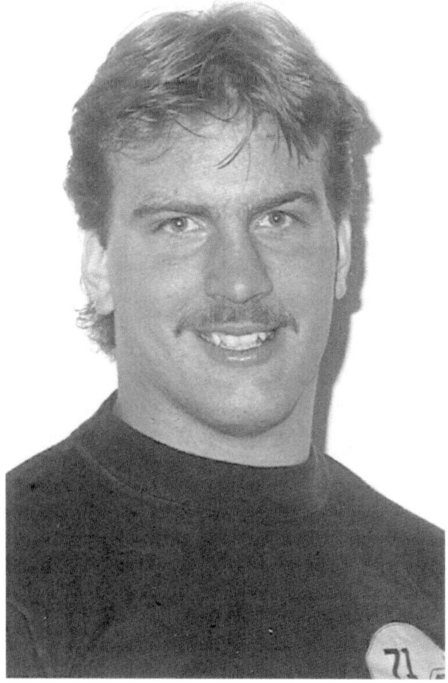

Defensive tackle Mark Garalczyk spent a lot of time in the opponent's backfield during his career. He was the MAC's Defensive Player of the Year in 1986 when he recorded 45 tackles for loss. He was twice named to the All-MAC first team.

A lifetime of service with the Western Michigan program earned John Gill the suitable title of "Mr. Bronco." Gill was a multisport star, earning 13 total letters, and a multitalented football player who could punt, pass, and run. After graduation, he returned as an assistant coach and later served as the team's head coach. He finally moved into an administration position where he remained for many years. The current press box at Waldo Stadium bears his name as does a WMU Scholar Athlete Award.

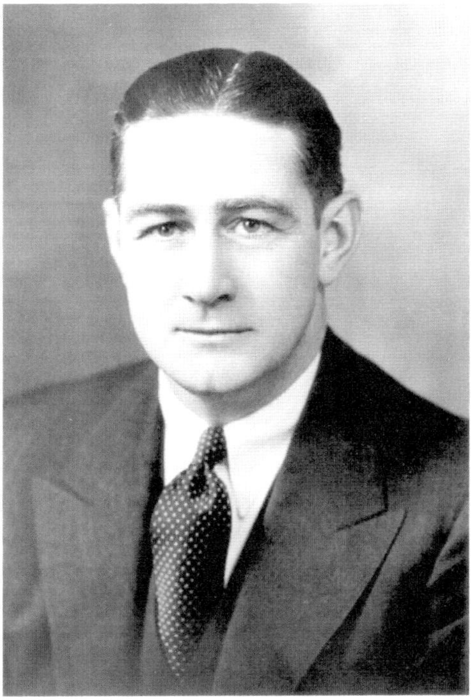

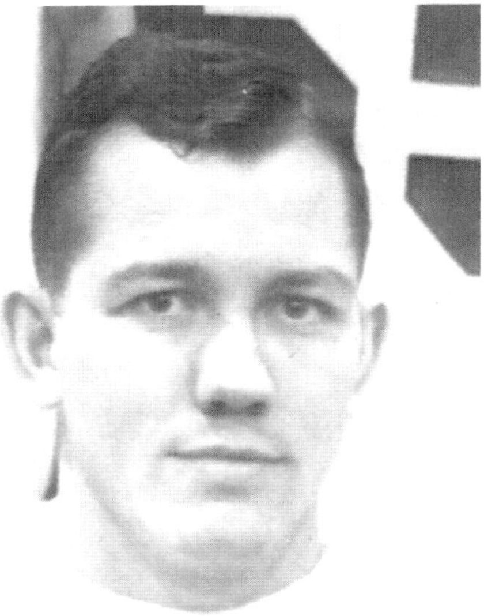

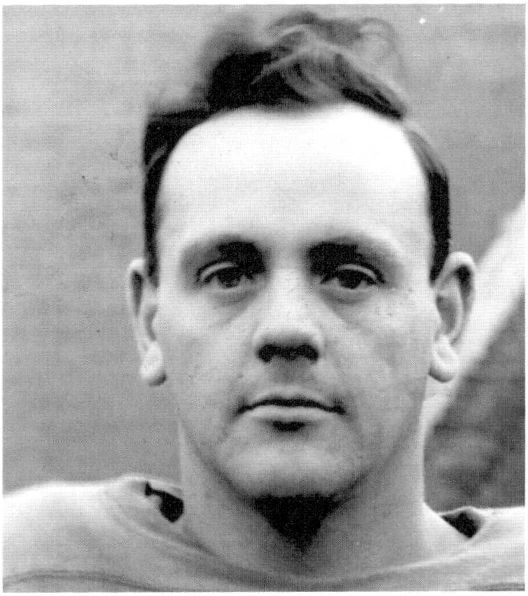

Fullback Art Gillespie (left) scored 15 career touchdowns and was always a threat to spark a highlight reel play with record-book quality rushing plays and kickoff returns during the war years. Norm Harris (right) ranks fourth all time for touchdown passes both in a career (35) and in a single season (18). He compiled 2,064 yards of total offense in his career.

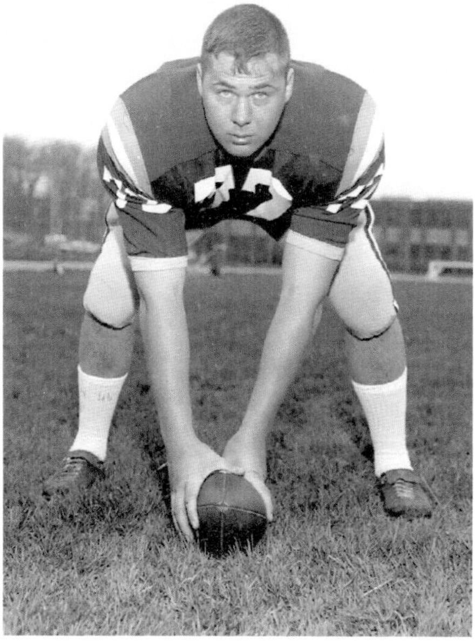

Center Gene Hamlin was an All-MAC first-team selection in 1967, following a second-team honor the year before. He played postseason ball in the 1968 Blue-Grey All-Star Game and later had a tour of duty in the NFL with the Washington Redskins and Detroit Lions.

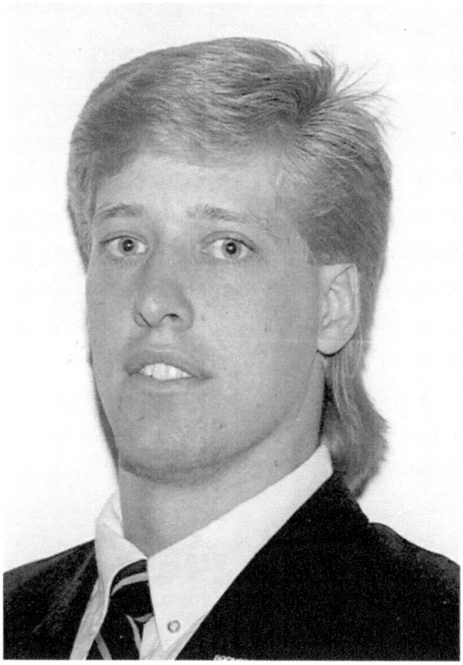

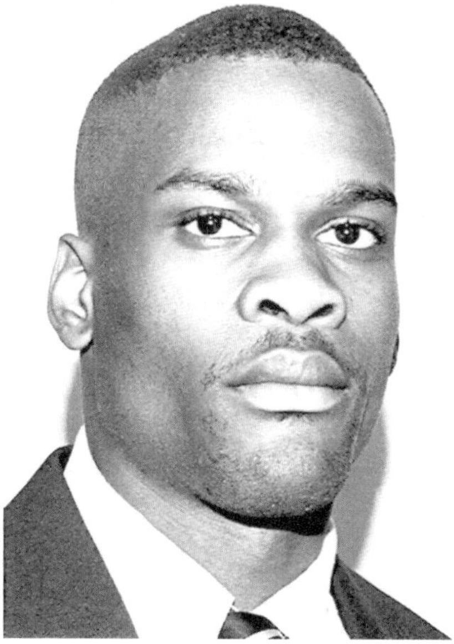

Kevin Haverdink (left) was recognized as a national talent by being named an Associated Press third-team All-American in 1988 to go along with his All-Mac first-team selection that year as well. Steve Hawkins (right) was an All-MAC first-team member in 1993 and selected to play in the Blue-Grey game.

SPLIT END JAMIE HENCE WAS CHOSEN TO the 1987 All-MAC first team and was an honorable mention in the Associated Press All-America list. Hence holds the record for receptions in a game, catching 16 against Ohio in 1987. He ranks sixth all time at WMU in touchdown receptions with 15.

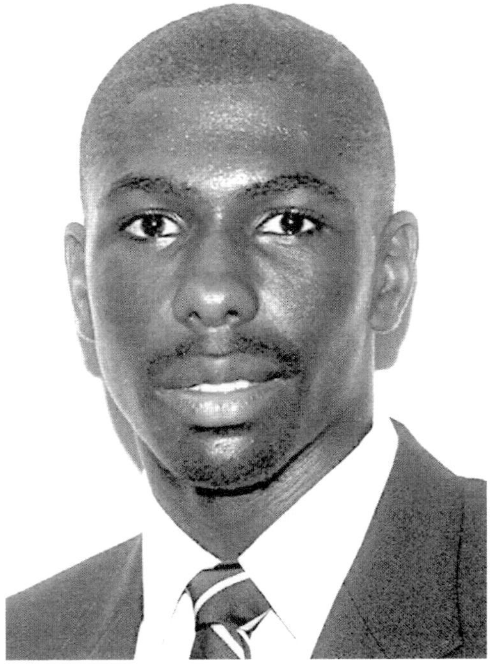

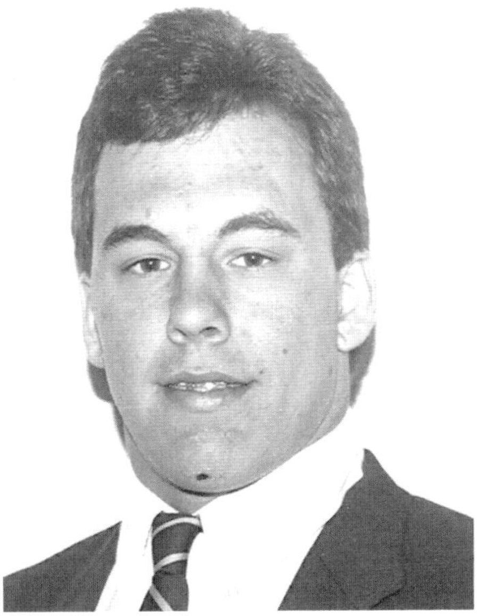

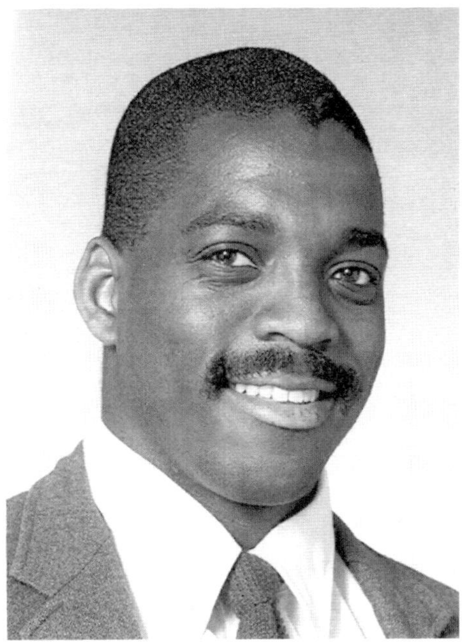

ERIC HOFFMAN (LEFT) WAS AN ALL-MAC first-team linebacker in 1988 and a second-team selection in 1987. He was runner-up for Defensive Player of the Year in 1988. He ranks third all time in tackles with 406. Fullback Bobby Howard (right) ranks fifth all time in rushing yards with 2,608 yards covered. He was a two-time All-MAC first-team selection in 1979 and 1980 while adding second-team honors in 1978.

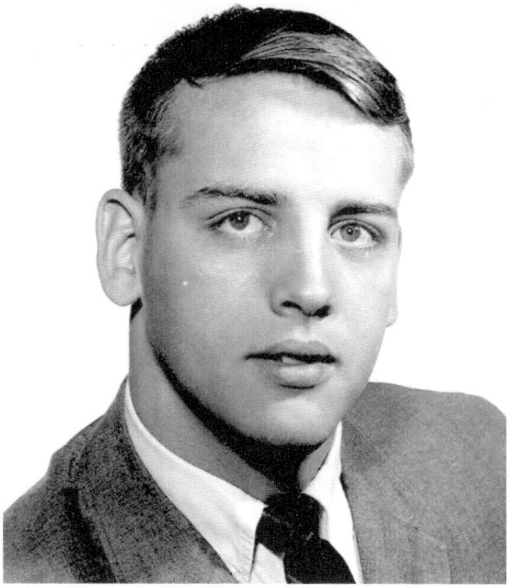

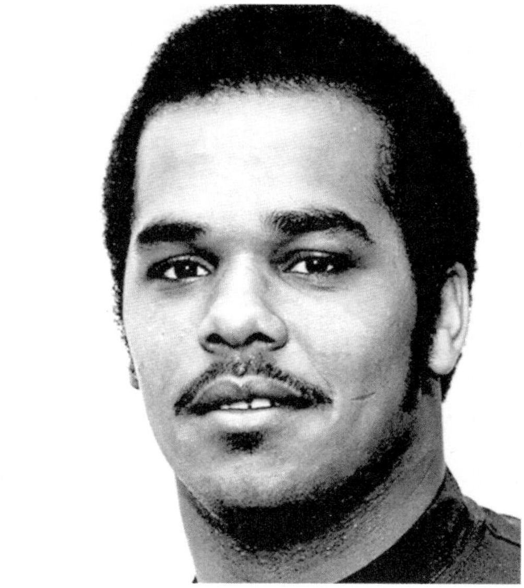

DEFENSIVE BACK DAVE HUDSON (LEFT) WAS named to the All-MAC first team twice (1967 and 1968) and to the second team in 1966. His 229 interception return yards ranks second all time. Allen Hughes (right) was a first-team All-MAC defensive tackle in both 1980 and 1981. He recorded 16 tackles for loss in 1981 and totaled 30 in his career.

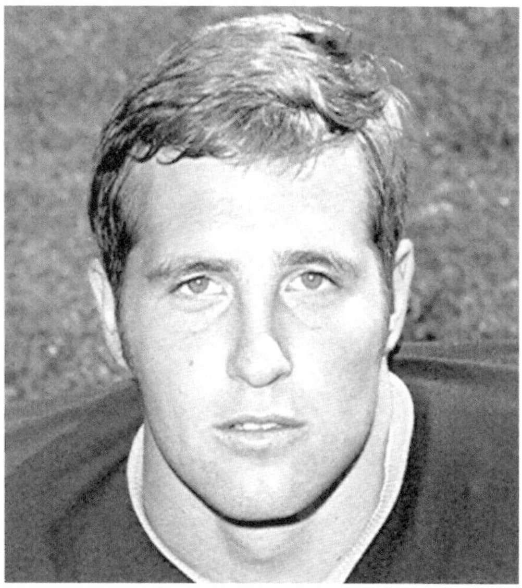

OUTSIDE LINEBACKER PAUL HUTCHINS (LEFT) was named to the All-MAC first team in 1991 and 1992 and was a second-team selection in 1990. Greg Igaz (right) was a two-time All-MAC second-team selection (1970 and 1971). From his linebacker position, he recorded 346 tackles in his career and ranks second all time in tackles in a game with 25 against Brigham Young University in 1970.

KALAMAZOO NATIVE GREG JENNINGS BECAME only the second Bronco offensive-skill position player to be named to the Associated Press All-America list when he received third-team honors in 2005. He accumulated a long list of record-book performances for career, season, and game totals.

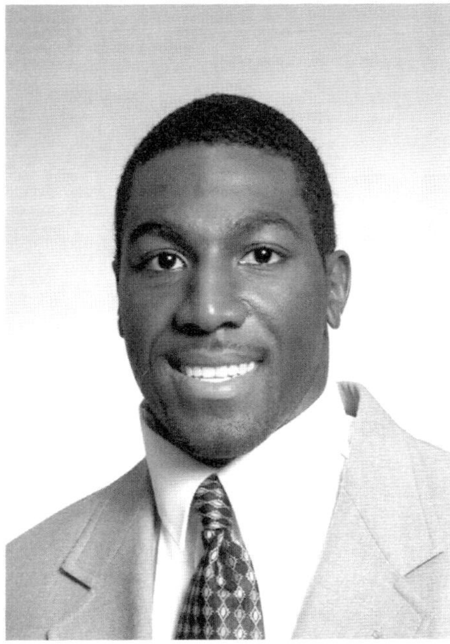

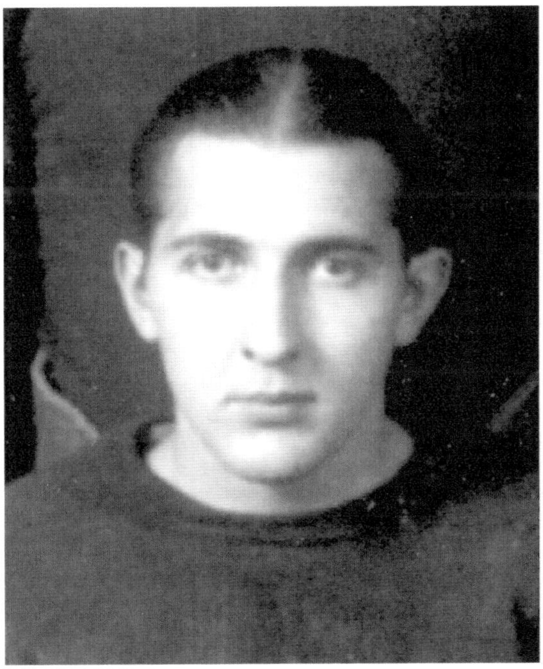

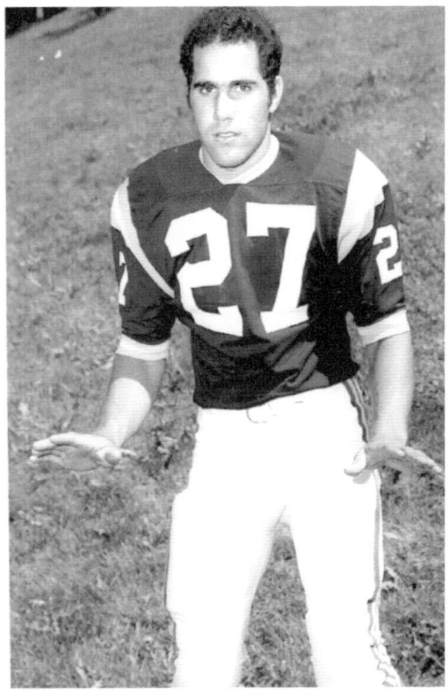

OSCAR JOHNSON (LEFT) WAS ONE OF THE premier tackles in WMU history. As a star on the undefeated 1922 team, he played both offense and defense with equal skill. An All-MAC first-team selection in 1972, safety Ron Karlis (right) was a master of sudden change. He ranks third all time in interceptions with 15 and first in interception return yards with 313.

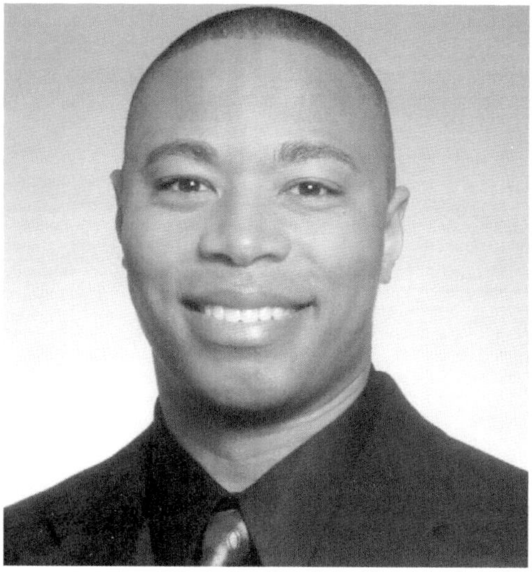

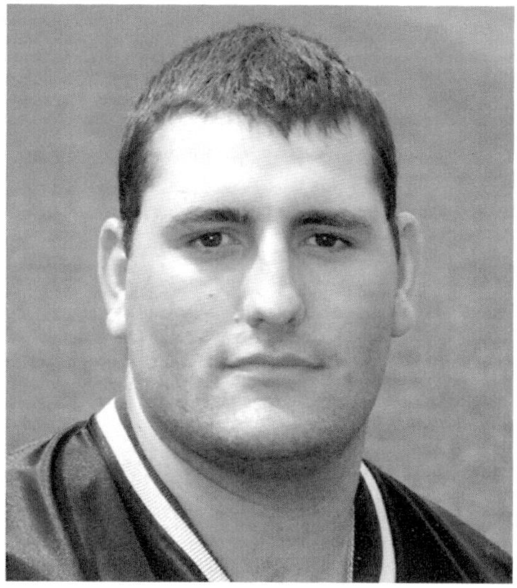

QUARTERBACK TONY KIMBROUGH'S (LEFT) collection of 4,055 career offensive yards and 2,465 season passing totals both rank in WMU's all-time top 10. Charlie Knapp (right) was a two-time All-MAC second-team offensive tackle in 1998 and 1999. He was invited to play in the postseason Blue-Grey All-Star Game.

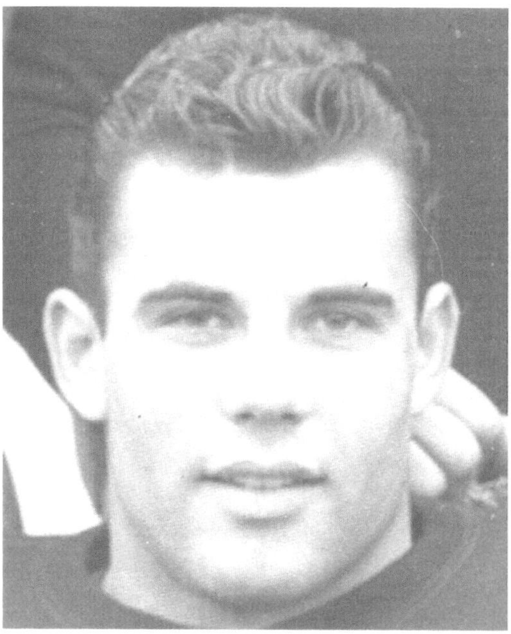

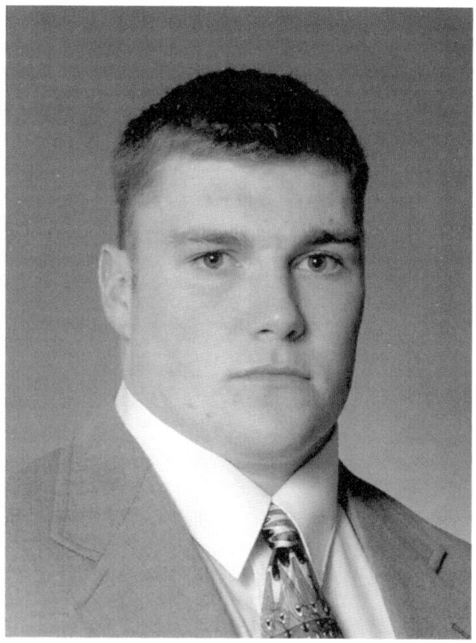

DAVE KRIBS (LEFT) IS WMU'S CAREER LEADER in interceptions with 24 and punt returns with 83. He recorded the first touchdown ever scored in Waldo Stadium back in 1939. Paul Lambert (right) was selected to the All-MAC first-team list in 2000 as a potent tackle for the West Division champion Broncos.

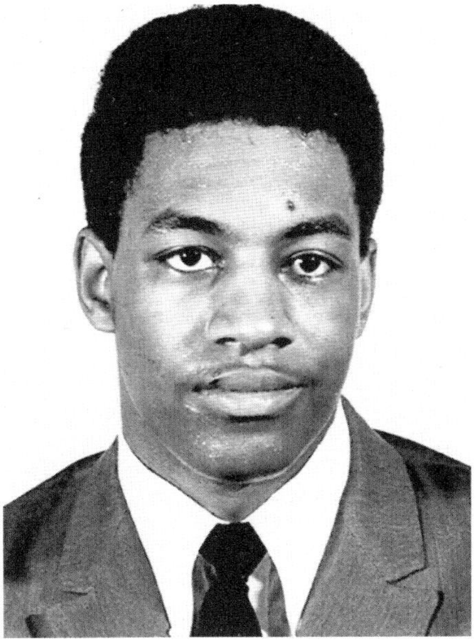

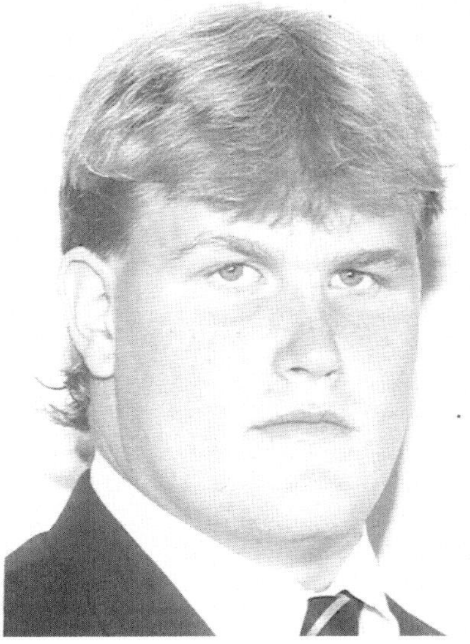

ROGER "RAMJET" LAWSON (LEFT) WAS THE Broncos' first ever 2,000-yard rusher. His 1,205 yards rushing in 1970 earned him an All-MAC first-team designation. Joe Lewandowski (right) was a three-time All-MAC second-team selection during his 1995–1997 career as a Bronco tackle.

FORMER BRONCO QUARTERBACK Tim Lester was one of the greatest quarterbacks to wear the brown and gold. He has returned to his roots and is currently coaching quarterbacks under head coach Bill Cubit at WMU. "Coach Cubit really made an impact on how I thought about and played the game. It took a while for me to adjust, but it made me a much better player." Now as Lester strives to apply that knowledge to the current crop of players, he advises them to "have a lot of gratitude for all the players that came before you that didn't have the same opportunities that you have today." The opportunities that he speaks of appear both on and off the field. "I appreciate all those people who might not always get the recognition they deserve, [such as] the administration, training staffs, academic services, equipment staff, coaches."

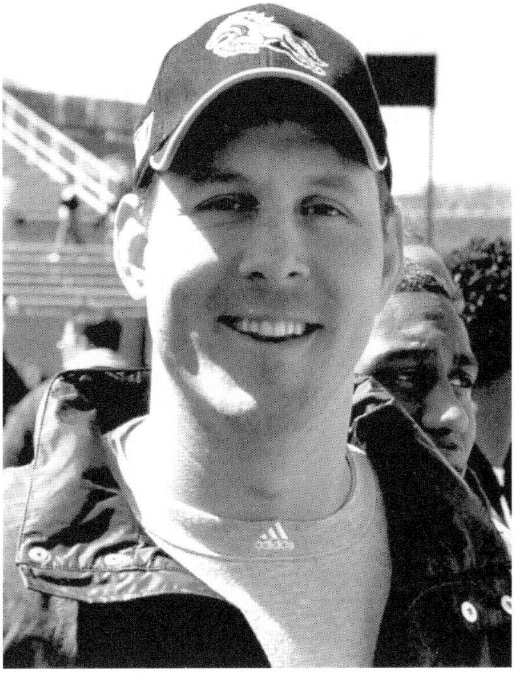

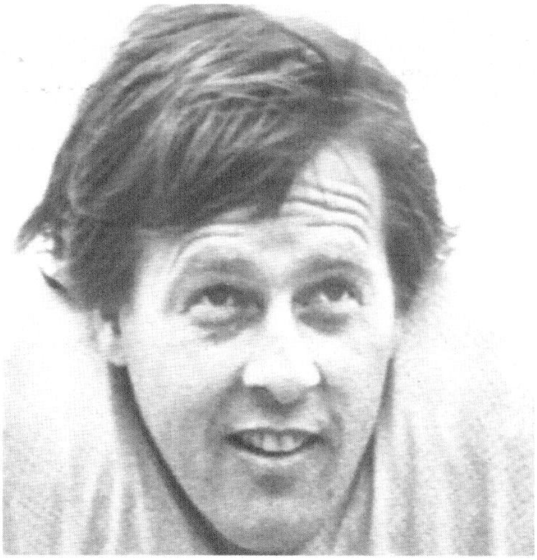

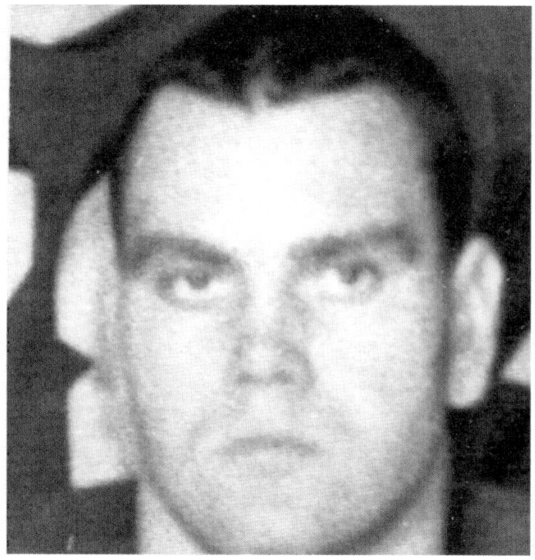

PUNTER DALE LIVINGSTON (LEFT) SHARES THE record for the longest Bronco punt, covering 86 yards with a boot against Kent State University in 1966. He was a two-time All-MAC first-team selection in 1966 and 1967. He ranks fourth in career punting average with 39.9 yards. Tackle Jon Lomakoski (right) was a 1960 All-MAC first-team choice and earned second-team honors the following year. His blocking helped earn WMU an Aviation Bowl bid.

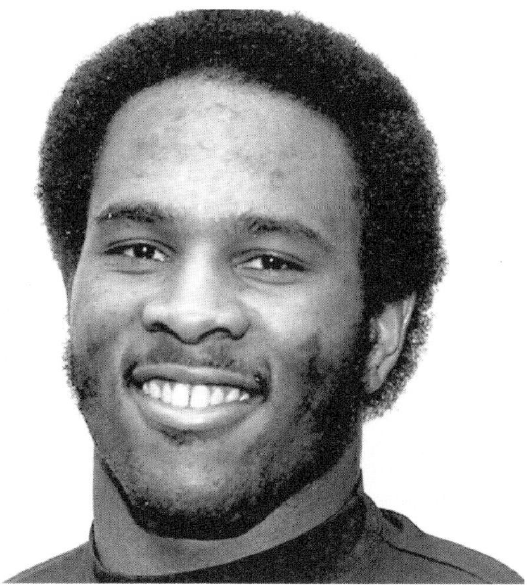

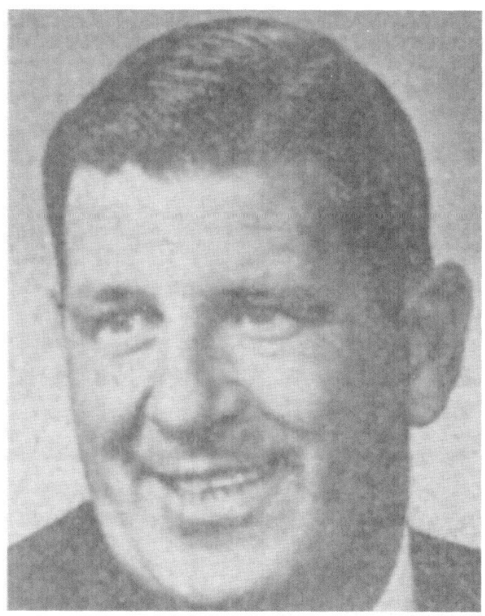

ERIC MANNS (LEFT) WAS A TWO-TIME ALL-MAC first-team member when his fine linebacker play earned him the honors in 1978 and 1979. His 186 tackles in 1978 is good enough for second all time in the WMU record books. As a member of the undefeated 1941 team, end Jack Matheson (right) was a team leader. He extended his playing career into a stint with the Detroit Lions.

JAY McDONAUGH PUT HIS NAME IN THE WMU record books by ranking in the top-three all time in passing yards with 6,148, completions (892), touchdown passes (45), and total offense yards (6,915). He was a second-team All-MAC selection in 1995.

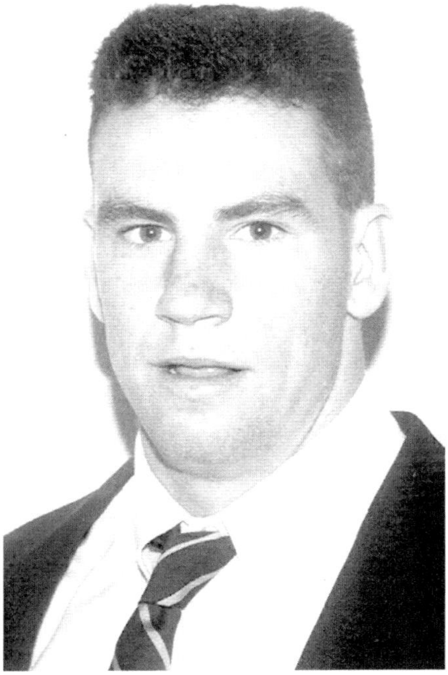

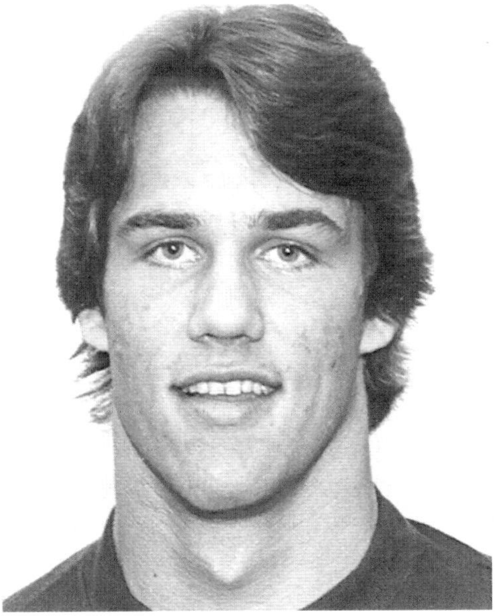

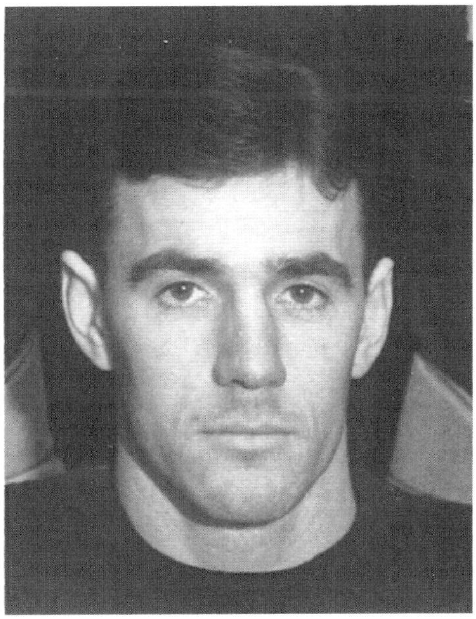

MATT MEARES (LEFT) WAS A FOOTBALL Coaches first-team All-America center in 1982. Twice he was named to the All-MAC first team (1981 and 1982). John Miller (right) was the squad's most outstanding back for three years. He was the team captain for Western's 1934 National Teachers College championship team.

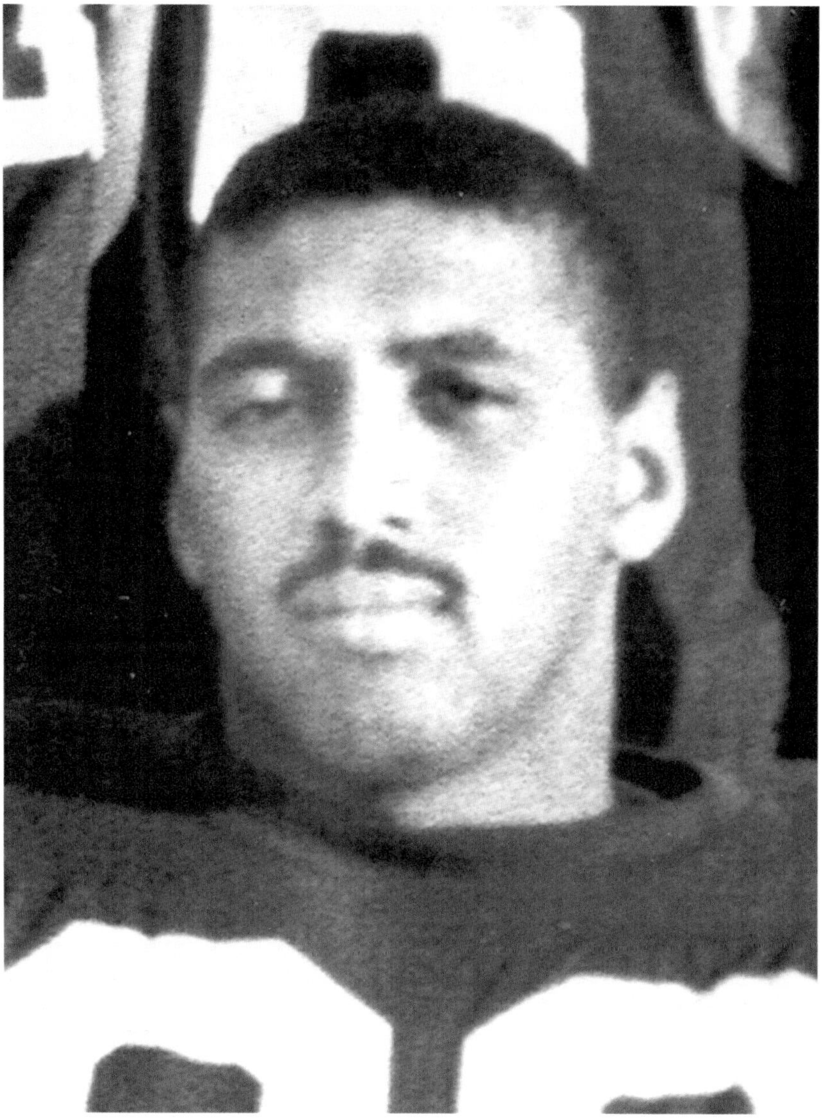

BEING SELECTED TO THE WMU ALL-CENTURY team was another in a long line of honors that have humbled former end Jim McKinley. "I have been very fortunate to have received all types of honors and awards in both of my careers—22 years as a college and professional football coach and 19 years as a businessman. Yet the two most treasured awards that I have received are being inducted into the Western Michigan University Athletic Hall of Fame and being chosen on the WMU All-century team." After his playing days, he went on to own McKinley Financial Services, Inc., the largest African American–owned insurance agency in the United States. "Statistics show that very few student-athletes will become a professional player. One purpose of attending college is to develop the total person for the balance of his working career. By becoming involved, this helps to develop and improve social skills that will enhance one's chosen profession for later life."

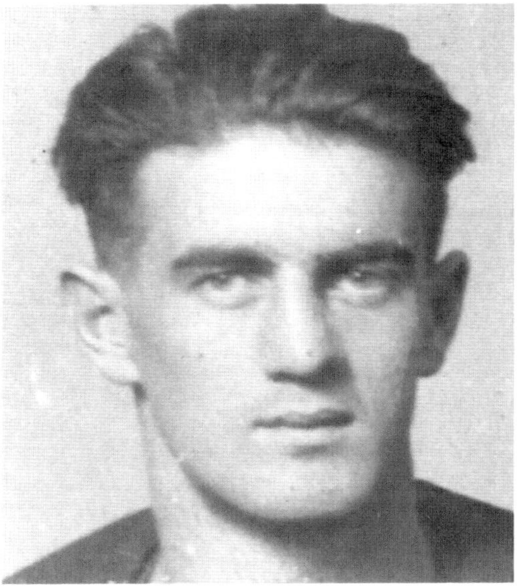

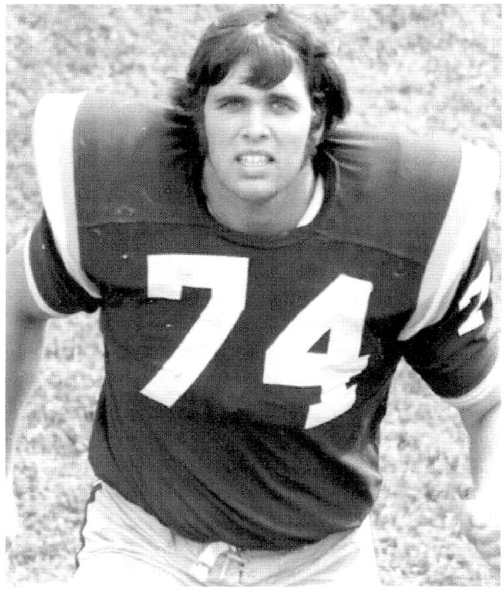

RUDY MILLER (LEFT) EARNED MORE ATHLETIC letters than anyone at WMU. He collected 14 such monograms and was cited for All-America honors by the legendary Walter Eckersall. Rocco Moore (right) was an All-MAC first-team selection in 1976 and earned four letters at WMU.

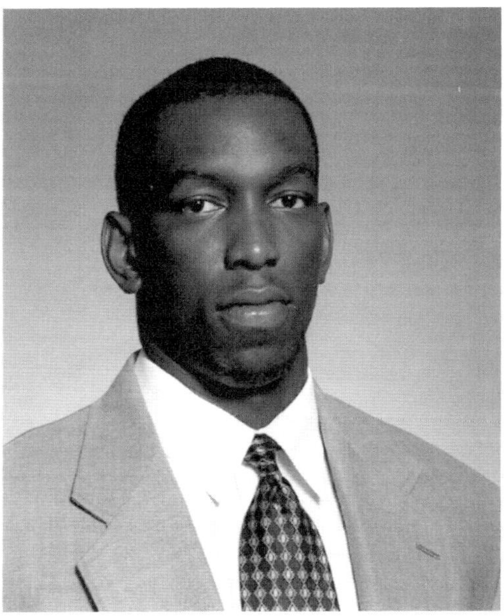

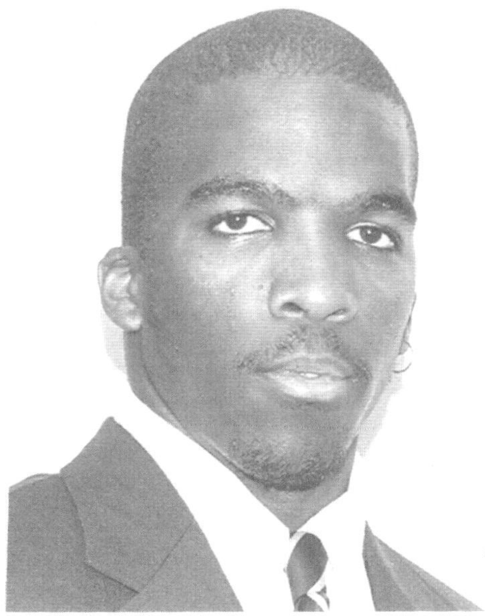

KENDRICK MOSELY (LEFT) RANKS THIRD ALL TIME in receptions with 163 and fourth in receiving yards with 2,042. He is WMU's all-time leading punt returner with 869 yards. Tristan Moss (right) was selected to the All-MAC first team in 1995. He recorded seven interceptions and 15 pass breakups in his final two seasons.

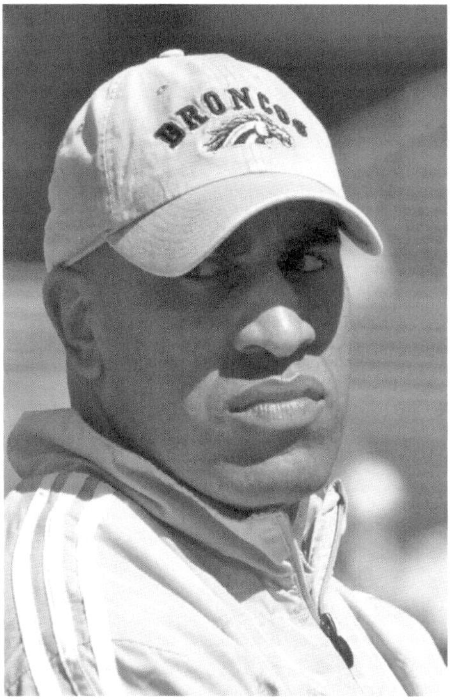

"PLAYING AT WESTERN PREPARED ME FOR THE NFL," says Jake Moreland, who played two years with the New York Jets and Cleveland Browns. "The way that we approached games, game-planning, preparation, and lifestyle were not very different from what I experienced in the NFL. The values, responsibilities, and leadership roles that I had when I played at WMU were the same no matter where I was or what I was doing." Moreland has brought his skills back to Kalamazoo as an assistant coach. "It feels great to be home. To have the opportunity to teach and coach football at my alma-mater is something that in my short coaching career will have a hard time being topped."

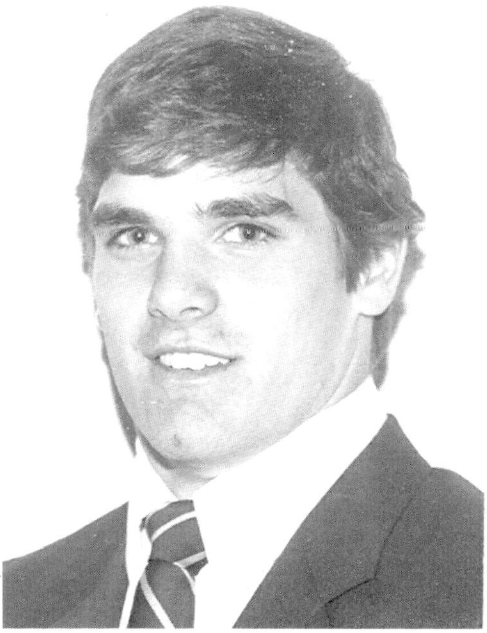

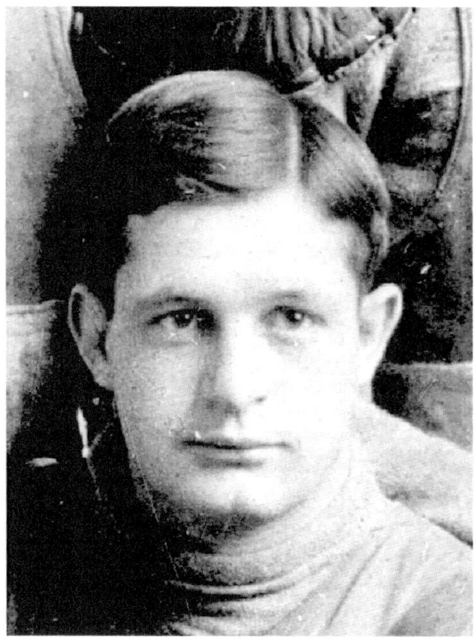

LINEBACKER SEAN MULHEARN (LEFT) WAS THE MAC Defensive Player of the Year and an All-MAC first-team member in 1990. He ranks second all time in tackles with 435. Melvin

"Tubby" Myers (right) was a player-coach who captained the 1907 and 1908 teams. He is regarded as the school's first great player.

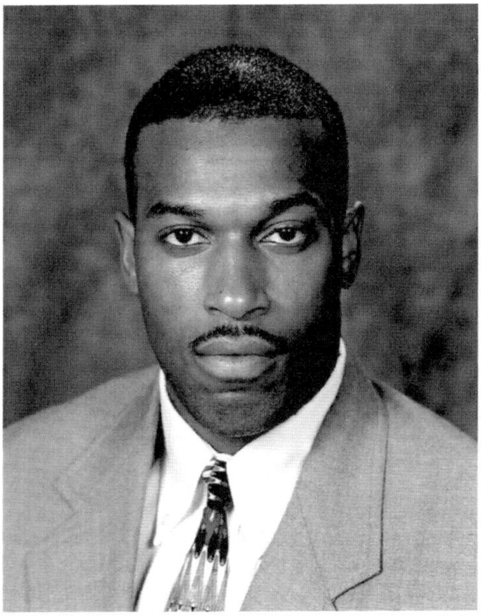

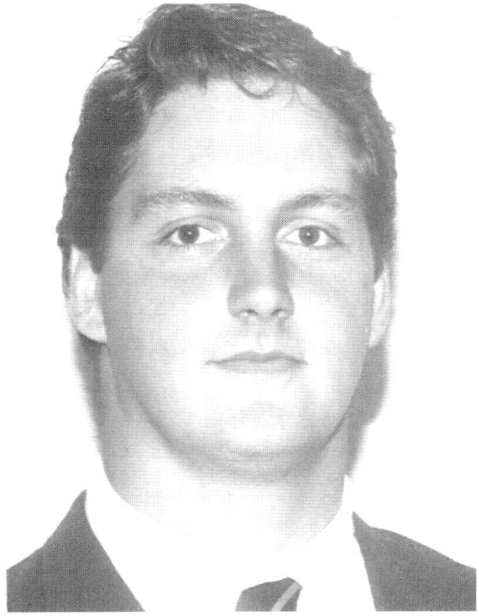

WIDE RECEIVER STEVE NEAL (LEFT) WAS named to the All-MAC first team three times (1998–2000), ranks first all time in receiving yards (3,599) and receptions (235), and is second in touchdown receptions (27). Guard Tom Nütten (right) was a 1994 All-MAC first-team choice. He participated in the East-West Shrine Bowl and Hula Bowl and played in two Super Bowls with the St. Louis Rams.

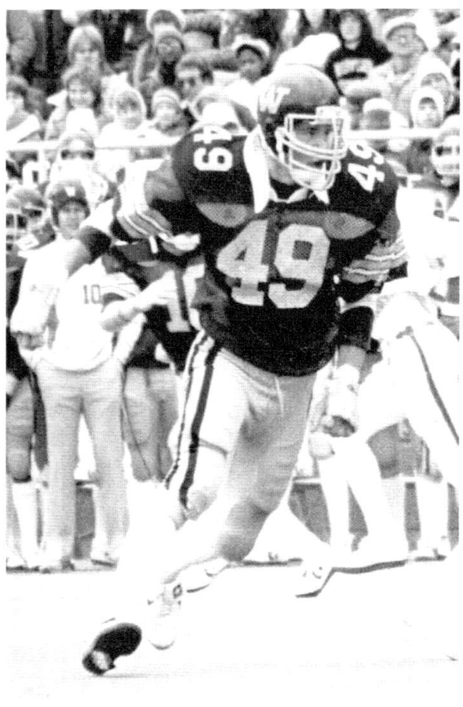

LINEBACKER JOHN OFFERDAHL WAS A TWO-TIME Associated Press All-American and named to three straight All-MAC first teams from 1983 to 1985. He was the MAC Defensive Player of the Year in 1985 and holds the WMU record for tackles in a career (694) and single season (192). He was named to five Pro Bowls during his career with the Miami Dolphins.

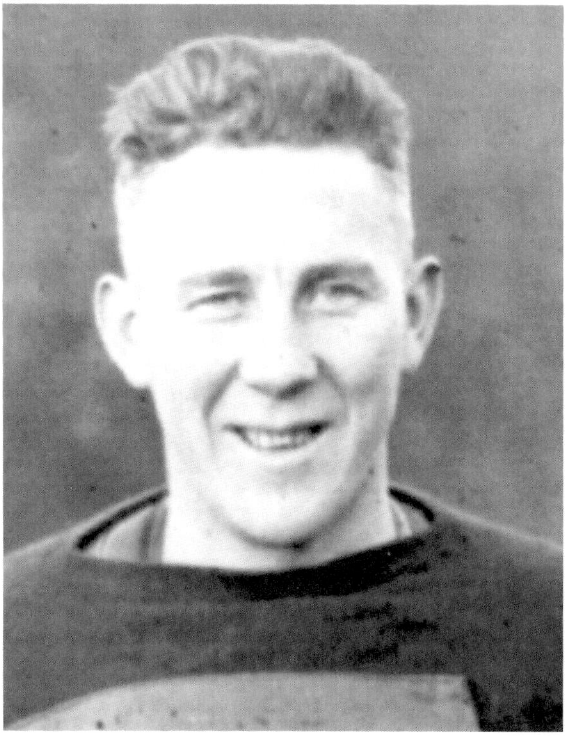

WALTER OLSEN PLAYED EVERY backfield position, ranks third all time in touchdowns (32), and holds the record for touchdowns in a game with 8 against Grand Rapids Veterinary College in 1916. He set a single-season record for total points with 138 in 1916 and ranks fourth all time in points scored (253).

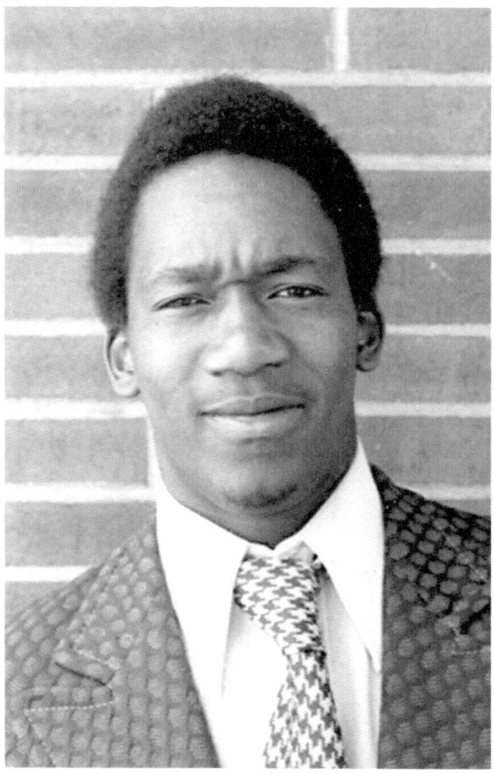

HALFBACK JEROME PERSELL RANKS IN THE top five in WMU history in rushing yards (4,190, second), rushing attempts (842, first), all purpose yards (4,394, fourth), touchdowns (39, second), single-season touchdowns (19, first) and total points (240, fourth). He was twice named to the Associated Press All-America team (third team, 1976–1977) and was the winner of three straight MAC Offensive Player of the Year honors, 1976–1978.

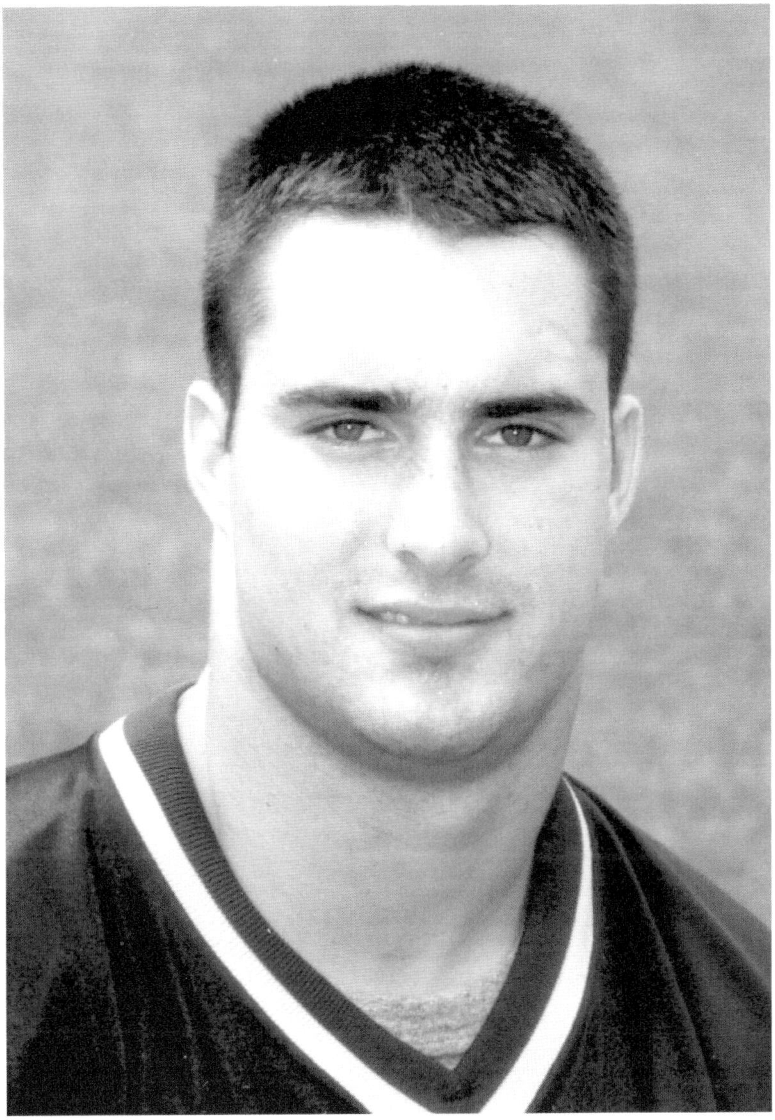

SCOTT NILES WAS AN ALL-MAC FIRST-TEAM selection in 1999. His advice to current Bronco players is "cherish every moment of your college career. Go above and beyond what is required to prepare you to be the best football player both physically and mentally. Your college football career will end in four to five years, and you will regret it if you don't give it all your best. You have the rest of your life to be 'normal' and do things 'normal' people do. Trust me, it's overrated. Nothing else in life gives you the feeling of playing at the highest level of college football in front of 30,000 or more." Niles realized his dreams when the Broncos faced the University of Florida in 1999 and he participated in the pregame coin flip. "It was always my dream to play at the highest level of college football, and taking on [head coach] Steve Spurrier and the Gators for a sold-out home opener in 'The Swamp' fulfilled that dream."

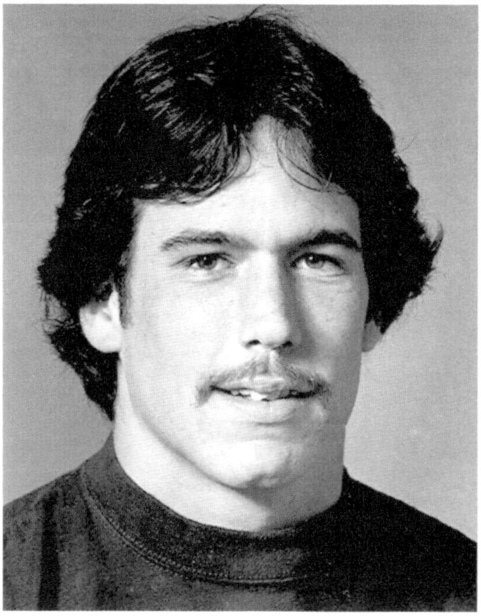

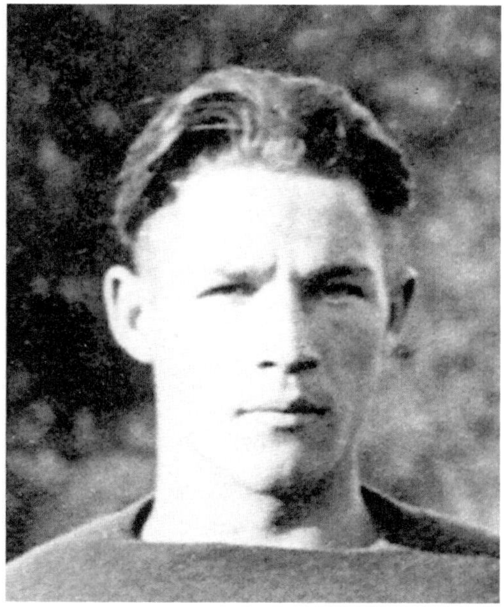

SPLIT END BOB PHILLIPS (LEFT) WAS A TWO-TIME All-MAC first-team choice in 1981 and 1982. He is fifth all time in touchdown receptions with 16 and recorded the second-highest single-game receiving yardage with 203 against Ohio in 1981. Halfback Harry Potter (right) was an honorable mention All-American on Walter Eckersall's 1923 team. He was the top runner on the undefeated 1922 team.

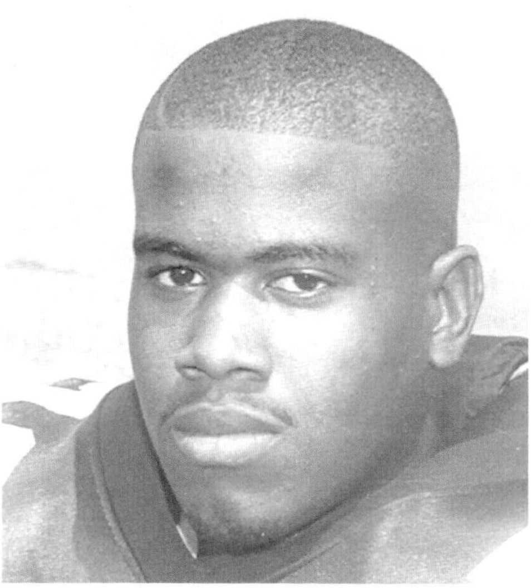

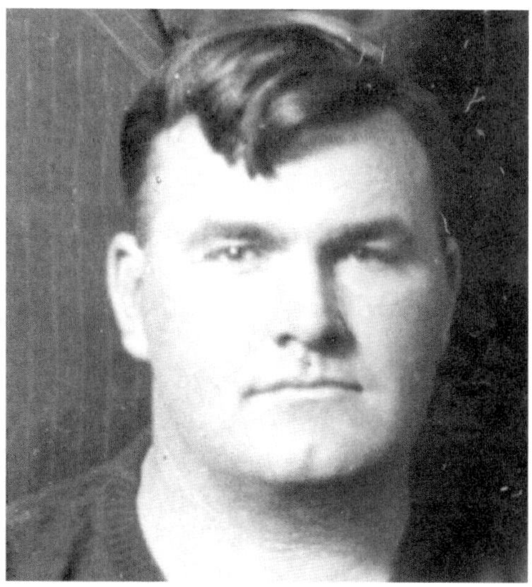

DION POWELL (LEFT) WAS A THREE-TIME ALL-MAC first-team defensive end from 1993 to 1995 and a United Press All-America honorable mention. Currently he ranks fifth all time for tackles for a loss with 39. Center Leo Redmond (right) captained the undefeated 1922 team and is considered one of the greatest centers in WMU history.

KICKER MIKE PRINDLE LEARNED AN EARLY LESSON after a bad game in his freshman year against Central Michigan University. Feeling the pressure from teammates, fans, and the media, he had second thoughts about playing. But he changed his mind saying, "I realized that I absolutely loved playing for Western. No one, not the media, fans, or teammates were going to change that." He rebounded to kick a game-winning field goal against Miami. "I was mobbed and hoisted. Unbelievable."

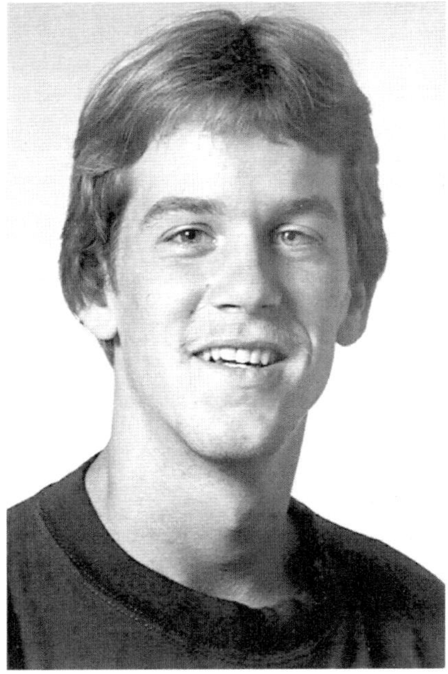

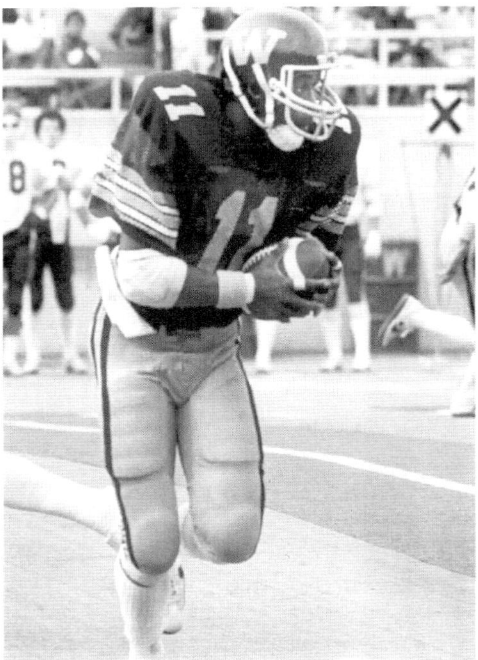

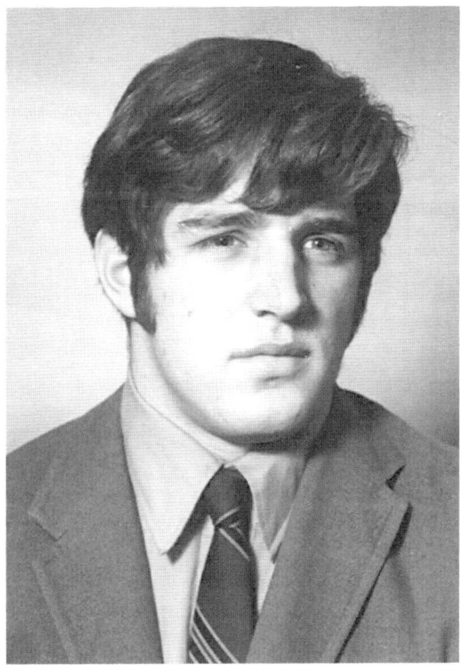

FLANKER CLIFF REED (LEFT) WAS SELECTED to the All-MAC second team in 1984. He recorded 3,812 all-purpose yards in his career and 1,741 kickoff return yards. Linebacker Dominic Riggio (right) was a two-time All-MAC first-team selection in 1972–1973. He was the MAC Defensive Player of the Year runner-up in 1972. He ranks eighth all time in tackles with 310.

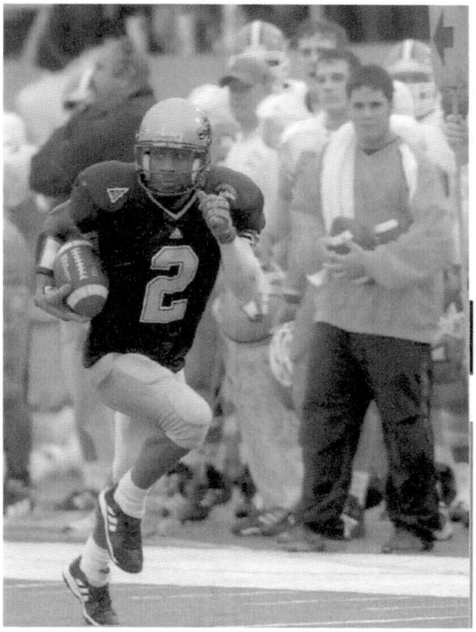

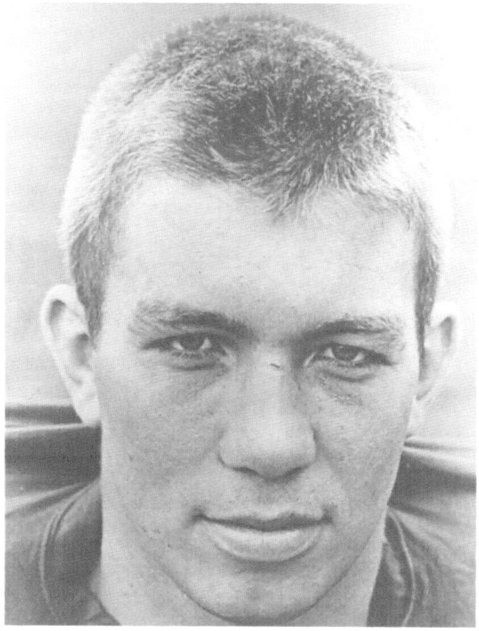

RONALD ROGERS (LEFT) WAS SELECTED TO both the All-MAC first team (2001) and second team (2000). He ranks first all time in pass deflections with 38 and fourth in interceptions with 14. Bob Rowe (right) was WMU's greatest defensive tackle. A member of the 1966 Associated Press All-America second team and the All-MAC first team, he was also a two-time MAC Lineman of the Year in 1965–1966.

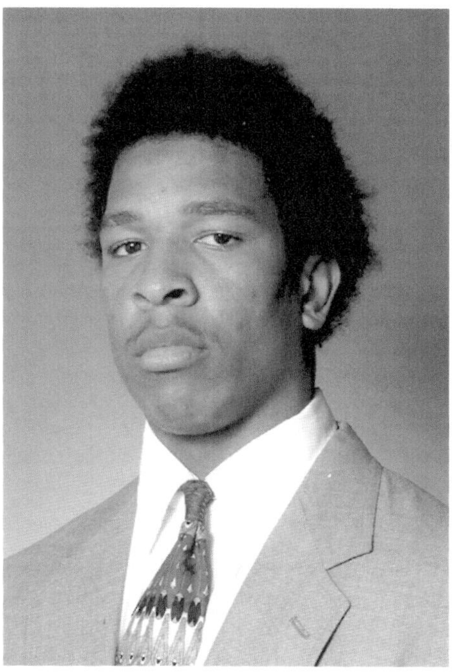

ROBERT SANFORD WAS NAMED BOTH THE MAC MVP and MAC Offensive Player of the Year following a stellar 2000 season. He was also on the All-MAC first team in 2000, holds the WMU record for career rushing yards with 4,219 and touchdowns (43), and ranks second all time in all-purpose yards (4,609).

In 2004, Tony Scheffler caught 53 passes and was named first-team All-MAC. Despite dislocating two knuckles in the 2005 opener and wearing a cast the next few games, Scheffler caught 57 balls and was again picked for the All-MAC team.

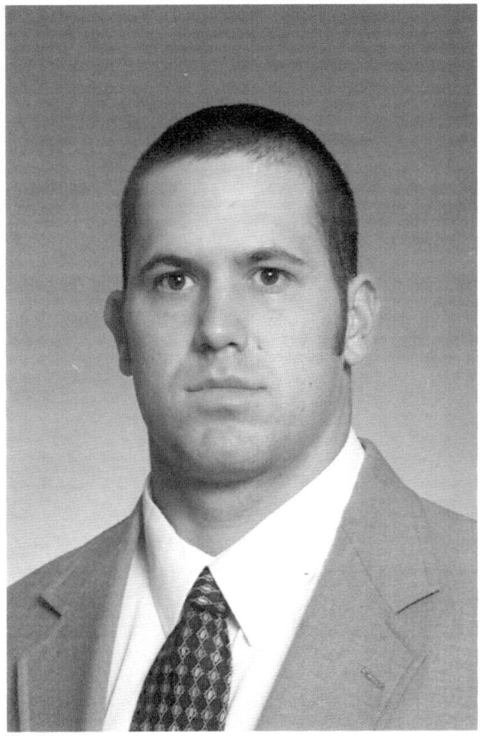

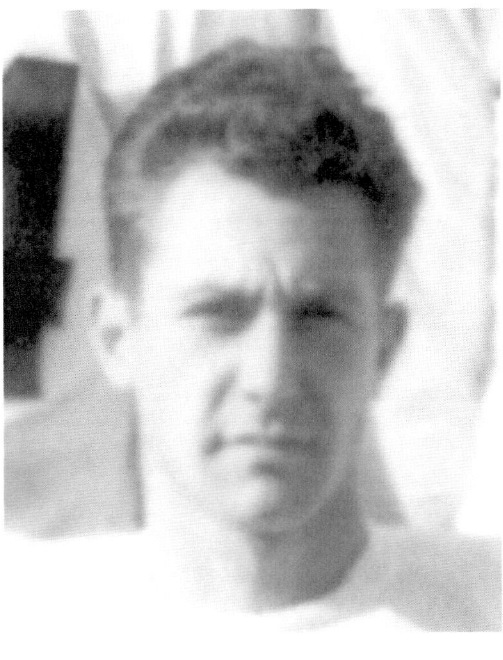

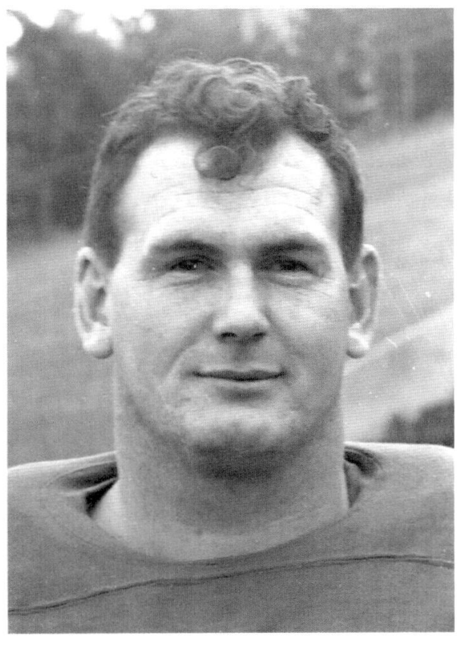

Carl Schiller (left) was one of Western's greatest ends. He caught 47 passes in 1947, which was the record until 1981. Chuck Schoolmaster (right) was a two-time All-MAC first-team selection in 1948–1949. He was the very first Bronco to capture All-MAC honors.

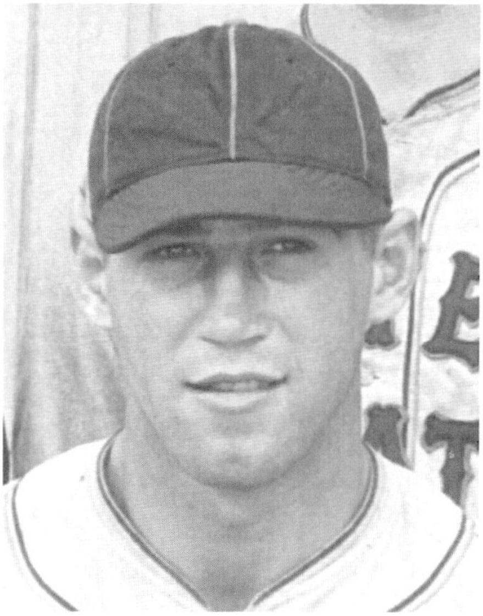

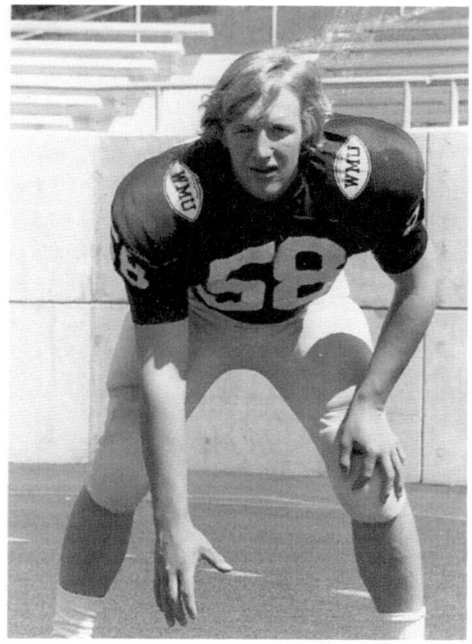

FRANK SECORY (LEFT) WAS A MEMBER OF THE National Teachers College championship team in 1934. He later played professional baseball with the Chicago Cubs and developed into a National League umpire. Mike Sitko (right) was an All-MAC first-team center in 1976 and a four-year letter winner.

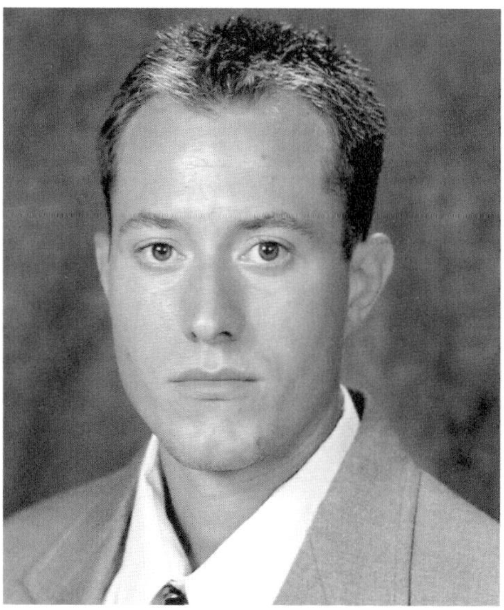

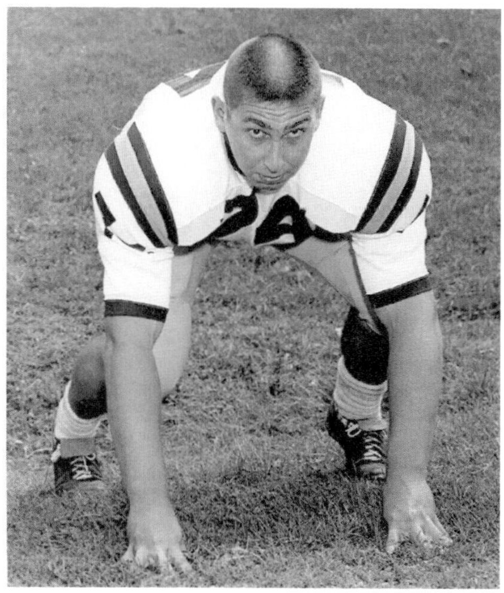

BRAD SELENT (LEFT) WAS A MAC SPECIAL Teams Player of the Year and member of the All-MAC first team in 1998. He is the WMU record holder in nearly every Bronco kicking category. Mike Siwek (right) was a member of the All-MAC first team in 1969 and All-MAC second team in 1968, was the Broncos' MVP in 1969, and participated in the North-South game.

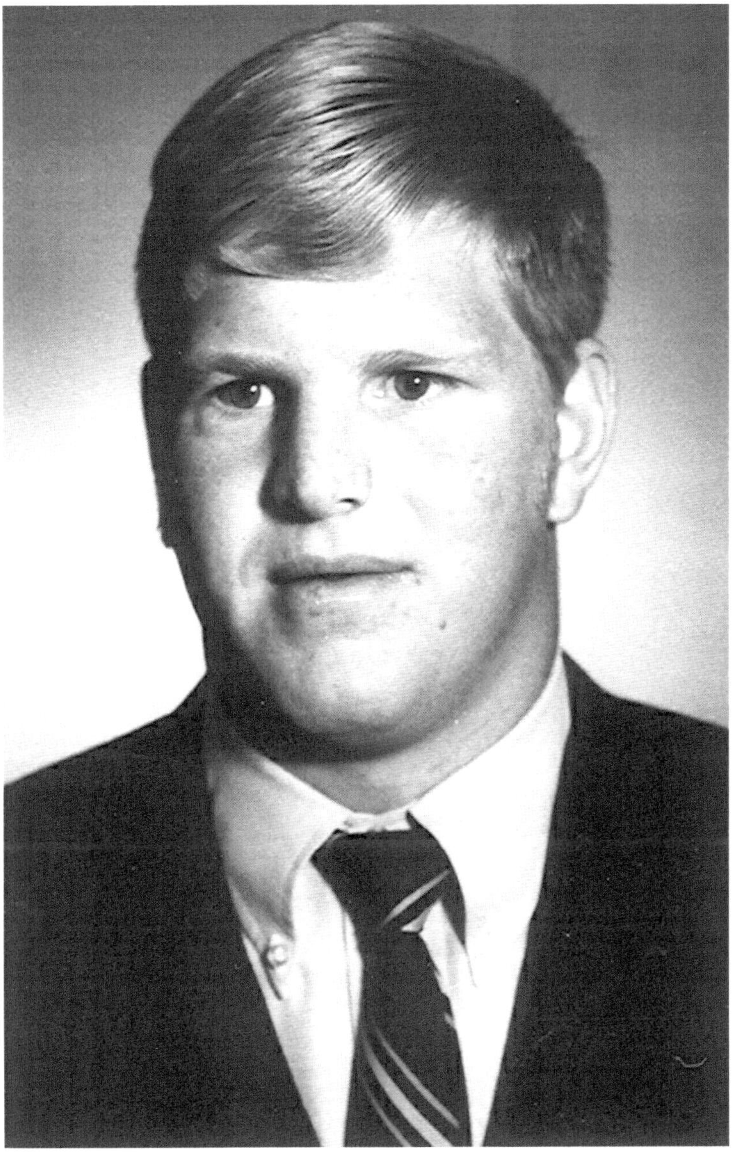

TWICE BILL SLATER EARNED All-MAC recognition, but it was one play that he remembers the most. "My sophomore year in the homecoming game against Marshall, I blocked a kick and fielded the ball just like a baseball infielder. In the paper I credited [WMU baseball coach] Fred Decker for the infielding skill. I ran the ball back for a touchdown. As a defensive end! The pride that the defensive team had, the respect that we had for one another during a game [was amazing]. We did not want to let each other down, and we played a as a unit. Those were truly specific game moments to remember." Along with Decker, Slater recognizes his defensive coordinator Bill Rowekamp as having the greatest influence on his career. "When you play any team sport at a high level, you learn a great deal about accountability, cooperation, pride, teamwork, and trust."

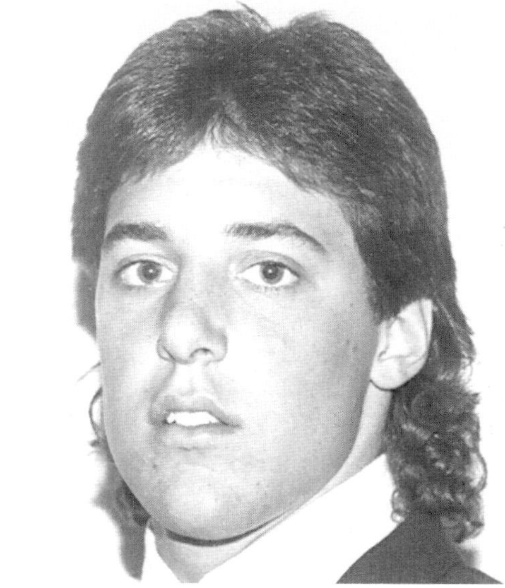

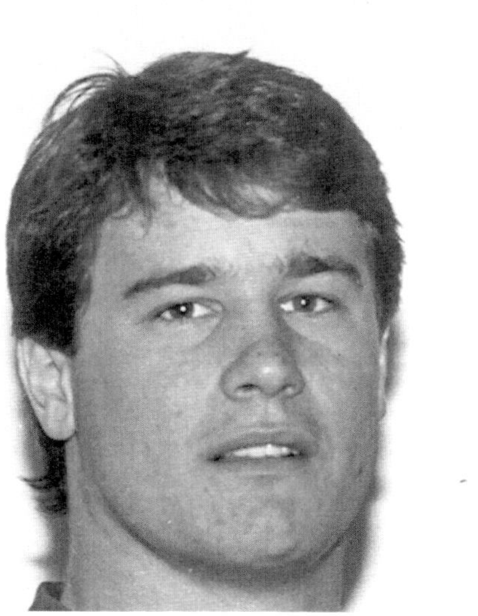

JOEL SMEENGE (LEFT) WAS A THREE-TIME All-MAC first-team defensive tackle in 1987–1989. He rates second in WMU history in tackles for loss (66) and sacks (34) and holds the record for forced fumbles (18). Kelly Spielmaker (right) was the MAC Freshman of the Year as a tight end in 1983 and member of the All-MAC second team. He recorded a third-highest receiving yards in a game versus Toledo in 1983 with 186 yards.

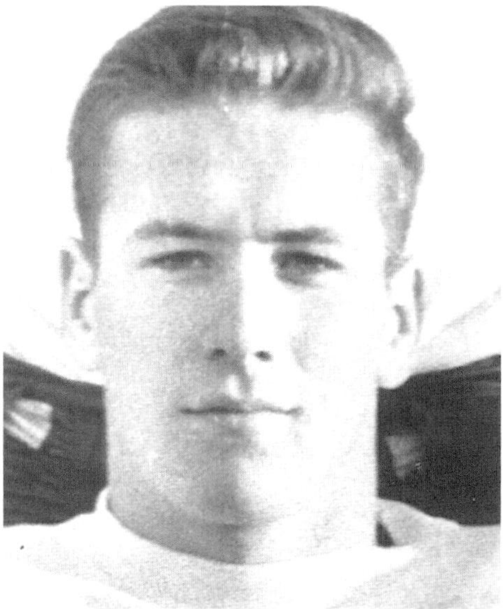

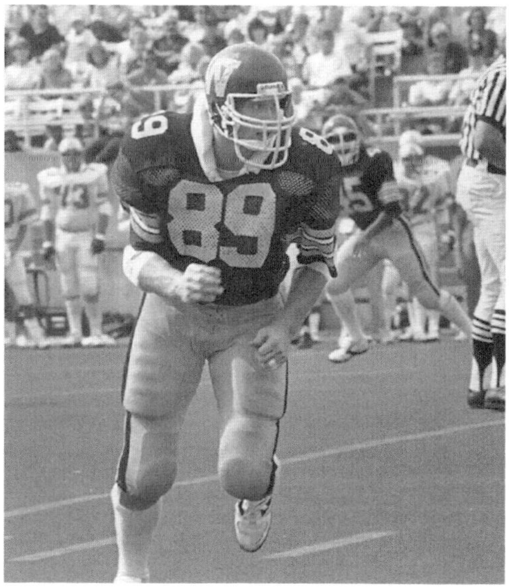

FLOYD STOLLSTEIMER (LEFT) WAS TWICE NAMED to the All-MAC first team in 1951–1952. He stands second all time in interceptions (15) and third in interception return yards (223). Roy Swoape (right) was a second-team All-MAC linebacker in 1985. His 42 tackles for a loss and 13 sacks in 1985 rank fourth all time.

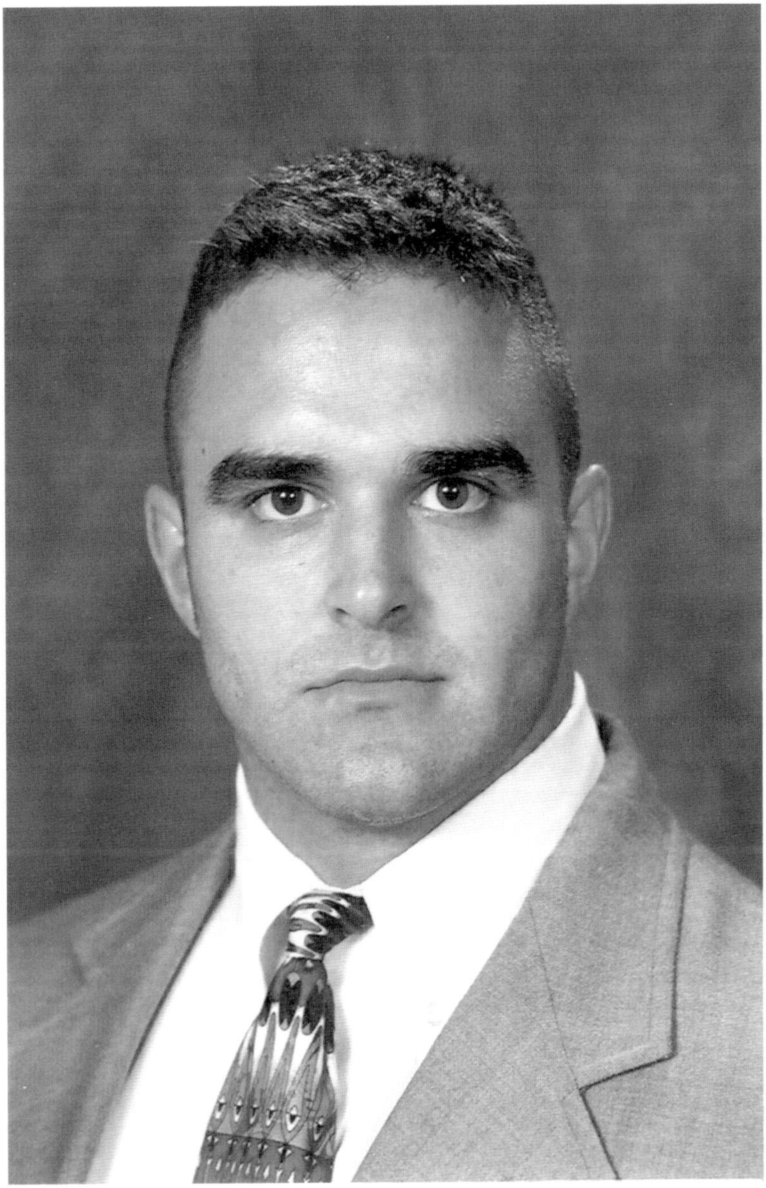

GARRETT SOLDANO, A 2000 All-MAC selection, recalls his experience at WMU as one of solidarity with his teammates. "You build not only camaraderie but lifelong friendships. You never want to let the other guy down in any situation. Whether that be at 6:00 a.m. during morning runs, when you were sweating and hurting all over and passing garbage cans that said 'spit or vomit here', or when the game was on the line and you give it all for your fellow teammates and your fans. I was impressed by my teammates on the scout team, especially the walk-ons giving it their all to prepare for the upcoming battle. They worked their butts off every week, even though they might not have a chance to play in the game. That impressed me, and they have my respect and gratitude."

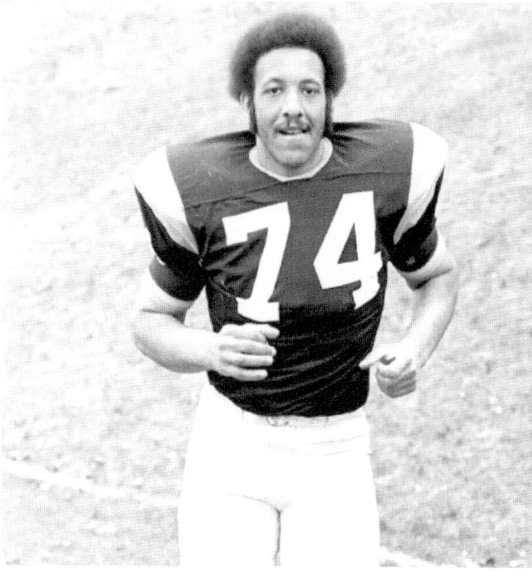

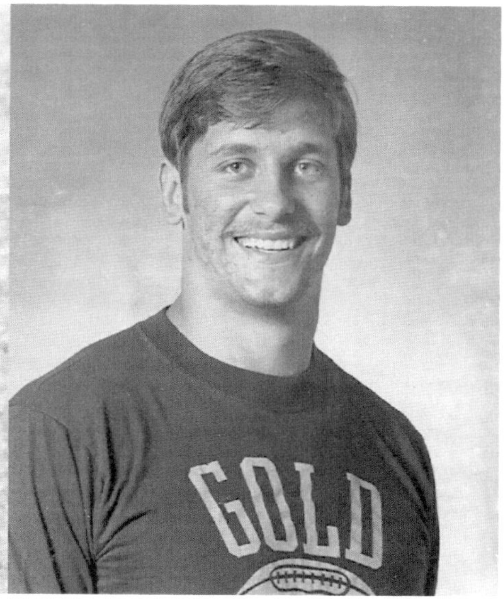

BERNARD THOMAS (LEFT) WAS A TWO-TIME All-MAC first-team defensive tackle in 1971–1972. He was chosen as one of the top-15 all-time Bronco players in 1980. Tom Toth (right) was selected to the All-MAC first team as a tackle in 1984. He played in the NFL for the Miami Dolphins and San Diego Chargers.

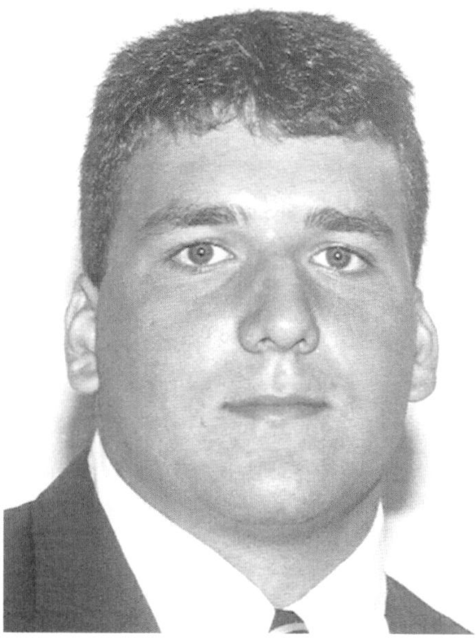
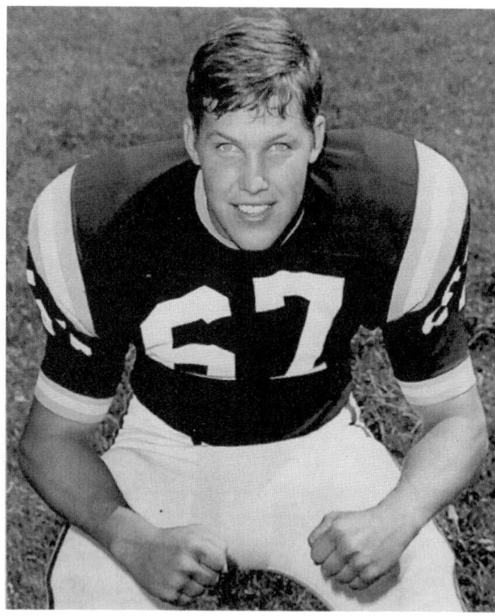

PETER TUFFO (LEFT) WAS A TWO-TIME All-MAC first-team linebacker in 1992–1993, and he ranks fourth all time on the Bronco record tallies in tackles with 382. Larry Ulmer (right) was selected as a third-team All-American in 1972 and twice chosen for the All-MAC first team in 1971–1972.

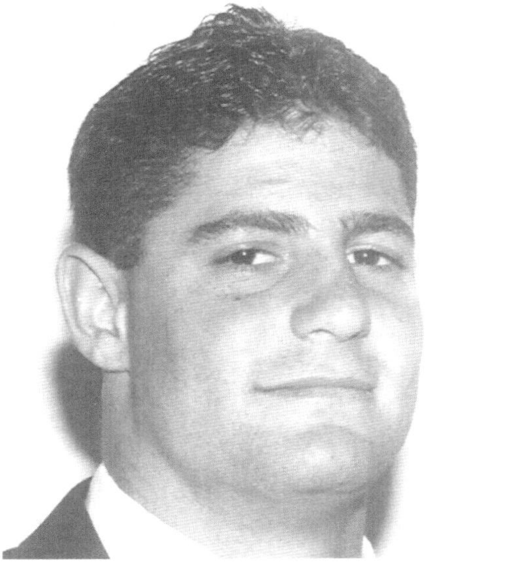

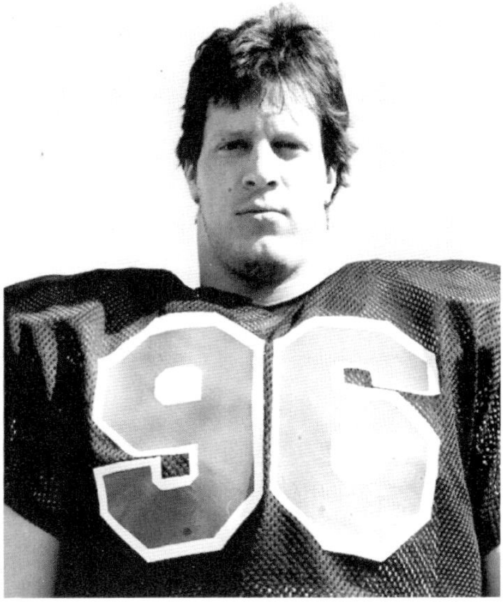

HALFBACK JIM VACKARO (LEFT) WAS AN All-MAC second-team selection twice, 1994–1995. He ranks second all-time in all-purpose yards with 4,446 yards and fourth in rushing with 3,045 yards. Duane Wilson (right) earned four letters from his tackle position for the Broncos from 1979 to 1982. He also played professionally in the United States Football League.

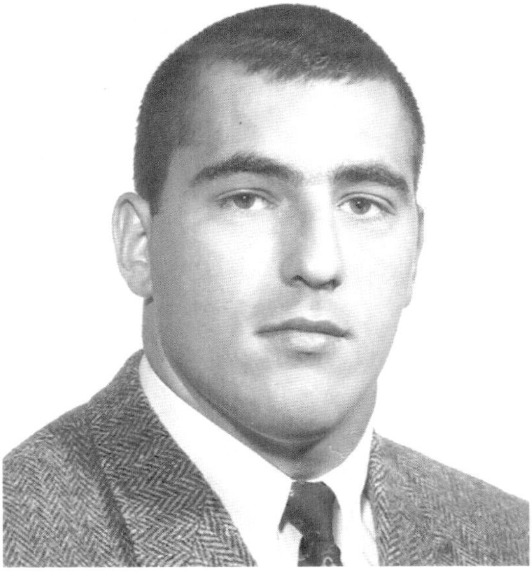

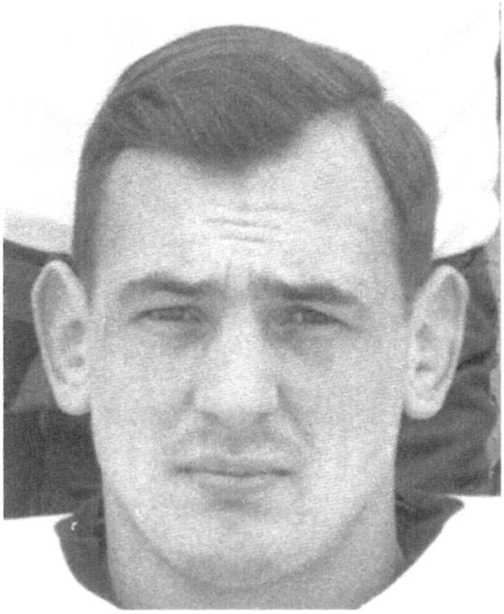

PETE WYSOCKI (LEFT) WAS A DYNAMIC FORCE for WMU and a 1968 All-MAC second-team member. He earned letters in 1966 and 1968 as a linebacker. Bill Yambrick (right) ranks second all time for interceptions in a season with nine in 1942, the year he was also named team MVP.

Consistent with our mission to preserve history on a local level, this book was printed in South Carolina on American-made paper and manufactured entirely in the United States. Products carrying the accredited Forest Stewardship Council (FSC) label are printed on 100 percent FSC-certified paper.

MADE IN THE USA